I've travelled the world twice over,
Met the famous: saints and sinners,
Poets and artists, kings and queens,
Old stars and hopeful beginners,
I've been where no-one's been before,
Learned secrets from writers and cooks
All with one library ticket
To the wonderful world of books.

© JANICE JAMES.

COLA COWBOYS

The men who regularly drive their juggernauts along the 14,000 rugged, turbulent miles of the Golden Road to Arabia are the tough, resourceful "Cola Cowboys". They need to be diplomats, bankers, linguists, mechanics and navigators. With only their vehicles, cargo and wits, each man embarks on an epic journey whose success or failure depends entirely on himself. They drive their way through ice-bound mountains, oven-baked wind-shifting deserts and possibly a war or two, to deliver a precious load worth up to a million pounds.

FRANKLYN WOOD

COLA COWBOYS

Complete and Unabridged

ULVERSCROFT
Leicester

First Large Print Edition
published February 1984
by arrangement with
W. H. Allen & Co., Ltd.
London

British Library CIP Data

Wood, Franklyn
    Cola cowboys.— Large print ed.
    (Ulverscroft large print series: non-fiction)
    I. Title
    1. Motor-truck drivers—Saudi Arabia
    331.7'61388324'09538   HD8039.M9525

    ISBN 0-7089-1094-7

Published by
F. A. Thorpe (Publishing) Ltd.
Anstey, Leicestershire
Printed and Bound in Great Britain by
T. J. Press (Padstow) Ltd., Padstow, Cornwall

Author's note

ALL cowboy stories contain the good guys and the bad guys, the white hats and the black hats, and both types of Cola cowboys have given great help in the telling of this tale.

Of the white hats, Bob Paul, co-founder of Astran, the first and still the Rolls Royce of Middle East trucking companies, Peter Cannon, Astran's transport manager, and Trevor Long, Astran driver and companion of seven arduous weeks on the nerve-wracking road, are especially thanked.

John Martin, whose idea this book was, would blanch at the idea of wearing a white hat because he has driven the Middle East routes a little differently from the Astran way, and sometimes worn a black hat of necessity. Now, as poacher turned gamekeeper, he is a fount of information. The first driver to run to Oman, he was awarded a medal by the Sultan for his services to the Oman Defence Department.

Appreciations to Gordon Pearce, one of the

first drivers on the run and a fine photographer. Thanks, too, to Stuart Heydinger. Also to Sheila and Matthew Wood who patiently waited at home to accept transfer charges telephone calls from all over the globe.

Like many an esoteric undertaking TIR trucking has its own slang. You will meet *Wombles*, Bulgarian State Transport drivers, so called after Uncle Bulgaria in the Wombles of Wimbledon stories. Then there's the *F-Troops*, Rumanian State Transport drivers who travel the world in convoy like an army cavalry unit under the command of a political commissar. *Willi Betz surrogates* are also Rumanians, they drive for German companies. There are *Alpine-Turks*, Austrian drivers who are not highly regarded professionally; nor are *Bubbles*, bubbles-and-squeaks, Greeks. Turks, deservedly, have a whole glossary to themselves: *Kamikazes*, suicidal coach and truck drivers, *Ursella Turks*, near relations to Kamikazes who drive for the biggest Turkish international trucking company, *Freewheeling Turks*, owner-drivers or those working for English companies driving trucks with British registrations at half English wages, *Zoomies*, Turkish guest workers in Germany who drive the cars they have bought in Germany home on German export Z-plates . . . one in every three never reaches home. *Tonkas*, a generic term for all Turkish trucks. *Rag 'eads* is the universal term for Arabs. And the journey is covered in kliks—kilometres. For British readers of the old school, eight kliks is roughly five miles.

Introduction

THE only way in is across 120 kilometres of virgin, untamed desert from the old British colonial fort, H4, in Jordan. The only way out at the other end is across 300 kilometres of fiercer desert, soft sand and howling shamals causing constant sand-storms; country no colonial settlers have ever tamed.

The trick is to crab across the desert, a remarkable driving manoeuvre: slightly jack-knife the tractor unit and tilt, flick the steering wheels in the right direction, then foot down, pedal to metal, and off like a bat out of hell. They move, these monster juggernauts, when they are unleashed; 120 kilometres to cover nonstop, sideways to slipstream the bow-wave of scorching dust. There is a sand temperature of 160° Farenheit outside, so pray to God that the air-conditioning doesn't pack up. Then 1,300 unremitting kilometres of the tapline, the world's most unforgettable road.

Driving the desert is like dirt-track

speedway riding a 46 ton monster with all 14 wheels going everywhichway simultaneously while wrenching, pitching and screaming to the other. Heaven help the careless driver who has failed to check his wheel nuts and torque-wrench them tight, a wheel can arrive at the other end with bolt holes doubled in size and worn to a perfect oval. Throw that wheel away, or you may not arrive at all. The road, when it comes, superheats tyres until they explode like firecrackers. It plays havoc with tyres, wheels, hubcasings, bearings, axles, transmissions, the fifth wheel joining the tractor to the trailer, havoc with the drivers' nerves. But hard driving is the only way to beat the desert.

When development engineers, living out their quiet, thoughtful lives in comfortable plastic offices at Scania, Volvo, Mack, MAN, Mercedes, Magirus Deutz, Daf, Erf, British Leyland, Ford, Dodge and every other great automotive engineering headquarters have nightmares they dream of drivers crabbing across deserts. They plead: "Straighten up and drive right, please. Slow it down, keep it steady." The drivers smile and say: "OK, guv, but it don't pay to 'ang about round 'ere, the rag'eads don't appreciate it, in fact, they don't like it at all."

Often chilling warnings are issued at border posts and military checkpoints: "Keep going. It is unsafe to stop with nomad tribesmen in the vicinity . . . do not go into tribal areas in the mountains, stay strictly on the marked route all the way."

From nowhere sinister black-clad bedouin will materialise, immobile and impassive on their camels. Also out of nowhere a Jeep-load of soldiers appear, automatic rifles brandished, mounted machine-gun trained on a loitering truck, they gesticulate wildly: keep moving, move on. And the other warning suddenly comes alive: "It is forbidden to stop or park within one kilometre of the pipeline. No excuses are valid." The soldiers show that they really mean it.

Across the vinyl-tiled corridors of those automotive works, in plusher offices than those of the designers, export sales managers smile and think: "Jesus, those boys can really burn 'em out, get a couple more containers of spares to the agents in Abu Dhabi, Riyadh, Dammam, Qatar and all points East. Keep driving, boys, its all down to the sheikhs, the rag'eads will pay, they've got plenty."

Today there is quite a lot of asphalt about, but ten billion dollars lays only a strip the equivalent of a strand of raven hair on a mile-wide linen sheet.

The enormity of the landscape, the unendingness of the sky, the silence, induce a feeling of curious unreality. The boys drive like speedway riders and like speedway riders they are travelling from nowhere to nowhere. They leave one dump to arrive at another having travelled through a dozen cassette tapes played on the cab hi-fi and a stream of conscious, subconscious, hypnotic, fantasising thought. The road runs straight as it is drawn on the map with no twists, turns or kinks; it is there before the eyes running to a perspective pinpoint in the far distance, nothing in sight, no hazards. Yet the route is splattered with mangled, burned-out wrecks. The accident rate is prolific, head-on collisions occur in statistically impossible conditions as sand-struck drivers run into each other.

A gruesome signpost in international colours and lettering points stright ahead "Qatar—500 kms", a thinner crossbar indi-

4

cates an intersection. Or does it? At the end of the crossbar where, in Europe or America, a vertical red-painted band would proclaim a cul-de-sac, here there is a pirate skull and crossbones—death either to the right or left. Drive straight ahead to stay alive, stray off the route and there is no chance of survival.

Suddenly, in the middle of nowhere, at the very heart of nothing, there appears an impossibly battered tin shack shanty. It emerges like a mirage through the swirling dust dancing and shimmering in the heat haze. The phut-phut of a two-stroke engine carries on the still, hot air. In the squalor surrounding the shack is a sign, all to familiar and all the more remarkable for that: "Coca-Cola—ice cold Coke".

The two-stroke works the refrigerator, but a hurricane lamp lights the shack at night; Coke quenches thirst at one-tenth the cost of pure drinking water.

Coke, Pepsi, Seven-Up, where the one goes the others are sure to follow: no other facets of Western culture have penetrated so deeply into the world's wildernesses. Coke, manufactured under franchise, has made more millionaires throughout the world than any other single product and also sustained more cults. Coke is a nectar, a celebration and a miracle under the blistering fire of a desert sun for heat-sapped "cowboys"—ice cold Coke when that relentless blaze in the sky has scorched the air in the deepest shade to 140°.

"Whoever brings Coke to a Godforsaken hole like this is either a nutter or a bloody genius."

To which a Coke salesman could properly reply: "Whoever brings a juggernaut to the same hellhole is either a nutter or a bloody genius."

So, if you are either very clever or mad, climb in the cab and come along . . . it is only a 14,000 mile ride.

But first, let us consider how it all began and how and why these huge articulated trucks and their idiosyncratic drivers ever came to be here in the first place. In the beginning, the fact that terra firma stretched from the continental Channel ports as far as Arabia and China had been ignored by freight forwarders. It was thought to be an impossible journey—the accepted way to the East was by sea. But when the Middle East boom began in real earnest tiny Arab ports along the Gulf coasts could not handle the traffic. Ships queued for 300 miles and waited up to two years to get into docks. Money was evaporating in the torrid heat of the Persian Gulf and Red Sea; ship owners chartered aircraft to fly out relief crews and bring home those exhausted by the tedium and boredom of month in, month out swinging round the anchor. Profits were being eaten away. Ashore, work was being held up because vital supplies were not getting through quickly enough, penalty clauses for late completion were being enforced, profits were, in fact, too often becoming losses.

Nothing galvanises the commercial world into exceptional action so much as a loss of profits and when it is a case of astronomical profits at risk the mood becomes one of Go! Go! Go! So the thinking became: "There is solid land all the way there, forget the mountains, forget the deserts, forget the vile, crippling winters and the intolerable heats of summer, get on the road and blast your way through."

By the same token, nothing galvanises enterprising truckers so much as the thought of the sniff of a big profit for themselves, so they did it—the hard way. Very few at first but increasing to a veritable host, the massive juggernauts began to roll along that Golden Road to Arabia. Nowadays a lot of people travel the road but that doesn't make it commonplace. Ed Hilary scaling Everest for the first time and Roger Bannister breaking the four-minute mile were sensational at the time. Today expeditions pop up the Himalayas every year and all world class milers clock under four minutes—but that still doesn't make it easy.

The first cowboys sorted out the problems, then they cracked the time barriers and delays, then they began to beat the ships.

One of the more remarkable aspects of the Gulf import boom was that as the inadequate docks clogged to a standstill, the governing authorities brought in teams of London and Liverpool dockers to shift the backlog; men who had become better known for their militancy and predilection for strike action than their working skills. They were paid fantastic wages, were not constricted by union rules and they cleared the docks a year ahead of the estimated time. Now huge container ships can be turned round in a couple of days. However, that has not solved the problems. The Arab mind is individualistic and often unfathomable operating in a labyrinthine tangle of misconceptions and taboos. The result is that now imported goods clear the docks and come to a full stop in the customs compound: it often takes six to eight months, sometimes longer, to get cargo out of Arab customs.

So the trucks have become even more vital giving a door-to-door customer service, customs clearance personally supervised by the drivers, and urgent consignments can be delivered on site in a fortnight to a month from date of despatch.

From necessity a great new trade route comparable with those classic routes of history such as the Hudson Bay trade, the East and West Indiamen and the wool clipper ships had been forged. Traders, especially in the early days, tended to regard their drivers in the guise of old-time merchant-adventurer captains like the ones who sailed from London, Liverpool and Bristol in the exhilarating days of the expanding Empire. Those men were astute sea-dogs of keen eye, sharp wits and polished profit consciousness who cast off on a favourable wind from their home ports to disappear over distant horizons for months and years on end. Until, one thrilling day, their sails appeared on the horizon and joyous, singing crowds assembled to meet them on the bustling quays and wonder at the exotic treasures crammed into their stout wooden holds. And sometimes they did not return and the Lutine Bell tolled in Lloyds of London to remark a disaster; there was no cast iron certainty in their adventures.

In a greatly shrunken world where little mystery was left, the modern-day merchant adventurers disappeared into a wilderness, a no-man's-land which civilization had skipped leaving a black hole in the world's communications system. They were alone and out of touch, they carried their sponsor's fortunes in their hands for better or for worse, for profit or disastrous loss. Then one day, in the manner of their predecessors, they loomed over the horizon in their trucks, sound and intact and the cash registers tinkled a merry tune of success and fortune.

In olden days black-coated scribes recorded cargoes and noted spoils in fine copperplate hands with quill pens while unsmiling Captain Blighs and similar Master Mariners built mansions on their share of the profits; the poor sailors got not a lot. But latterday scribes needed a computer rather than a quill with which to handle a vastly more complicated world. In the great ages of the buccaneers and adventurers, providing the ruling king or queen got a fair whack of the profits and the merchant princes got a good return, commerce was a simple, uncomplicated affair. Now it needed specialised, complex minds to cope with innovations like the EEC, rapacious Turks and squabbling Arabs and Jews, you couldn't just run them through, cut 'em down, give 'em a broadside, you had to deal with them on their own terms.

1

THEY do not look at all like truck drivers. Who ever saw an average group of truck drivers trotting along clutching prissy, expensive executive brief-cases? Beautiful brief-cases made from the finest leather with aluminium and stainless steel fittings and combination locks, made to grace the first class compartment of a train, or even the back seat of a Rolls, rather than the cab of a mud-spattered, oily juggernaut. And purses, they are carrying purses the size of a lady's handbag—truck drivers with handbags, preposterous!

Yet that is the way today's super-haul trucker must travel, with a brief-case packed full of vital documents and a purse crammed with hard currency—the essentials of international movement in this day and age.

So they climb from their cabs and hurry to the customs offices to clear papers, passports and pay taxes as quickly as possible. It is a routine which will take place dozens of times before they arrive at their destinations.

It is a rough, hard and dangerous road to the Middle East, classified as one of the most rigorous truck routes in the world. Yet the physical hazards of the road in the form of formidable mountains and deserts, fearful winter weather when the truck engine freezes solid while it is running and desert heat, when men die just by stepping out of the cab, is the least of their worries.

The constant, ever present fear is: is the paperwork right? As in most intrinsically exciting and dangerous undertakings, the real problems, the ones which cause the most trouble, are not necessarily the ones which seem most obvious. There is more danger in an office at a border than in the mountains with bandits.

Q is the quintessential letter of the alphabet along the golden road to Arabia. In its spoken singularity or written out large in blazing capitals—QUEUE—it dominates all strategy: life is spent avoiding, planning to avoid, plotting to cheat, scheming to dodge and being eventually stuck in a queue—a three, four, five day queue; a 10, 20, or 240 kilometre queue. Queues to defeat the bravest spirit, queues to temper the fieriest impatience, queues to gently die in.

14

As Q comes after P in the alphabet, so P for paperwork comes before Q for queue at international borders. Paperwork causes interminable hold-ups with delays which stretch to days and weeks at a time. Queues can begin as minor irritations in civilised West Germany and culminate as nerve-searing frustrations in the heat, dust and squalor of disorganised Middle Eastern countries. The driver is the sharp end of the business but he is a blunt instrument without a paper-wizard backing him up at home.

Which is where the computer scribe and the ubiquitous brief-case become important. That brief-case contains a portfolio of documents any one of which, if it were incorrectly made out, could bring the journey to an abrupt end at any point along the route. A mistake could—and it has often happened—result in the total loss of truck, trailer and cargo. So it needs a sharp brain to organise the paperwork before a wheel is turned.

Astran's Ewe Ploog is such a man who troubled to find his way around the Common Market paperchase and has never looked back. He plays the paper game with a relish that only a true-born German could. All the niceties and finesses appeal to his highly-tuned Teutonic mind but he is an untypical German, slim, twinkling-eyed and full of laughs—he can afford to laugh where others can't.

A new client, hard-headed and impatient, but innocent of the complexities and mysteries of Brussels-style red-tape and the Arab bureaucracy, telephones to say: "I've got a rush consignment for the Gulf and I want it there quick. Will you shift it for me? I'll leave it to you."

"Yes," says Mr. Ploog, "but first we must check your documents to see if they are right . . ."

"Of course they'll be right, I've been in this game man and boy and I didn't get where I am making mistakes."

"Good, then we'll have to get the documents legalised."

"Legalised, of course they'll be legal, we're not a bunch of fly-by-night crooks." There is a touch of outrage in his voice.

"That's fine," the patient Ploog continues, "so there will be no trouble in obtaining a certificate of origin of each item in the consignment."

"The stuff originates here, I've manufactured it."

"Well, all you need to do then is to get it authenticated, take it to your local Chamber of Trade and have each item sworn, certified and stamped by them."

"The lot? Each individual item? What a nonsense."

"Yes, the lot. Then get a separate certificate of origin written in Arabic and English and we will take that to the Arab—British Chamber of Trade to be sworn, certified and stamped."

"Written in Arabic? You must be joking."

"Yes, I'm afraid so. Then send your documents to us and we will take both sets to the embassy of the country of destination for separate swearing and stamping so that customs at the other end will release the consignment on arrival."

"That's bloody dozens of forms."

"And it's only the beginning," Ploog gently explains, "next you must swear that the goods are not of Israeli origin, nor do they contain materials or parts of Israeli origin."

"I've just eaten a Jaffa orange, do you think that will wreck the deal?" the client asks.

"Don't leave the pips in the container," Ploog advises and he continues, "conserve

17

your strength because you will now have to complete the TIR and CMR forms."

"What on earth are they? Intelligence agencies?"

"They are Tourists International Routiers and the Contrat de Transport de Merchandise par Route, and both are vital," says Ploog.

"French!" the client exclaims. "Trust the bloody Frogs to get a sticky finger in the pie, I'll bet they're taking a cut for themselves to bolster their hauliers like they do their farmers."

"Take the CMR form first," Ploog advises, "this is the International Consignment Note which reads, 'This carriage is subject, notwithstanding any clause to the contrary, to the Convention of the Contract for the International Carriage of Goods by Road (CMR).' From the French—Convention Relative au Contrat de Transport de Merchandise par Route—CMR. All 24 sections must be completed."

"Sounds like a day's work."

"As follows: 1. Sender (name, address, country) 2. Consignee (Name, address, country) 3. Place of delivery (Place, country) 4. Place and date of taking over goods (Place,

18

date) 5. Documents attached. 6. Marks and numbers. 7. Numbers of packages.

"Still with me, eh? 8. Method of packing. 9. Nature of goods. 10. Statistical number. 11. Gross weight in Kg. 12. Volume in M3 . . ."

"How many more? I'm losing count."

"Half way there. 13. Senders instructions. 14. Instructions as to payment for carriage, carriage paid, carriage forward. 15. Cash on delivery. 16. Carrier (Name, address, country) 17. Successive carriers (Name, address, country) 18. Carriers reservations and observations . . ."

"Observations, that's nice. Are there any limitations on the type of observation you can make? I could think of a few," the client comments.

"Be patient, we're coming to the end, the end of this form, that is. 19. Special agreements. 20. To be paid by: Sender, currency, consignee carriage charges, deductions, supplementary charges, other charges. Established in . . . 22, 23, 24, signature and stamps of sender, carrier and consignee. That's it for the CMR, the TIR form must match perfectly."

"But naturally—unmatched forms, God

forbid, worse than wearing brown boots with white tie and tails," customer responds.

Ploog recovers his breath and explains further: "It is vital that the CMR and TIR forms are identical. It's no use the CMR stating 735 items and, by mistake, the TIR listing 734, we have had loads turned back for just that kind of typing error. "

"Ah, well, I'll leave you to it." The client is losing patience.

"But that's not all, there must be a complete customs declaration on every item, in duplicate, and a copy of that must be sent to the Department of Trade for the monthly and annual statistics on imports and exports . . ."

The client by now is mumbling: "It seems an awful lot of form filling just to send a simple cargo to a new customer in the Gulf. I want to send him the goods, not write a book about it."

With forced cheerfulness Ploog tells him: "So far those forms have only got us through Europe. Now you will need a full cargo manifest for the Arab countries and that will have to be duplicated in Arabic."

Exasperated, the client protests: "But they've got the other CMR form and all those certificates of origin, what do they need a manifest for?"

"The cargo manifest is to verify the CMR form."

"Let me get this straight. You fill in umpteen forms, get them certified three times and stamped and then you get another set of forms and duplicate them just to prove that the first lot have been properly certified? This could go on for ever. It could go on until we are all certified insane."

"It probably will," says Ploog.

And he adds: "Oh, by the way, you'll also need a Certificate of Shipment for the customs with details of the ferry, the time and numbers of the trailer and truck . . ."

Click . . . brrrrrrrrrrrrrrrr.

"He's gone," Ploog smiles in sympathy with the departed client's understandable irritation, and before I had time to tell him that if his cargo is heavier or longer than the regulations permit, he'll also need an exceptional load certificate. Still, I don't want to put him off any more than I have done already."

What Ploog didn't mention as well was that if he failed to include a document stating: "To whom it may concern: we hereby certify that this company, Astran International Limited, and the vehicle carrying the cargo mentioned below is not of an Israeli concern and is not mentioned on the Arab blacklist. The vehicle is not scheduled to call at any Israeli port en route to its destination," the whole shooting match might as well stay at home.

The man with the executive brief-case and purse in the customs at Dover is a bit special too, he needs to be to handle the paperwork, money, diplomacy, banking, repairs and driving as well. On some workaday afternoon he will have slipped from the crush of wage-slaves hurrying along the road outside an unremarkable transport depot to become a man apart in a very different life.

At the depot he will collect his brief-case and money, usually about £2,000, depending on how far he is going, in sterling, dollars, Deutschmarks rather than travellers' cheques which can be difficult to change on- the remote back roads of Europe and Asia and will be too costly at border banks.

His truck, spruced, polished and slick as an air hostess at the beginning of a flight, will be waiting, trim shining, mirrors glistening, chrome agleam but geared to run more than half way round the globe. He will listen with ears acutely tuned to each and every sound within and without the vehicle, he will test and sense the feel of clutch, gears, accelerator, air pressure, brakes, air-conditioning unit and every device built into the complex assembly. His ears will stay acutely attuned for miles until the rhythms of the machine match those in his mind.

He will be thinking several thousand miles ahead for "when the driving really starts" with the technicalities of potential disaster much in mind. He will tell you in a stream of semi-conscious thought: "You don't know how easy it is to lose your brakes . . . on a big mountain that can happen in two seconds . . . and you burn 'em out . . . the brake shoes like on an ordinary car get hot and when they get hot they go soft . . . then you get brake fade and all that . . . once you've lost 'em you can't get 'em back, you'll never get 'em back, it's impossible . . .

"Then you're rollin' and nothing will stop you . . . when you get to a certain speed in a truck you can't change down, it won't go in the gear . . . it will only go in gear when the revs are in the green section anyway, so if you try to change when you're rollin' all you do is end up in neutral and roll faster, free-wheeling . . . in Britain we have a three line braking system so the dead man's handle operates the tractor and the trailer, on the Continent with motors like the Magirus Deutz the dead man's only works on the trailer, which is good because it means that on a big mountain you can alternate the brakes . . . give a touch of the dead man's, then a touch of the foot brake, which is bloody good because you're never overheating all the brakes at once . . . plus you've got the exhauster . . . which is the exhaust brake . . . a button on the floor by the clutch or accelerator . . . you put your heel on it and it shuts off the manifold and blows the gasses back into the engine . . . it retards the engine . . . you need a lowish sort of gear and a lot of revs, the more revs you've got, the better it brakes . . . that's very good on a big V10 or V12 when you've got two banks of five or six . . . it's not so effective on a straight six . . . but the big American trucks and straight sixes have a Jake brake . . . the Jake brake is a similar principle to an exhauster but better on straight sixes . . . the Yanks use it a lot because a lot of American trucks don't have braking on the front axle . . . but once one of these things starts rollin' there ain't nothing you can do about it . . . you head it over the side and get out . . . jump . . . unless you want to go down with it, like a captain with his ship . . . Dave Anderson lost his brakes on a Turkish mountain, he tried to stop by running into the concrete posts at the side of the road . . . he knocked three miles of posts down, then he was dead lucky because the hill stopped going down and began going up . . ."

So the *feel* of brakes, exhausters and so on, the actual sense of *rightness* about the vehicle, is essential if the trip is to be accomplished with any degree of peace of mind. A driver worried about his machine is a danger to himself and the public. There is, too, apprehension of the consequences of failure, not the all too obvious final consequence which is ever present, but the hassle of accident. John Martin was on that mountain when Dave Anderson lost his brakes: "That hill suddenly going up saved him. But in those countries you pay for whatever damage you do. You pay for damage to people and property or they won't let you leave. You don't swap names and addresses and show insurance certificates, you pay or stay—concrete posts come expensive anywhere, so it costs plenty. You make sure in your own mind that every little thing is right and working properly. Only a bloody fool goes into the mountains with a doubt in his mind. Some bloody fools do and you see them splattered at the bottom of ravines all the way along the route."

Looking good, they say in the yard, the truck smart and purposeful, the paperwork clipped and neat, engineering and administrative expertise combined to efficiency. But the driver's eyes can scan everything and he might nit-pick. Lingering in half-thoughts in the recesses of his mind are vague memories of delays, excruciating frustrations of inexplicable hold-ups and arguments in incomprehensible languages because of some minor error or mechanical fault.

A niggle in England can escalate to a crisis at any of the 48 customs points encountered en route; a faulty document, a lack of sufficient ready cash, a mechanical failure has frequently resulted in the total loss of half a million pounds' worth of cargo, tractor and trailer—just gone and irrecoverable.

The sign on the back of the trailer and truck—TIR painted in white on a blue background—marks the vehicle as one apart from run of the mill local traffic. It means that this is an international truck running under the Tourists International Routiers convention and agreements and, as such, entitled to the privileges of those agreements at the customs points of all countries which are signatories to them.

The sign certifies that the cargo will have been checked and sealed by the customs at its point of departure and, providing that the seals remain intact and there are no signs of interference, no further customs inspection will be necessary en route. The TIR forms will be accepted as proof of the cargo and all matters relating to it.

In the case of "tilts"—tarpaulin covered trailers—TIR tapes (strong wires) are threaded through rings in the tarpaulin and matching eyelets welded to the trailer sides. The vertical tapes from the top of the back of the trailer, where the flap opens to allow access, are connected to the horizontal wire which runs round the base of the trailer and these wires are joined in the middle at the back and sealed with a lead customs "plumb". As long as that plumb is intact and the wires unbroken, the cargo cannot have been interfered with.

The drivers are known as TIR men as a short way of saying international drivers: TIR is a badge of pride, it shows that the driver knows his way around and a little bit about the job.

One other distinguishing mark sets the driver a further degree apart, a squat oblong box on top of the cab—the air-conditioning unit which almost certainly means that he is a "Middle Easter".

The pull to the ferry port, Hull, Felixstowe, Harwich, Dover, Folkestone, Newhaven or wherever it may be, is a local trip and doesn't really count. Some companies, like Astran, only license their trucks to run overseas because they do not think that travelling 30 miles on British roads every five or six weeks in a 14,000 mile journey warrants the hundreds of pounds per vehicle it would cost in British tax. So they run their trailers to the ferry termini using British taxed tractor units for the short haul to the docks where the Middle East unit takes over for the Big Pull to the Gulf.

For some, however, the local trip can have its excitements. When the great oil boom mushroomed virtually overnight and desert sheikhs, awakening from centuries of sleep and indifference to their fellow mankind, rushed like so many sons of Croesus and Midas to buy up the world, what they needed most of all was heavy mechanical equipment to manipulate the deserts, sand dunes and salt-flats of their unlovely homelands to make them habitable. They cried out for any "heavy gear" that would push, pull, dig, level, excavate, fill in, grade or carry. Anybody who had an earthmover in the Middle East in those days had a fortune at his fingertips.

Michael Pearce had delivered a couple of trucks to Qatar and knew the profit there could be in it so he recruited some friends "to do themselves a bit of good" in the business and make a quick killing. He arranged with Munirul Hasan, a Pakistani entrepreneur established in Qatar, to buy in England three battered, secondhand TK Bedford trucks, an ERF and a Seddon with a big Cummins engine in it, load them with Bray shovels, diggers and similar equipment and drive them down to the Gulf.

It was an omen of what was to come when one of the Bedfords which Mike had just collected from the dealer burst into flames on the hill outside Hemel Hempstead and he had to jump for his life. Nevertheless, they assembled their shabby seen-better-days fleet and parked it ready for an early departure in the big car park outside the Robin Hood Hotel, in Clacton.

On Sunday morning wives and girl-friends—and in one case, both—gathered in the pub for a tearful goodbye. All the dramas of a fond farewell were duly enacted, hands wrung, backs slapped, "good lucks" and "take cares" properly spoken before the convoy set off for Felixstowe, 25 miles up the coast, to catch the ferry on the first stage of its epic 7,000 miles expedition.

Four miles from the pub the police were waiting and stopped them to examine the vehicles—and the drivers. The law complained about the vehicles' tyres, brakes, lights and general mechanical condition; they further complained that the heavy diggers and shovels "seemed likely to fall through the trailer bottoms"; they found fault too with the documentation which, to a policeman's eye, "looked funny, not quite genuine"; finally the police complained that only two of the four drivers in the convoy had valid

Heavy Goods Vehicle Driver licences and furthermore one of those without such a licence was also banned for three years from driving anything. So there, at Weeley Bridge, the excursion came to a premature stop with 6,996 miles still to go.

Back in the Robin Hood before the farewell party had even begun to think of breaking up, the sardonic publican, Lew, said: "That was a bit quickish, you haven't even had time to get a decent suntan."

"Some rotten bastard must have shopped us," said the bemused Mike.

2

FERRYBOATS are very special to TIR truckers. They lend a suitable air of occasion to setting out on a long trip and bring down the curtain on coming home. However, this short ferry trip can cause a measure of bizarre confusion later in the trip.

Down in the wild country beyond Adana, in southern Turkey, where ungovernable Kurds, armed to the teeth, still freely roam the mountains, five grizzled ancients squatting round the stewpot nursing their hookah pipes refuse to believe that the strange trucks are British and have driven from England. A child's atlas is produced to prove their argument and they point to the English Channel. With smiles and much merriment they say through the interpreter: "There is sea between Inglisi and the rest, how can you drive such machines across the sea?" To these men of the mountains that is an end of the matter, notwithstanding the fact that Turkey itself runs some of the finest ferries in the world, the limits of their horizon are the surrounding mountain peaks . . .

The ferry is the break with normality, the one place where the public comes face to face with the super-haul men and their intimidating vehicles—which look so much more enormous in the confines of a ship's hold than on the open road. When the juggernauts have been gulped through the great whale-jaw doors of the ship to squat in its belly, with private cars clustering like voracious hooded crows round a sheep's carcass, the action aboard begins in earnest. The human content of the vehicles is sucked up narrow companionways and passages into the digestive system of the vessel where their currency can be ingested at breakneck speed in bars, duty-free shops, dining saloons, casinos, discos and one-armed bandit areas. The ferry profit lies in this activity.

The TIR truckers keep themselves apart. They receive special treatment because they travel regularly and pay a great deal of money to do so. On the return journey they will be given access to the crew's bathrooms, some ships have special clubs for them knowing that they need sleep and rest.

The Middle East driver, who has made the

trip more times than he cares to remember, comments with a smile: "The warning notices say, 'Keep clear of the propellors,' they should hang one over the bars saying, 'Keep clear of the wankers.' The propellors can't get at you, the wankers can."

He warns: "Watch out for 'First Trippers' wearing new Dutch clogs and sunglasses. Somebody has told them that's the proper gear for the job, so they buy the shoes and the shades and set themselves up as desert drivers when the nearest they've ever come to it is watching Peter O'Toole in Lawrence of Arabia at the local Odeon cinema."

Everybody has to be a "First Tripper" sometime but how they behave on that testing introduction often determines how they will succeed later. Experienced drivers are willing to help beginners, but only those who help themselves; there is not much room for manoeuvre along this road, nor is there time to spare. In spite of the weeks of waiting and hanging about, which the job entails, curiously, every minute counts.

The old hand adds: "Particularly watch the ones who are all big talk and buying beer like the brewery was going bust tomorrow. You'll soon see them parked in a lay-by in Belgium numbed out of their minds and sleeping it off."

Experienced drivers have a couple of glasses then get their heads down—they know the score and sleep comes precious.

"I'm turning in," the old hand says, "remember, steer clear of the wankers, most of them couldn't drive a nail with a club hammer let alone a big articulated truck."

They form a curious and diverse group, the regular ferry travellers, with accents from every region and class and attitudes from the extrovert to the downright secretive.

In the corner, the quiet man says nothing and seems to see nobody except for the slightest acknowledgement for recognised friends. A countryman, a strangely soft and gentle character in a raucous company, he is not a man for strangers. His attitude is partly natural reticence and partly wariness. He drives "tricky loads"—live animals—and no cargo is more emotive. Livestock trucks cannot be disguised, they have a distinctive, unmistakable look about them: this man has spent his working life being hounded by animal protection societies and charities, and there is no fiercer creature to be found than an animal protectionist at bay. They have ambushed his truck, laid siege to his cabin aboard ship, chased him across the roads of Europe and sabotaged his vehicle—sometimes to the acute distress of the animals inside.

It doesn't deter him, he runs a good firm and the ferry crew help him. His truck is always stowed amidships where there is least movement. On bad crossings he never leaves his charges, if the weather blows up during the voyage, the crew call him. He takes little time off and will not let anybody else drive his rig. "Well, they don't understand animals, do they? Can't be expected to," he explains in his soft, burred accent. "I've got a load of pedigree boars in this time, for the south of Italy, some beauties among 'em, four on 'em sold for £11,000 apiece, rest of 'em fetched £4,000-£5,000 each. Lovely beasts, for a breedin' farm down there. Should be a nice run."

There are other emotive and volatile cargoes on the car deck as well, modern cargoes which would confound John Masefield's sea-going imagination in their variety: tankers of explosive fuels, lethal gas and toxic chemicals which need to be driven by men of infinite care and skill and, by contrast, refrigerators filled with 20 tons of ice cream for the children and families of a sunbaked sheikhdom in the desert. Cargoes reflecting every facet of human life; the software and the hardware. And their destinations paralle Masefield in stretching the imagination. They extend from the capitals of Europe to places like Istanbul, Ankara, Amman, Baghdad, Basrah, Teheran, Kuwait, Riyadh, Dammam, Doha, Abu Dhabi, Jiddah, Muscat—the magic of the ferry is that it is the gateway to the world not just, as once they claimed, the gateway to the Continent.

3

FERRIES arrive in Belgium which is useful for Middle Easters because it is the nearest point to Aachen and access to the German autobahn network and a flying start across Europe. But nobody wants to remember Belgium, it is the most forgettable of all countries. And the most boring.

They speak two languages in Belgium, the Flemish speak Dutch and the Walloons speak French, probably because neither group can bear to listen to the other. On top of that they have in Brussels, capital of the country and headquarters of the EEC, the undoubted bumph metropolis of Europe. Nine-tenths of the documents in the truckers' executive brief-cases originate in Brussels and the problems that they, or the lack of them, cause are legion.

This paperwork has, in fact, created a whole new industry—but not under the auspices of the Brussels bureaucracy. This is a slightly less formal affair and its products are known universally along the line as

38

"moodies" and "Micky Mouse" papers. A lot of drivers travel on moodies or Micky Mouse documents when they find official ones difficult to obtain. These are forgeries the quality of which can vary from the brilliant to the ludicrous. A Yugoslav official held a "permit" to the light and declared: "Nix good. We have not yet started printing our permits on Basildon Bond paper."

Forged permits are available for all purposes and countries. The more permits and documents Brussels produces, the more the moody boys rejoice, they can always produce a near perfect facsimile.

Maybe it is the way you arrive in Belgium which colours the view of the country. The way in is by Ostend or Zeebrugge, usually in the early hours of the morning. Early morning is a godless time at any port: the dockside cranes are dead, shunting engines quiet and stilled, office windows blank. Reflections of lights shimmer in black, oily waters—it is as if the last man to go home hours earlier had forgotten to switch them off.

This is a dismal time, you are cold from sleep half fulfilled and relinquished too soon. A trail of bright, red tail-lights rolls from the ship's car-decks to stretch in a glowing stream along an approach road as a reminder that life goes on despite the depression in the pit of the stomach emanating from some ill defined source. What is the time? Is it an hour on or an hour off? Is it the same time? Does it matter?

An hour into Belgium there comes the first indication that trip 5113 will be a bastard run. Suddenly it has the smell and taste of trouble about it—quite literally, since diesel where it shouldn't be leaves an unpleasant smell about the hands and penetrates the taste buds. Trevor Long's truck, Lavinia, has blown a diesel pipe. She is a Scania III and called Lavinia because she is recognised as a perfect gentlewoman who has purred her way through 500,000 kilometres over mountain and desert without complaint. She has shown the fortitude, unflappability and strength of character associated with gentlewomen. Now she has blown a diesel pipe. It is not a big thing but it is annoying and something that the most searching servicing cannot reveal. A thin pipe pumping oil at the phenomenal pressure of 3,000 lbs per square inch year in year out for hundreds of thousands of miles is entitled sometime to give up the ghost.

The procedure is simple, jack up the cab

and look for the leak; put the jack handle into the hydraulic pump on the chassis under the rear of the cab and pump, gradually the whole cab tilts forward to expose the engine. Diesel cleans all metal and paint it touches so the gleaming area on the cylinder block under the pipe shows which one it is. Unbolt the old one, bend the spare to shape, which can be a tricky job in the wet and dark and bolt on the new one. This is simple enough, but knowing what has gone wrong is the important thing and that is largely a matter of the driver's instinctive diagnostic ability.

The usual rule of the road is that breakdowns happen at the worst possible time and worst possible place, so this is an exception in that it happens on the open road with adequate parking conveniently close. Which was not the case when Chris Bedder and John Martin broke down in Belgium and caused minor havoc.

They had collected a Belgium-built vehicle for delivery to Oman. This was an Inco-Mol geophysical vehicle—a massive machine seldom seen by the public since they usually work in remote areas far from public roads. These monsters are built to work the roughest terrain, cross impassable deserts and

41

climb Matterhorn-class mountains, consequently they are not very handy on a busy highway. This brute had five-feet diameter Caterpillar wheels, six-wheel drive, a 480 hp Deutz engine under a bonnet so long that it really needed a lookout posted on the front. It was designed with twelve wheels but with all of them fitted it was too wide to fit any road or pass through any border control en route to Oman, so a vertical spindle had been welded on the back and the extra wheels stowed on that for transit. Zealous engineers had also equipped the vehicle with several sophisticated safety devices which, well intentioned and clever as they were, proved a pain in the neck at the start of its journey East.

Circumstances combined so that Chris and John found themselves driving the monster into the centre of Brussels at the beginning of the city's rush hour. Brussels has an extensive and heavily used tramway system. At 4.30 in the afternoon they stalled the contraption in the middle of the tram tracks straddling a triple junction. Soon trams were forming long crocodiles in every direction and blocking all the intersections but the geophysical wouldn't re-start. After twenty minutes, she gave a splutter of life and jerked 20 yards to what seemed to be a lay-by, then she cut dead again. The lay-by was, in fact, the city's main taxi rank and a dozen cabs were trapped in it. By now there was utter confusion and John comments: "It was the only time I ever saw anybody come even half alive in Belgium. They were actually getting quite agitated."

In the middle of the chaos Chris said: "I'm hungry, let's go get a bite to eat."

John replied: "*Eat!* At a time like this? You must be a raving lunatic." But still the geophysical would not budge.

Angry police arrived and the Brussels cabbies were getting quite bad tempered, so John reconsidered. "Eat," he said, "that's not a bad idea, let's go before they lynch us."

They told the chief policeman that they were going to seek help from head office, jumped into an untrapped cab cruising the streets and instructed the driver: "Eats. Good grub. Nix rubbish. Quiet. Comprenez?"

The restaurant was set in a clump of trees close by the World Exhibition site. They had to ring the doorbell to gain admission. A footman let them in. Through the vestibule they glimpsed a marble hall, on a table in the middle lay a whole roast pig with an apple in its mouth and ruffled white frills round its neck. The table was piled with lobsters, a dozen dishes in aspic, fraise du bois—there was a distinct touch of class about the place.

The two Englishmen were in their driving gear, slacks, sandals, flash shirts, a bit loud but not scruffy, nobody minded. The wine waiter recommended "a special from the French end of the Rhine valley, a private chateau, very fine".

John recalls: "It was a king of a wine, magnificent. We settled for fresh lobster soup and I couldn't resist a Dover sole. A Dover sole in Brussels, it eased the homesickness."

A party arrived at the next table apologising for being so late. In English the diplomat hosting the party explained to the head waiter: "There are the most terrible traffic jams in the city. An enormous machine has broken down and the drivers have disappeared, the police are searching the city for them."

John summoned the wine waiter and told him: "I think we'll have another bottle of that plonk, we might be here for some time."

Later, by telephone they established that the trouble with the machine was probably a shut-off valve. Inco-Mol had tried to make it Arab proof, since Arabs are inclined to run all machinery full belt until it burns out. They had installed a fail-safe valve to stop the engine if it overheated; it was working a little too zealously and she was cutting dead as soon as she warmed up.

Back at the vehicle they told the police guard: "Engineers, come repair machine, OK?" Then they disconnected the faulty valve, asked the guard if the drivers had been found yet, climbed in "to test", started up and roared off into the night.

In those days the route TIR trucks had to take dropped into the centre of Brussels, the by-pass flyover was not strong enough at that time to take their weight; so light traffic flew past the city while the heavy mob dropped in to tangle with commuter traffic. It caused considerable confusion and not a little annoyance, for truckers actually hate cities and the traffic jams they know they create in such places. They like a simple life and a clear road.

With Brussels thankfully cut out of the drive by new autobahns, the trip through Belgium is straight, pedal-to-metal stuff until Walli Stop is reached. Walli Stop is the first of the many intelligence posts along the route, a place where those coming back stop to relay what is going on down the road and those going out stop to listen. It is part of a grapevine which extends 7,000 miles through 17 countries and is one of the more inexplicable mysteries of communications since whatever happens at one end of the line, a fortnight away in driving time, somehow manages to reach the other end in a couple of days. It may get garbled but the information is often accurate enough to be useful.

The name originated from Walli who used to run the place in the early days. The drivers got to know him so it became "Walli Stop" which is now emblazoned in white wrought iron on the outer wall of the cafe.

Today there is talk of snow in Rumania and Bulgaria which—hopefully—must be nonsense. The accepted wisdom of the job is that snow doesn't fall until January or February and this is November. You don't listen to alarmist talk, particularly if you have forgotten your snow chains.

Then the Sex Machine arrives with his new woman which disturbs a number of people because she was quite a disturbing lady. She is a Yorkshire lass of chunky build, with square features framed by short, dark, well-cut hair in a deceptively casual style. But her most immediately striking attributes are her eyes, which are very lively and full of good humour to match her smile. In her trucking gear she looks unisex until she moves with surprising feminine grace and lightness revealing a plenitude of young womanhood.

What disturbs the other drivers is that the Sex Machine always manages to pull extraordinary girls with special attributes and flaunt them in front of others who are less fortunate. It is pure jealousy.

"Get the grub, love," says the Sex Machine with the casual assurance of a man who feels himself fully in command of the situation, "Two eggs, bacon, chips, coffee, two sugars."

He knows the impression he is creating and the thoughts in every other driver's head so, without looking up from his copy of the *Sun*, page three, he says: "And get this, she bloody drives as well. She's got her actual HGV licence, now beat that."

There was clearly no beating it so the driver from Birmingham voices the feelings of the rest when he says: "You jammy sod."

"Where y'going, anyway?" he adds.

"Baghdad," the Sex Machine announces triumphantly.

"Baghdad!" the Birmingham driver expostulates with contempt, "that's your third Baghdad in a row. How come you get all these bloody locals while we get the Abu Dhabis and Dohas? Have you been creeping again? Kissing the boss's arse?"

After his meal, the Sex Machine rubs it in. He commands the girl: "Bring the truck round, love, we'd better make a move." They leave with him sitting in the passenger seat, his feet on the dashboard, a cigar between his lips and reading *Penthouse*. "Makes you want to throw up," says the driver from Birmingham.

Germans know all about automobiles, more so even than do the Americans. They have organised and catered for them in ways which they have perfected and refined since Hitler constructed the autobahns and built a million or more beetle Volkswagens to run up and down them. They have made motoring in the Fatherland easy and comfortable, though possibly a little compartmentalised.

Germans like a place for everything and everything in its place, so Teutonic logic dictates that commercial vehicles are strictly for business and private cars essentially for pleasure. Thus since Monday to Friday are days ordained for toil and Saturday and Sunday days decreed for holidaymaking it follows that no commercial vehicles should be allowed out on holiday days. They ban heavy goods vehicles from the roads on the latter days which means that many truck drivers find themselves "weekended" at German borders or in lay-bys, unable to move from Friday evening until Sunday midnight—much to their chagrin and the delight of the population. This regulation takes half-a-million juggernauts off the highways for an unwelcomed rest. Officially the reason is to clear the highways for holiday traffic, particularly during summer months—which seems extreme considering the size and capacity of the road system.

Extreme, that is, until you witness the volume of traffic a weekend produces all over Germany and realise that no German driver would consider going anywhere unless it can be reached at 120 mph in a family saloon and 150 mph in a turbo Porsche. And a weekend runabout isn't any fun at all without a monumental multi-car pile-up along the way.

If you ever mistakenly imagined that the disciplined German nation is drilled to behave well on the roads, disabuse yourself of that false notion. An autobahn in poor weather produces as much motorway madness as anywhere else in the world but at twice the speed. They knock over cars faster than skittles in a 10-lane, 10-pin bowling alley on a big match night. It is just as bad as Britain, France, Italy and Spain except that the Germans lift the mangled victims from the wreckage faster with helicopter blood-wagons and clean up the mess quicker.

However, in ordinary conditions the great roads are so easy to drive on that you can actually relax and enjoy the scenery. There are truly dramatic roads with such features as the great bridge spanning the Mosel Valley, towering high above matchbox mansions with ribbon-thin rivers and roads tracing silver streaks across variegated fields, orchards and vineyards. The Germans put their wealth into splendid mansions and opulent villas which enhance the views.

But amid their plenty and wellbeing these Germans create traps for the unwary motorist. If you wish to enjoy the advantages of the German lifestyle then you must pass their initiation tests: like keeping an eye open to spot the hovering helicopter sitting directly above you and checking your speed.

Unexpectedly: "Polizi—STOP!

"What's the problem?"

"Speedink."

"Rubbish. How do you know? There's been nobody behind me for hours. Anyway, I wasn't speeding at all."

Unsmiling, the policeman points skywards and a persistent chop, chopper noise tells that your number has been called—pay up and smile.

The story goes that, in the days when British drivers treated German laws in a cavalier fashion, preferring to pay up and carry on, those doyens of the run, Dick Snow, Geoff Frost and Georgie White, were all pulled in together for speeding. The police officer held them at the roadside and summoned his superior.

The local police chief, delighted that his subordinates had at one swoop pulled off the remarkable coup of grabbing three of these troublesome British truckers who so plagued his life, rushed to the scene to supervise operations and crow over their downfall. He spoke good English and thought he knew a lot about the baffling British sense of humour. The arresting officer told him that the culprits were called Snow, Vhite and Frost.

"Snow, Vhite, Frost," the police chief mused. Then he stopped. "Snow Vhite Frost," he murmured reflectively and the light of realisation dawned in his eyes.

"Snow, Vhite, Frost," he bellowed in triumph, "they're yoking, arrest them."

But the far more serious obstacles for drivers to negotiate and overcome in the Fatherland had come in places such as the Reeperbahn in Hamburg; Ludwigstrasser in Hanover; certain very fruity byways in Frankfurt, West Berlin and Munich; and innumerable beer festivals, with Oktoberfest in Munich the Beecher's Brook of the German Grand National debauchery course. Some drivers, they say, have a season ticket to the fleshpots stamped on their transit permits.

A car is a strong male aphrodisiac and a truck is an immensely more powerful stimulant for a man through its sheer size, power and mystique. The driver, the loner in the high cab looking down on nyloned knees and thighs in passing saloons, is distanced from womankind by the very macho image of long distance trucking. He is the man of mystery bound for faraway places with strange sounding names, a king in a tough, hard talking, hard drinking, hard living industry. What further isolates him is his travelling nature. Truckers get randy in their isolation, it is something the general ambience of the business induces. But randy travelling Albions are often thrown off course by the German attitude to sex, it is too easy and comes on a plate.

Sex on offer German fashion certainly threw two drivers who are known by their nicknames Broomstick and Tombstone. They arrived in Frankfurt with a pocketful of Deutschmarks and other currencies on their way to Doha. "About two-and-a-half thousand quids between 'em," the grapevine intelligence had it.

Broomstick was so called because he was a thin, wiry, rather emaciated character, and Tombstone because during an unfortunate altercation outside a rowdy hostelry somebody had dropped a paving stone on his face. "Christ, I thought they'd buried you when I saw you with that on your kisser," commented a fighting friend. The two of them were no angels, they stopped in Frankfurt looking for fun, sex and beer and hang the consequences. In that city there is no lack of opportunity for lads on the loose.

It ought to be explained that German whores are in a class apart. Without doubt they are the finest looking girls of their species to be found anywhere. Each one walks in the proud manner of a graduate of the Lucy Clayton School of Fashion and Modelling. They are classy, expensive dressers wearing nothing but the latest fashion in the way its designer visualised it should be worn and displaying the gear to its utmost sexiness. Buying a German whore is like buying a living Vogue fashion plate. They look so good and beautifully turned out that it is difficult to recognise them as whores. So the conversation in the bar goes:

"Is she on the game?"

"She can't be, never."

"I'll bet she is, she wouldn't be here if she weren't."

"Bollocks, look at the gear she's wearing, and that bloody hair-do has cost a week's wages."

"Well, ask her. Hold your glass up and wave it at her, if she comes over, she's on the game, if she doesn't, she isn't and you were only being sociable."

But a whore is a whore the whole world over no matter how good she looks and she does not have gold for a heart, she has a cash register.

Broomstick was a fast car freak which proved to be his downfall. He saw this girl patrolling in a Ferrari, a brilliant red and gleaming car, and that was good enough for him. The car was magnificent, the girl had to be a cracker. If she was good enough to be able to afford a car like that she must be a bit special. What he really wanted was a ride in the car, if he had treated her like a taxi there would have been no trouble.

Tombstone, on the other hand, just liked the girls. It was his first trip abroad apart from the Costa Brava and Marjorca and he could not believe the extraordinary display of available talent paraded before his bulging eyes. For a time he sat like the proverbial street urchin with his nose pressed to the cakeshop window—until he pinched himself into action.

The two met again in their hotel room in the waning hours of the early morning. Broomstick returned with his Ferrari floozie, one of her companions and a couple of bottles of champagne, which doesn't come cheap in Germany, to discover that Tombstone had not been playing a male version of Cinderella toasting her toes by the kitchen fire. He, too, was organised en famille with two exceedingly decorative companions and a case of champers.

So the bubbly sparkled and the fun flowed, and flowed and flowed again until it collapsed in an exhausted, bedraggled heap on the giant beds they provide in German Rasthauses.

At breakfast, round about two o'clock the following afternoon, Broomstick asked: "Got any dough with you, Tombstone I must have left mine in the room?"

"I must have left mine there too," said Tombstone.

They searched the room to the point of thinking about unpicking the duvets, but not a penny was to be found. There were plenty of champagne corks, leadfoil coverings, empty glasses, cigarette butts with varying shades of lipstick on them, but no money.

"The evil bitches have rolled us," exploded Broomstick, filled with rage and indignation at the perfidious nature of the female sex. "Two-and-a-half thousand quid," he wailed.

"We'll have to telex for more," said the sad Tombstone.

"Don't be a berk," replied Broomstick, "we're only in Frankfurt, we haven't even had to fill up yet, and one being rolled is feasible, but two gives the game away. They're not bloody idiots."

So they sold all the spare tyres, the snow chains, the spare half-shafts and sundry other gear to raise the money to pay the hotel bill and leave enough spare to continue along the road.

"We'll do some business along the road and fiddle enough to reach Istanbul, then we'll telex for extra cash," ordained the more experienced Broomstick.

They were in the car park preparing to leave. Broomstick was in his cab recapping route instructions to Tombstone through his open window in case they were split by traffic on the way out of the city. Suddenly his eyes darkened and glazed, he hammered into gear, revved his engine and thundered forwards before the astonished Tombstone and other sympathetic onlookers could mutter goodbye.

The truck hurtled across the park making no attempt to turn into the exit lanes. They watched in silent amazement as it careered towards a line of parked private cars, shimmied a quick left, slithered right, straightened up and shot through a gap in the line of parked saloons to come to a shuddering stop with the sound of rending metal and shatering glass.

"He's gone bloody bananas, the mad bastard," they said and broke into a gallop across the tarmac dodging and buffeting bemused bystanders.

They found Broomstick with a beatific smile on his face, under his front wheels lay a familiar, but somewhat mangled, red Ferrari Pinafiori with a stunned woman beside it— she didn't look half as well-groomed as once she had.

"Don't 'ang about, Tombstone," said Broomstick, slipping into reverse and carefully manoeuvring between the parked saloons, "fuck off a bit sharpish before the gauleiters turn up."

His smile broadened and he gloated: "Revenge is sweet."

Sugar also is sweet. And sugar, we're told, is a killer, listen to dieticians talk about it. Put it in a petrol or diesel tank and the vehicle will not go very far; put it in your beer and it can have the same effect upon you.

Chris, Dave and John were weekended in Rasthaus Irshenberg, Wendlestein, or so it said on the menu, contemplating the extreme hardship and discomfort of a Middle East trucker's existence and wondering why the blazes they bothered doing it.

As they glanced across the shimmering expanse of the Chiemsee toward Gstadt on the lake and surveyed the nearby Alpine peaks—ruminating on the various alpine ski resorts and holiday playgrounds they were about to traverse in the course of a day's work, wondering which one to stay at and if one could offer better entertainment in the accepted après-ski style than the other, with the drawback that it was only October and not yet the skiing season—they were idly dropping sugar lumps into their beer glasses to bring it to a foaming head in the British manner. German beer does tend to go a bit flat.

They agreed that in winter the ski resorts were so thick with crumpet that you could easily break a leg watching it without the bother of going on the ski-run to do it, and dropped more sugar lumps into their drinks.

A German, his curiosity aroused, approached with great formality, clicked his heels together and asked: "Excuss plis, for why you drop sugar into your bier, it puzzles my friends."

They told him why and demonstrated the effect, he was enthralled. So too were his friends. All ordered extra steiners and sugar lumps from the kitchens: in no time at all it became the night of the fizzing steiner. It was so popular a new pastime that the kitchen brought out a five kilo bag of sugar lumps and everybody joined in.

Soon there was dancing and much slapping of knees and heels until, five kilos of sugar later, the dancers were missing their knees and heels. A few managed to miss their thighs, spun round and fell in a heap on the dance floor.

The formal German had become much less restrained and quite loud with it. He bellowed: "It is Oktoberfest, we will all go to Munchen and make the bier really fizz."

He commanded cars to be called, all the remaining stocks of lump sugar to be taken from the kitchen and loaded up and the expedition headed for the festival city where they toured each and every bier keller dropping sugar lumps into steiners all round.

It became the fashionable tipple that particular Oktoberfest.

The Englishmen taught their new German friends to sing the popular ditty. "Sugar in the morning, sugar in the evening . . ." and so on. It became a sort of theme song for the festival.

Oktoberfest is a testament of sorts to German efficiency. Munich is the only city which has a special machine to suck up sick from the pavements and station floor after the drinking becomes really serious. A stranger knows when he is beginning to enjoy the fun the moment the German oompah bands on every corner begin to sound like the Boston Philharmonic.

"Three questions," Chris demanded of the girl next to him when he woke up. "What's your name? Where am I? And what day is it?" She couldn't remember who the hell she was or where, but she glanced at a newspaper and thought it was Saturday.

"It can't be," said Chris, "yesterday was Sunday."

"But that Sunday was six days ago," said the formal German in the bar, adding, "I don't think I like your sugar in the bier very much, it makes you drunk. I don't get drunk when I take bier straight."

Chris, Dave and John looked at each other with resignation and in unison conceded the point: "We're weekended again."

Despite the hazards of excess speed, sex and general sin, motoring through Germany is good. Though it is predictable in that you know exactly where you will be at any given time if you comply with the law. Drive the regulation speed for the regulation hours and you will be the regulation distance further along the road at the exact regulation time— and you will be so regulation bored by it all that you will not recall one kilometre of the day's trip.

That distance is, by law on the Continent, 450 kilometres which is almost exactly the distance from Aachen to Wieskirchen, the second major intelligence post we call at.

There are lots of Brits and Dutchmen pulled in at Wieskirchen.

Ray, a thoughtful, reflective man, is telling a story. It is so bizarre that nobody interrupts.

"I've been doing Europes and done quite well out of it. I had a cracking job, Birmingham to Lisbon with a good return load. I got down this road, half way to Lisbon, the roads are not much cop but this wasn't bad, then I hit this bit where they were doing a tremendous amount of construction work. It was Saturday and there were massive graders and rollers and all that gear lying about unattended because they were all off for the weekend.

"There were diversion signs all over the place, I couldn't make out which was which and there was nobody to ask. So I followed what looked the most likely road. Then I came to this village, it looked deserted but there was one bloke in the street. I couldn't speak a word of Portuguese and he couldn't speak English. I kept yelling, "Lisboa" and he pointed straight ahead. But all I could see in front was a big hill, there didn't seem to be a road.

"So I motioned that I was going to try to turn round and go back. But, no, he got very excited and pointed straight ahead. I thought "He lives here, he ought to know" so I went on. A couple of kliks along it opened up into a track, it was obvious that a lot of big trucks had been running down it, so I reckoned he must be right and that this was a diversion.

"Then round a corner I came upon a great

tunnel in the side of the hill. I thought it couldn't be right, but the truck tracks ran into it. Then I found that I couldn't turn round anyway, there was no room at all and it was thick, deep mud either side of the track. So I drove on into the tunnel.

"By God, it was rough. There was no proper floor, it was still rounded with a hard ledge either side for the trucks to run on. It was obviously not finished, they hadn't put the road in yet. It went on and on until it turned two corners like an angled letter S flattened out. Well, there was no way of going back, I couldn't reverse round those bends, I was blind at the back.

"And there was all sorts of gear left in front, I had to keep getting out to shove it on one side or down the ditch in the middle to get past. I thought it was never going to end, I'd been in there for half-an-hour. And then, round the last corner, I saw a pinprick of light. I tell you, my heart leapt. It got bigger and bigger and I put my foot down a bit as it got nearer. I had all my Cebies on, spots and heads blazing.

"At the end I suddenly saw a private car parked right in the middle of the track just outside the tunnel. Getting closer, I realised that it was a police car. Marvellous, they would be sure to know the way—if the police don't, who does?

"I didn't want them to move off before I reached them, so I gave them a blast on the air-horn. It sounded like Gabriel's trumpet in that tunnel. The car doors flew open and two coppers jumped out. They looked down the tunnel, jumped back in and blasted off as if their pants were on fire. The miserable swine.

"They were out of sight before I drove out into the sunlight, I blinked a bit before I was used to it, but I could see that they'd gone to the left, it seemed the only way, so I followed until I came to a little village a few kilometres down the track. It was the bumpiest ride I've ever made, I thought the springs had gone at least a dozen times.

"In the village square, an excited crowd had gathered, they were shouting, arguing and gesticulating like only a Portuguese crowd can. The police car was just disappearing round the corner. When they saw me, the crowd stopped in its tracks then backed away. I was getting a bit bloody terrified by this time, I wondered what was going on. I stopped and they surged round the truck jabbering like mad, I couldn't understand a word or a gesture until the local Roman Catholic priest arrived.

"They parted and let him through, he was wearing a big hat, like they do, and he spoke perfect English but with an Irish brogue thick as a Paddy from Dublin, it was music to my ears.

"He asked me 'My son, where have you come from?' I told him from up the road back there.

"He said, 'They told me that. How did you get on to that road?'

" 'Through the big tunnel, the bloke at the other end said it was the only way, he was insistent.' The priest shook his head and took off his hat and said, 'My son, you have just driven six kilometres along the sluice tunnel of the main dam for the biggest hydro-electric scheme in Portugal. You have terrified two policemen and a whole village who believed it to be impossible'."

Ray smiles in memory of the incident and adds: "The priest told me later that the old fellow at the other end thought I was delivering a load for the site. He wasn't to know."

The experienced Middle East drivers nod

to each other and one comments: "You'll be all right, Ray, you'll fit in. You're the type who'll make it work down there."

It does indeed take a curious breed of man with extraordinary resources to make it work in the Middle East and any collection of Middle East drivers has more than its share of curiosities.

Take the very first man on the run, the man who started it all, Bob Paul. Nobody could have had a stranger career: he is one of the very few doctors—are there any others?—who completed training and took his degree at Guy's, the great London teaching hospital, married a ward sister he met there, then took up long-distance lorry driving as a full-time occupation. All he had retained of his medicine is his bedside manner.

His friend and former colleague Mike Woodman's career runs in parallel: a qualified dental surgeon with a flourishing practice, he threw it all away to join Bob Paul and together they began to haul heavy trucks from Europe to Arabia and the Orient at a time when the roads ran out completely at Istanbul and there were no signposts or directions. They founded Astran which is still running.

Neither of them was an experienced driver. Gordon Pearce was and he joined them in the early days. "Those were the good old days," say other drivers who joined the circus, "if anybody on the trip suffered a headache, hangover, broken limb, toothache or a slight dose of clap they felt reassured with Bob and Mike in the convoy, and Gordon could always run you safely to the nearest hospital if it was serious."

Independent of Astran, Chris Bedder was a strange sort of fellow to be on the great overland run—being a deep sea diver by trade.

Bobby Brown, who scored a number of firsts on the route, made his name as an all-in wrestler appearing often on television under the name of Vincent Randell and as Adrian Street's tag partner before he took up Middle East driving.

And still they come, men from all walks of life and professions lured by the strange attraction of a precarious, back-breaking way of life: Terry Tott, bass guitarist with the pop group Showaddywaddy, Leo Smith, drop-out company director, Andrew Wilson-Young, public schoolboy, ex-turkey farmer Kim Belcher with his degree in chemistry, a physicist, a former bank robber, a teacher—

the list is interminable of all those under the spell of the Big Haul.

Snap decisions are the rule, there cannot be much hanging about if schedules are to be met. Right, let's go: top up with diesel in Furth-im-Wald on the West German-Czecho-slovakian border, spot of nosh and a couple of drinks there, then the Commie Bloc . . . ugh!

The holiday is about over, this is when the kissing has to stop.

4

ALL that ever comes from time, experience and mistakes is proof positive that mankind, by nature, is masochistic to the point of self-destruction. Which is why every driver arriving at the Communist Bloc border at Folmava, Czechoslovakia, asks himself the question: "What the hell am I doing here again?"

The Communist Bloc produces a dreadful sinking feeling in the pit of the stomach, a sense of inevitable despair, an intuition that whatever you are about to do is already too late. The die is cast, there is nowhere to go except forward when all instincts tell you to go back while the going is good.

We leave behind the West German border town of Furth-im-Wald with its air of cosy domesticity, its extensive gardens and comfortable villas and, above all, its blazing lights which light up the entire valley in a warm glow. In our stomach lies the superb cuisine of the Station Hotel—goulash soup and hot crispy rolls, Châteaubriand and asparagus tips. We have made the most of our last taste of West German affluence. At the small border post the German officials are relaxed and friendly. They whizz efficiently through the paperwork.

The customs chief thumbs through his ledger. "Two or three Englanders in front of you, went through a few hours ago. They were asking about you. Have a good journey, my friend. See you soon."

The two-inch diameter red and white pole swings up bouncing on its counterweight, the guard smiles. "Goodnight, good journey."

We roll and suddenly everything is darker, much darker. We are full of the gloom and foreboding which wells up within the soul on this two kilometre trek across no-man's-land into the Marxist dream. And what is revealed in the sweeping headlights is enough to dim the gleam in a free man's eyes.

A great swathe of open land cuts through the forest trees and brushwood, clean as the track of a mop across a kitchen floor in a Flash detergent advertisement—and just as artificial.

Dragons' teeth tank barriers fringe the edges of the swathe. Barbed-wire fences, neatly placed yards apart follow the contours of the countryside, between them lies ploughed, rolled and harrowed flat land, the soil of fine enough tilth to record the footprints of a furtive fox on his nocturnal prowl. Beyond the barbed-wire, the machine-gun watch-towers stand stark and menacing against the night sky. Underfoot, the treachery of anti-personnel mines, above, the scrutiny of watchful, impersonal eyes.

But the dragons' teeth defences are angled *inwards*, the overhangs on the tall barbed-wire fences are tilted *inwards*, searchlights on the towers are mounted to sweep along the barriers and *inwards* towards Czechoslovakia.

The sign says "The Socialist Republic of Czechoslovakia—welcome."

A red and white customs barrier bars the road. But this one is of solid steel nine inches by six. It is mounted on concrete blocks some four foot square, but it is hung to open *inwards*. It slots into a recess on the inwards side of the block, it will not open outwards towards West Germany. A bubble-car could crash into the Socialist Republic of Czechoslovakia—a Centurian tank would have difficulty getting out.

The soldiers swing open the barrier. Driven accurately, the wheel hubs will squeeze through with nothing more than two inches' clearance on either side; the chances of anybody slipping out are slim indeed. The soldiers with dogs scrutinize the truck from the shadows.

The Czech visa is in quadruplicate with two photographs on separate pages, three are retained at the entry border, on no account lose the fourth page for you will need it to get out. If you are staying in the country you must state who you will be visiting, where and why. Then you need another quadruplicate form to come back through the country on your return journey. The actual visa stamp is in your passport and must be stamped in and out to be legal.

At this particular time the Czechs are happy, most of the vast European—Middle East traffic is running "Commie Bloc" through Czechoslovakia, Hungary, Rumania and Bulgaria because their Warsaw Pact allies, the Yugoslavs, have made a momumental cock-up and seriously underestimated the number of Transit Permits they would require in the year. And the Austrians have put up their transit taxes and restricted their permits to further cut down the traffic along that route.

This means a steady income in hard currencies for the Czechs who desperately need it and can scarcely believe their good fortune.

The Yugoslavs, meanwhile, perturbed at the loss of hard currency revenue, are having it "put about" that if you turn up at any Yugoslav border there will be "no problems, we'll fix you up with a permit on the border, just pay for it and go through".

But it isn't as easy as all that, the brief-case full of paperwork specifies the route and cannot, without risk, be deviated from. The carnet de passage, CMRs and triptyches for the truck and trailer are explicit, so it has to be "Commie Bloc". Triptyches are temporary import and export licences to take truck and trailer through a country. Technically the vehicle is imported at the entry border and exported at the exit border, the main purpose of the triptyche is to prevent the vehicle being sold during transit. A bond is lodged with the RAC in London for British vehicles and if the regulations are broken the country where the breach takes place can claim against it. The driver carries a book of them, half the document is torn from the book on entering and the other half on leaving.

It is very easy on this border with little or no hassle; they love people coming in, it is just that they hate them going out, particularly if they are Czech citizens with itchy feet.

The soldiers are fresh-faced kids or sallow-faced youths and sheepish in demeanour, awkward with their automatic weapons and confused with their surroundings. They lack the arrogant self-assurance of the West's young soldiery, they do not look as potentially brutal and shamble about at a perpetual disadvantage. And they scrounge for cigarettes all the time.

The whole Warsaw Pact alliance scrounges cigarettes. An army on the scrounge for cigarettes destroys its image of military effectiveness and discipline. It becomes a pest. The answer may be to post a notice in the cab in the manner of shopkeepers reluctant to give credit: "Please do not ask for cigarettes as a refusal might offend."

The rosy-cheeked young officer, perusing our papers, is a pleasant young man, keen to show his superiority and broadmindedness. Clean cut, with shiny boots, he is far removed from the rabble of scrounging militia under his command. "Good evening," he says and smiles with delight at overcoming that first formidable hurdle of the language barrier. "English? Where you going?"

"Saudi Arabia . . ." but the reply is too quick for him, he glances at the carnet and reads aloud: "Sowdeea . . . Kuwait."

He nods reflectively and comments: "It is a long way, a long way. You work government? Big company?"

"Some do, but these boys with us are owner-drivers."

"Owner-drivers," the idea amuses him, "they own themselves these vehicles? They do not belong company?" Clearly it is a preposterous notion so he smiles in the manner of a man who can take a joke and doesn't mind having his leg pulled and repeats slowly: "Owner-driver . . ." Then he jokes: "You rich men, very rich men?" He laughs spontaneously and carefully notes the Dutch clogs, jeans, T-shirts, anoraks and selection of bizarre headgear worn by the drivers, now he knows they are joking. "But these vehicles cost very much money." We tell him that truck and trailer cost about £40,000.

He relays the information to an officer

colleague who clearly considers the English very jocular fellows—£40,000 indeed!

To add to the comrades' confusion the Birmingham dambuster arrives and leaps from his cab in a state of agitation. "'Ere, d'y know what I 'ad for me dinner in Furth?" he asks with outrage in his voice. Then he answers himself. "Chicken, bloody chicken, can you believe that? I didn't think till I was half way through it, bloody chicken. The Kraut next to me had it on his plate and it smelled that good—and I couldn't read the bloody menu. Chicken!"

He splutters in disgust. "Chicken! The rag'eads' staple diet, I'll get nowt else for the next six weeks and I have to order bloody chicken for my last meal in Germany. All that steak and pork and schnitzels and I have to order chicken. I must be goin' soft in the 'ead."

The young officer is bemused. "Had your colleague bad food in Deutschland?" he queries.

"Bloody chicken," snorts the dambuster.

A dishevelled man walks from the shadows of the outgoing bays: six days' growth of stubble, tired, strained eyes, a layer of black oil and dirt under his fingernails, his hands stained with oil blemishes which cold water washing has failed to remove. His clothes are mud-splattered and soiled. Under the bright lights of the customs inspection bay, his truck is a monotone brown/grey all over, no numbers, nationality plates or company names are discernible under the overall mud coating. His complexion is as brown/grey as his rig. But we know he is English, you can tell.

He says: "It's a bastard, bloody snow at this time of year. It's thick down Rumania and there's a bit in Czecho and I've no bloody snow chains. These roads are a pig at any time but under the snow you can't see the bloody holes. I did two springs."

He draws deeply on his cigarette and adds: "You can't go Prague and use the motorway all the way down. That road between here, Pilsen and Prague is motor-cross in good weather, you'll never get through in snow. The only way through is via Klatovy but the silly bastard Czechs don't tell you there's a 3.1 metre bridge just outside Klatovy. There is a back road round to Pilsen but by the time you've done that you may as well have gone down Brno. That Prague's a pig as well. They've changed the TIR route and routed it under a 3.5 metre bridge. There's another bridge 100 metres further down which they've made a diversion—that's 3.1 metres. They're bloody brilliant, these Czechs, I'm going to buy them a tape measure for Christmas."

Listening drivers frown, the minimum clearance needed for a big rig is 4 metres.

So it is down to Domazlice, right to Klatovy and then follow the signs to Ceske Budejovice, keep that in your mind, say it slowly, Ceske Budejovice, watch for alternative spellings, but, most of all, watch for signposts, they don't come all that often along these roads.

Czechoslovakia is a black place to drive in. The quartz halogen headlights search out a village. It seems to crumble and peel before us, there are gaps in the houses where the plaster has fallen away. There is no life, no lights in the windows, only shadows from the beam cast by the truck lights dancing over the rubble facias of the buildings; a gleam in a window is merely the reflection of the headlights.

On the left stands the military barracks, unpainted and flaking as well; a solitary soldier blinks in the approaching glare and scurries through an opening. There are no lights in the barrack windows, no lights in the guardroom, there is no one about. It is eight o'clock in the evening and the place has shut down.

The road runs between an avenue of trees. Suddenly the suspension begins to rumble, the cab lurches and the lights swing, the cab rocks and shudders. It is a strange, uneasy feeling after Western Europe's smooth rides, but this is what a suspension is for, let it get to work. And it is going to work desperately hard, harder than could ever have been conceived by engineers accustomed to Western roads where a change of surface is considered affront enough to warrant a warning notice and enormous signs shout at drivers: "Beware Ramp". The roads will get no better except for a few sparse miles of showpiece motorways. Often they will dis-integrate into no road at all, but a potholed, fissured, rock strewn cattle track. There will be hundreds of kilometres of cobblestones laid by peasants and serfs of some twilight, bygone age who resented their enforced toil; cobblestones for horses and oxen, cobble-stones which have sunk out of sight or been forced upwards by a winter frost; great patches where cobbles used to be but have long since been removed to shore up some tumbledown hovel; cobblestones covered by alien tarmac forcing their way through to the light of day again.

The drivers say that the Russians have a miracle of road building technology, the only known machine which can resurface a road and lay the asphalt round the potholes—and they have perfected it on their satellite country's roads.

For the truck this driving is the equivalent of going 15 punishing rounds with an automated Muhammad Ali and being on the end of every jab, hook, cross, uppercut and never knowing when the big one is coming. The driver cheats, he lets the truck soak up the hammering. He sits on a £500 seat, moulded perfectly to the contours of the spine and thighs, balanced and tension sprung, scientifically stressed to smooth out the roughest ride. So all he suffers is the mental anguish of seeing, hearing and vicariously feeling the beating his truck is taking.

Night driving, sitting high, nine foot above the road, with an unimpeded view and spotlights to supplement powerful head-lights, reveals a detailed landscape. Piece by intimate piece it rolls into view to be examined in its isolation without the distraction of surroundings. It is an unfair viewpoint, there are no compensating factors to relieve the tawdry or to conceal the dilapidation. This is a country which has disinvented paint, which has allowed itself to slip into squalor. A country where the economy is crumbling into piles of rubble alongside the road. Rubble in the country lanes, strewn around the villages and piled in great heaps in the towns. But it is not the rubble of the building site—this is the rubble of the demolition crew.

Eight o'clock, nine o'clock, coming up to 10 o'clock and there is not a car in sight, not a moving object, not one seen since taking the road from Folmava. There are no lights in the dwelling houses save for three glows in three dim windows—windows with tattered rag curtains slung on bow-shaped string. People? The soldier, yes, he was there. Were there a couple of shadowy figures slinking into an alleyway back along the road? Maybe, or were they just shadows from the beam?

This cannot be right. Wake up. Maybe the

people all live at the back of the houses. But you can see the back of the houses on the bends and there are no lights there either. There *have* to be people somewhere.

These shadows, they're prancing about like lunatics in front. The lights are bouncing off the road, the bumps are throwing great long patches of black. It will be better when we get out of these trees. A bump like that doesn't help, hell. The shadows come up like blank walls ahead.

Holy Jesus, Christ help us. We can't stop, the back's swinging, we'll jack-knife. Slap the lot on. Too late. Gun her, gun her. Get through the bloody box, get over to the left. What the hell's on the left? Never mind that, gun her, foot flat down, get the turbo in, for Christ's sake get the turbo in. We're off the road drive side but she's holding. That's the turbo in. Oh blessed, blessed whine, she's levelled up.

What the holy hell was that?

Unbelievable! It is a donkey cart, piled 12 foot high with maize. Not a light, not a blink in sight. Jet black on a jet black road under the trees. We can't see him in the mirrors, there's not a sign. Who would drive a donkey cart without lights down a road like this? Only a Czech peasant.

A small searchlight suddenly appears ahead. It is a police or militia check point. The check point itself sits high above the road, the wide windows give a perfect view in every direction. Mounted on the outer walls facing each way are two floodlights. Part of the military detail are on lookout in the high command post, the others are manning the bariers at ground level. They are flashing hand torches so that they make a continuous arc of light. Move to the right. Switch off the spots and headlights, switch on the cab light, hold your passport in the left hand clearly in view.

People are here, ordinary people not militia. They stand in a disconsolate group huddled together by the check point wall. Two Skoda cars are pulled in to the side of the road, bonnets and boots open to the skies; a soldier with a lamp probes their innards. A man, hands above his head, leans against the wall supporting himself with his raised arms. His legs are spread apart; he stands in the classical attitude of the oppressed and humiliated, the underdog who cannot move until instructed. His travelling companions keep their eyes averted from the militia. A sinister atmosphere pervades the whole tragic little cameo.

The man in the upper room scrutinises the truck cab, peers into the sleeping compartment through the opened curtains, cranes forward to look on the floor. This is a people check, a search for unauthorised passengers or stowaways. The truck is clear, so, on a nod from his companion aloft, the soldier at ground level waves the truck on, flicking his hand almost irritably. Quick, quick, quick, don't loiter, move away, this is a private affair, a domestic issue, do not pry, look the other way and drive on.

But we must linger for at least a few moments more, two private cars which have been stopped on the other side of the check point are reversing in the narrow road to turn round. They have been sent back, their occupants sit still and numbed, they show no resentment or even reaction. Czechs in their own country are ordered by their own countrymen to cease their travelling, denied the freedom of their own roads. They move off ahead of us.

Their dim rear lights gather speed, shudder as gears are changed and settle down to lead us at moderate pace along the road. The road opens up but the sense of indignity persists, it seems to hang around the tiny, under-powered, inadequate vehicles running home with their tails between their legs.

This is too slow by far, our big Scania wants to roll, she is struggling resentfully in this gear at this speed. The Skoda and Lada cannot manage much more, performance is not one of their qualities. The car does not have the same commanding interest in the Eastern Bloc that it has in the West and consequently lacks any degree of sophisti-cation. However, it does carry status: the status of privilege and party importance, the status of being able to get on with the system; the status of succeeding in the black economy; the status perhaps of being the first sign of the emergence of an acquisitive society. What else can a resident of the Marxist world own?

But as a product it is a pretty crude, old-fashioned one by Western standards though much beloved by Western truckers. The police drive them. "Put your foot down and suck 'em up the air intake," say drivers like Trevor Long. "A touch on the accelerator and a Commie police car is a memory in your blue-tinged diesel smoke. You can outpace them and leave them down the road before thinking about changing up into fifth. And, of course, they have difficulty reading Western plates, that's if they can see the plate at all under the mud." Now we overtake the returning Czechs.

Soon the dull, receding headlights reflected in the wing-mirrors drop out of view and the darkness takes over again, relieved only by the glow of the trailer lights.

Hell, a bloody signpost. Did it say Ceske? Too fast. The sign flashed by half read and it almost certainly will not be repeated, possibly not for another 10 kilometres. Why did we not see that sign? We didn't see it until too late because it was not illuminated nor was it a reflective sign, it didn't light up in the headlights. Simple, they don't do that out here, you know that.

That is it! That is what is wrong. There is no street furniture to speak of, nothing beyond the absolutely essential. It is so minimal, in fact, that the average cluster of signposts in an English surburban high street would easily accommodate 20 miles of Czech highway.

Nor are there any commercial advertisements on the streets, not a hoarding nor a billboard. No wonder the road signs feel out of place in such a visually sparse environment—who would ever imagine that they could miss the visual impact of posters, the garish razzmatazz of vulgar capitalist messages? But be fair, there are roadside signs, 1930s style fretwork cut-outs of hammers and sickles, red stars, paintings of clear-eyed solid citizens all staring heavenwards—everybody depicted in a Communist poster looks aloft for a ray of hope.

Ceske Budejovice rolls under the wheels in the guise of a mini-metropolis with street lights, double yellow lines and "Keep Right" signs on bollards, but rapidly reduces itself in status on closer acquaintanceship.

A once handsome provincial town of some standing with wide thoroughfares, commercial buildings, banks and places of refreshment, it has slipped from its former elegance to follow the universal fashion of "Socialismus"—the Czech word for Communism. It now piles its rubble in mounds in the gutters.

Coming up to midnight everybody is drunk which is par for the course in Marxist Europe and nobody takes a lot of notice. The drunks are bullied and pushed around by the harassed forces of the law who, the drivers say, are also drunk but who stand up straighter because their overcoats are thicker. There is a lot of pushing and shoving and people suddenly walk into the middle of the street. The lights are out in the apartments but on in the streets which adds some extra dimension of life to the scene.

The TIR route is clearly, unmistakably marked. Splendid. Straight ahead to Brno, under the railway bridge; the sign is alongside the bridge and the bridge is marked 3.7 metres plus. And it is quite a plus as there are wires running under the bridge which gives us an additional thrill in that we can knock the bridge down and at the same time cut the lights or stop the trams. Police confidently wave us on.

No thank you, we will not rely upon such assurances, no offence meant, but we will find an alternative route round the railway. There is adequate room enough to reverse along the main drag, miss the tram tracks and piles of rubble, swing her and head right into what looks like the town centre.

BRRUMPH! The sound of an explosion. And it echoes all around in dozens of little brrumph, brrumph, brrumphs. What lights have been on in the apartments go off; everybody who was walking in this direction abruptly turns round and walks away.

The rear off-side back tyre has blown: it has had a pounding on the roads from the border and the tram lines were probably the last straw. But it is a super-cube and super-cubes are notorious for blowing. Super-cubes are universally hated and all drivers detest pulling them.

The super-cube is a stepped trailer; instead of a level, flat base from front to rear the super-cube breaks in the middle so that the rear end of the trailer is carried on smaller wheels than those of the tractor unit. This allows greater headroom at the rear end and more capacity for bulky but lightweight cargo. The derivation of the name is self-evident—super cubic capacity. It may be a smaller tyre but it is still big enough to go off with the sound of a good-sized bomb. A juggernaut tyre is made of steel and rubber inflated to eight atmospheres, about 130 lbs per square inch which is a very considerable pressure when you consider you put 22 to 28 lbs per square inch in the tyres of your private car.

An exploding juggernaut tyre can be a dangerous thing if you happen to be near it. The militant young Mr. Peter Hain, then leader of the Young Liberals, once led a campaign to stop juggernauts on some route or other. He threatened that he and his supporters would slash the tyres of any juggernaut which transgressed the territory they felt should be inviolate. They were saved in the nick of time by officers of the traffic police who warned that if they did, in fact, succeed in slashing a tyre (which is a difficult thing to do through that thickness of rubber and steel) they would almost certainly lose their heads in the resulting explosion.

Back in Ceske it has now started to rain, the wet stuff is coming down by the bucketful so hard that it bounces off the road and so cold that it freezes the back of the neck and stings the back of unprotected hands during the arduous business of re-building the wheel.

In this circumstance there is nothing for us to do but rebuild the wheel. Undo those ten massive wheel nuts by jumping on the cranked spanner; release the hub, smash out the retaining rings; smash in the flap over the new tube and tyre, it will never go in, never; smash it with a heavy hammer keeping a good distance in case it flies out; belt the hell out of it until it snaps into position; lift it until 10 holes match the position of 10 bolts on the axle bearing, tilt it to the correct angle to slide on to the bolts; try to stop the slimy, slippy rubber sliding from the grip of mud-caked hands; squeeze and coax the extended valve tubing from the inner tyre through the small hole in the outer wheel otherwise we cannot blow up the inner tyre; twist on the nuts and tighten with the cranked spanner; connect the airline and blow in 130 lbs pressure; on our backs again under the trailer as the water soaks through our clothes, release the jacks; secure the blown tyre on the roof rack; stow the gear. Let's get out of this Godforsaken hole and find somewhere to park up.

We travel down the road for another 36 kliks.

"P", the sign says.

"TIR", says the other sign. A veritable glut of signs.

We take it carefully into the lay-by. Check to see if the surface can hold us, check to make sure we can get out once we're in, check the overhang of the trees for height and, most important, check for telephone wires or electricity cables. "They sling them anywhere, nobody cares out here and some of them think it is possible to squeeze a 13 foot high truck under a 10 foot high cable sagging to eight foot in the middle."

Nurse the engine, don't switch off, let her idle: there are very fine rubber seals inside the works, let them idle gently into rest, it protects them and prolongs their life.

The "off" switch on every known truck is a built-in standing joke perpetuated by all manufacturers, none have ever been known to work. Why should they? These engines need no electricity to work, they fire on pressure once the battery has turned them over. So heel the exhauster brake button which, when the drive wheels are stationary, will shut her down.

God, it's quiet, the blackness overwhelms everything, it seeps through the windows, fills the cab and sits heavily on the eyelids. Better if there was somebody else here, a couple of other friendly trucks to keep us company.

Quit worrying. But there are people out there and you never can tell which way they are going to jump. Soon you will know that they are around the truck. There's a tell-tale snap of a twig underfoot, a slight roll of the suspension as they ease themselves up to attempt to peer into the cab. You might have to lean forward from your bunk, flick the lights on, touch the starter switch, they will think you are moving off and a soft thump will tell that they have dropped off and retreated into the all consuming dark. They are everywhere, the night people, all over Europe, Turkey, Asia. You don't often actually see them, you don't want to see them; if you give them the opportunity to see you, then it is too late, the probability is that you will have failed to secure your cab properly . . . .

"I woke up and looked straight down the barrel of this Russian rifle. I didn't give a damn about the nationality of the gun at that moment, that muzzle looked the size of a railway tunnel. They had picked the lock, I didn't hear a thing. I can't remember exactly what I thought, I couldn't think. I couldn't see the face behind the gun, all I could see was that gaping hole. I was lucky, they just took the money, £1,200, watches, radio, camera, all that sort of gear. I do not know why they didn't shoot." That happened to colleague Trevor Long. He was lucky, over the years a lot of drivers have been shot.

Nobody was ever arrested, they seldom are. Trevor explains: "Now I have had a secret safe built into the cab where I keep the bulk of the running money. But I always have a couple of hundred on hand so that if it happens again I've got something to give them. That often keeps them quiet, but it has got to be something a bit substantial otherwise they tend to get very nasty."

And there are also official people out there: the watchers. They too are nocturnal creatures, quiet, secretive and unpredictable. Men of mean countenance and cold eyes who have no friends other than their immediate colleagues—and few real friends among them. They are custodians of their country's secrets and, under regimes which rely on secrecy for survival, they are men of power. It is a power which induces terror in those confronted by it. The transgressor in the West at least rests assured that a part of the system is fighting for him and whatsoever rights he may have. Not so with these gentlemen of the night and gun who can exercise their power in an almost impenetrable barrier of secrecy. Such secrecy, in fact, that the accused often has the greatest difficulty discovering exactly the nature of his transgression.

But they can be beaten. Say nothing, do nothing and use the system to beat them. The one thing which "Socialismus" cannot cope with is obduracy or sheer bloody-mindedness coupled with indifference: an amused shrug of the shoulders, a blank stare of incomprehension reduces outraged Communism to spluttering impotence.

"Well, fucking shoot me then," says the weary trucker slumping over his steering wheel in an attitude of aggravated frustration, "you got the shooter, you got the bullets . . . and I ain't goin' nowhere. But do me a favour, put a notice in *The Times* sayin' 'No floral tributes or wreaths, send the money to the Robin Hood boozer, Clacton, for a decent piss-up for the lads.' What a bunch of berks," he confides to assembled colleagues, "look at the geezer wavin' the shooter about, 'is bloody arm will drop off in a minute."

Nothing is so futile as an ineffective show of force. The gun waves more slowly, it is jabbed less aggressively, doubt spreads across the officer's face, the realisation of imminent total foolishness brings caution into his attitude until he is obliged to retreat to reconsider his stance.

"Worried? Why should I be worried?" asks

the Englishman. "I've done nothing wrong. If they want to make a cock-up, then they can put it right . . . or they can shoot me, there ain't nothin' I can do about it."

The two attitudes are wholly incompatible but necessity makes strange bedfellows. This is the way to the Middle East, the only way open, so the truckers need it. Truckers bring hard currency and the Socialist states will put up with virtually anything to bolster shattered economies.

The jaundiced eye is a lamentably poor observer: there must be something good, something with a tinge of warmth, something remotely happy to see, feel and hear. But where? In the light of day there is little improvement.

A landscape minus human beings where they ought to be chills the spirit. Only three human images are given universal public display, two dead and the third aloof and remote: Marx, Lenin and the incumbent local Comrade Boss. In every village and hamlet their photographs alone look out over the sad, dilapidated streets; in the towns their images on a bigger canvas scan a wider vista. And what do those aesthetic, intellectually severe features look out on from the vantage points of their prominence other than a crumbling society in ruins?

Shop after shop is empty of goods save a few jars of jams, local honey and bottles of beetroot. Mostly they are closed. Sometimes a bedraggled, disheartened and haggard-faced queue has formed outside a shop where a delivery is expected. A butcher's shop seems to be open but the counters and shelves are bare. There are no vegetable stalls, no baker's windows filled with crusty loaves and confections.

Incongruously a village sports a fine asphalted car park, white lined into parking lots, trim, neat with room for a couple of hundred vehicles. A single, solitary ancient and rusting tractor is parked there, the white lines are unsullied by tread marks.

There is no bread in the shops, no cars in the car park: so what to make of Radio Moscow's English broadcast at this very moment in time? At dictation speed the news reader tells us: "Soviet and Communist Bloc grain production this year reached an all-time record and surpassed set targets. The Soviet Bloc is now the world's biggest grain producer and produces more than one-fifth of the world supply."

He then quotes a series of adulatory press comments on the Lada car from various Western capitals including the *Morning Star* in London: "The car is praised for its fine finish and very low petrol consumption. In excess of one million Lada cars were exported last year mostly to Communist Bloc countries which makes it the biggest selling car in the world."

But the air waves carry a different story a few minutes later from different stations: London, Munich, Madrid and even the ever-loud Tirana, all report a Moscow announcement by President Brezhnev. He tells the world's media that the harvest has failed for the third year running and fallen short of the target of 230 million tons by 52 million and the prospects for next year look even bleaker. The same stations quote official sources in Prague reporting the introduction of rationing at a level lower than at the end of the war in 1945. Yet on poster, film, television, radio and on banners slung across roads the Big Lie is perpetuated for home consumption—success through wonderful Socialismus.

Good cheer: in a lay-by on the left, we spot three Brits, a Swede and a Dutchman, somebody must have the kettle on. Young Beth has brought along a home-made birthday cake for Leo to celebrate his 43rd anniversary. A cake to inspire Gavin and Harry to crack a bottle of duty free Chivas Regal to lace the teas and coffees in honour of the celebration. Suddenly the world looks a better place, perhaps we should stay here all day.

Beth is a talented lady, a good cook and a tough cookie. She has assimilated the run perfectly in the couple of years she has been doing it to be with Leo. Her extreme youth has probably allowed her to absorb the hardships and pressures and retain her striking femininity; she can change character from donkey-jacket and dungarees to disco dress in an instant. Alert, sharp as icicles at the borders, quick-witted in putting down awkward officials, she still keeps a laugh bubbling just beneath the surface. She had the inborn ability to be fully accepted the first minute she appeared on the scene and this is a man's world in the best, and worst, macho and anti-feminist sense.

Yvonne, nearly twice her age, is the one filled with wide-eyed wonderment and showing traces of culture-shock. Even at this early stage of the journey it is a long way from

100

Southport, Lancs, the elegant Lord Street and a centrally heated villa, freezer, television and mum to look after the kids. She is travelling with her husband, Albie Keeghan.

She came because she was bewitched by the romance evoked by exciting names: Budapest, Sofia, Bucharest, Istanbul, Babylon, Damascus—all rich with the sweet smell of adventure. She had to see it if only once, she could not bear the vicarious excitement of letters and postcards from Albie, she had to experience it for herself. Now she is learning to live with the culture shock and the experience. She too has the advantage of humour and a laugh that could crack an egg at 500 yards.

Leo pulls a big fridge and fridge drivers are the loneliest men on the road. Nobody will pull up with them at night because the fridge motor must be kept running at all times. It is a small, independent diesel engine attached to the front of the fridge container—nobody can sleep parked near a fridge truck.

It is a strange and exotic trade, great fleets of fridge trucks run from Liverpool, Hamburg, Amsterdam, Paris and Malmo carrying the frozen delicacies of Europe to the desert kingdoms: ice cream, chocolate

101

bars, asparagus, peas, eggs at just the right critical temperature so that they come out liquid and runny when cracked into an omelette in Jeddah, Riyadh and Kuwait where the temperature in summer reaches 120° to 140°. Alien foods for alien palates in an alien environment at an astonishing cost.

The lay-by is in a village and the trucks have attracted locals from their hideaways intent on some trading. Food? Cigarettes? In return they know a garage where there is diesel for "good" money, a finger points to a driver's purse. One Brit and the Swede elect to go along with the local black market leader.

"We don't want to turn up mob-handed, let them suss it out then we can make a note," the other drivers say.

In a couple of days, if the deal works, location, price and availability will be firmly committed to several memories. If it is a good deal and free from hassle it will achieve the distinction of a code name in the truckers' vocabulary: "I topped up at Leo's party place, no problems."

A Brit observes: "Actually, this could be a good spot. A top-up here on the way out will get you into Rumania and it could be very useful on the way back—get you half way through Germany if not further." He means half way through Germany on one-third price fuel which piles the profit on the trip.

The further into the Communist Bloc you go the more you need fuel and the less problems there are to obtain it. Rumania and Bulgaria are "stitched up". "No problems". The black market has superceded the official economies of these countries, it has gained such momentum that police, militia and officials have been sucked into the system and either comply, turn a blind eye or go short. In a couple of days everybody will be dealing on the "black" as a simple fact of survival.

Without the black market, profits on the run would be ruinously slashed, a belly-tank is vital to profitability: side-tanks hold 180 imperial gallons, a belly-tank takes 400. To fill up in Germany costs £980, on the black market the price is £255-£355 depending on the deal struck. Turkey has put up the price of diesel to almost European levels, so you allow £600 to fill all tanks if necessary, possibly more. Then, of course, the Middle East prices are ludicrous, 3p or 4p a gallon. To fill up in Arabia costs only £20. The problem is to bridge the wide gap between expensive fuel and the give-away stuff. So the equation is simple: a tank-full multiplied by seven, 10 or 12 miles a gallon depending on motor and weight being pulled and how much can be bought on the black. Make allowances for running speed, weather conditions, hold ups . . . the answer is a long, long way for very little or blow the cream off the profit by overspending on fuel.

A thunder of juggernauts moving off rested and refreshed from a social stop is an event: the air is shattered with the concerted roar of 2,000 horsepower roaring in unison, the snort of gears and hiss of airbrakes. Then silence.

They space themselves out along the road, the good drivers, that is. Nobody likes running in convoy, everybody prefers to make his own way and take his chances as they come up. Drivers like space to overtake, to cruise at ease, and to belt it up a bit when the road conditions permit. Towns are diabolical, villages a headache, and overhanging buildings, low bridges, dogs, pigs, cattle, kids darting and old folks shuffling into the road . . . The open road is what juggernauts were made for and that is what they like.

The Czech motorway runs from Prague to Bratislava, a fine, modern road fully up to

Western motoring standards. Coming on to it from the backwoods shattered cart-tracks is like eating cream caramel after a packet of crisps—smooth and quiet; or washing with toilet soap after using a pumice stone . . . It is riding on silk, purely sensuous, physically indulgent.

Brno stands alongside the motorway looking much like a typical town planner's cockup: grey tower blocks rising to isolate residents from neighbours and their environment and create social problems. Here Jimmy-the-One has set himself up as a one-man social unit to help deal with and alleviate the effects of those problems. He has diagnosed the root causes of social disenchantment and alienation as deprivation, lack of the good and glossy things of life and lack of the wherewithal to pay for them.

His philanthropy is not limited to Brno, it extends to Bratislava, Plovdiv, Bucharest to name but three of the outlets for his notable single-handed altruism. All citizens are grateful and love him dearly.

He has set up Littlewoods and Marshall Ward mail order clubs to bring the benefits of the consumer orientated world to these suffering souls but since there is no official mail service or currency exchange to facilitate these transactions he acts as agent, collector and postman himself.

"They can pay me in any bloody currency they want," he explains, "it's all money and it's all convertible into something else, that's what money is all about."

He adds: "I'm oiling the wheels of industry, commerce and international good relations. In a few years the governments will all be following my example. If they found out about me now and how I operate, they might not understand. They would probably bang me in the nick, but every pioneer has had to suffer. So I take good care that unnecessary suffering shan't be inflicted on me, I couldn't let my customers—patients—down.

"So just take a quick shufti down the road and let me know if the law's 'anging about, there's a good lad."

The arrival of the glossy, 1,000 pages-heavy catalogues sends a thrill of anticipation through the flats where the customers live. It is a major event in their lives, a glimpse of a world they will never know but which they can briefly enjoy through the enticing photographs so brilliantly displayed. A world of magic, riches, delusion and fearful temptation, yet a world they can enter and make tangible through the medium of profligacy and decadence—a world they would love to join.

Though not necessarily join as defectors from their own society because defectors are a rare species in the Communist world, no matter what the hawks in the West would like to believe. Home is home anywhere on earth and the territorial imperative overrides the urge to get away; the outside world terrifies rather than tempts them.

Curiously they find Western affluence offensive, it doesn't attract them as a way of life after what they have grown up with. As many of those who "escape" to the West choose to return home as elect to stay. They speak to you in dozens, the ones who have worked in London, New York, Hanover, Munich, Bradford, Miami, and earned, to them, great riches, and come home of their own free will.

But still the catalogues have the aura of sin about them like forbidden fruit illicitly acquired. And the goods when they arrive, glossy as the catalogue photographs, add a touch of exotica to drab surroundings.

Jimmy-the-One involves nobody else in the running of his business, he brings in all the goods himself which results in many a glassy-eyed confrontation with officialdom while the commodities are in transit.

However, Jimmy-the-One has ever been a man to stand his ground in the face of hostility and adversity.

"Vas is zis? Quartz-electric alarum clock and tea-maker . . . Teasmaid?"

"I like a nice, hot cuppa when I get up in the mornin'—and that goes for the coffee percolator, an' I keep two or three in case I 'aven't got time to wash 'em out properly. Nothin' ruins a good cup o' tea or coffee more than a dirty pot. Didn't your mum teach you anything?"

"But these clothes are vimen's clothes and vimen's underclothes as vell . . ."

"Listen, Sunshine, your job is to collect customs and taxes. I don't ask you about your personal 'abits, so don't ask me about mine. This is a customs point not a court of morals, I'll wear what I bloody well like to wear in the privacy of my cab, I won't go paradin' round your dirty streets in 'em."

"But 10 sets?"

"Are you callin' me a dirty bugger? I like a

nice clean change every day, sometimes twice a day, and a spare set in case it rains. And you don't get launderettes every 'alf mile down here, mate. That's if you know what a launderette is, you ignorant sod."

And Jimmy-the-One advises all newcomers to the run: "Never let them push you around, son, or you're lost. Give 'em a bit of stick now and again, it keeps them in order."

He is, in fact, the Mr. Chips of the Middle East run and has taught more "scholars" all they know than any other driver. "Runnin' with Jimmy-the-One," say the older drivers, "you come out well-schooled. You never need go wrong or short of anything, he's a professor at the job . . . and he can drive a bit as well."

Tourist Czechoslovakia is unrecognisable from the workaday, backwoods country. The motorway is a rest cure, a half-day holiday before the onslaught. It runs smoothly, straight and true with only gentle curves and undulations towards the prosperous south linking the great cities. A show-case road for the visiting, holiday-making Western world with motorway services and smart hotels, food aplenty and gift shops modelled on the motorway/autobahn equivalent of Hilton plastic, which the tourist industry universally assumes is what visitors require. Of course they do, so let us not be critical except, perhaps, to observe that a tourist holiday in any and every Communist country is, perforce, a holiday in blinkers.

Out of high season this civil engineering feat could claim to be the most unnecessary major road in the world: count the vehicles travelling either way in a one hour's drive, going your way that means the ones that pass you or you pass and those you can see ahead and behind. Midday onwards, on a Thursday, cruising at 80 kph, a total of 57. Perhaps that is unfair, so consider a return journey, 1500 hours onwards, Friday, same average speed, a total of 112, 87 of which are foreign vehicles, German, Dutch, Austrian, Swiss and a couple of Frenchmen.

A motorway is about as exciting as flying airline standby to New York. Navigate your earthbound Jumbo along its predetermined course, the landscape moves, not you; count time in monotony and prepare for landing; all the tedium of flying except in this case land-fall is in Bratislava among the inevitable mounds of rubble and your luggage isn't lost.

In the process, set the automatic cruise

hand throttle, foot off accelerator and steer with your little finger, a touch of the little finger will keep her straight and level. But the driver isn't steering as such, he controls a hydraulic ram set between the steering wheels which does the hard work of shoving the wheels around, fingertip control, flick and the ram will straighten her out. In a matter of minutes you begin to think about going walkabout round the cab, or brewing up, or reading a good book, or doing a crossword, or thinking about women, or . . .

Such a state of mind was the Baron's undoing. He was called the Baron because he had his coat-of-arms emblazoned on the doors of his cab and was noted for his nerve, panache, sense of fun and streak of ripe vulgarity.

It was the time when an Arsenal football star had increased his fame one Saturday afternoon at Highbury by dropping his shorts and underpants, bending forward and displaying the two perfect half-moons of his rear anatomy to fans who had disapproved of his play, or it could have been the club directors, it matters not.

The Baron was smarting under some fancied insult or ribaldry from two Astran drivers who, he felt, had "put one over him" earlier down the road. They were following him and, he imagined, quietly chortling to themselves at his embarrassment.

So he set his hand throttle to cruise at 10 kph less than the usual cruising speed thinking: "They won't wear this for long, they'll soon lose patience and then the flash bastards will come roaring past and I will show them my contempt".

Inexorably they closed the gap until they were sitting on his rear lights. He watched them in his mirrors and prepared himself for his coup de grace, loosening his belt, dropping jeans and underwear around his knees.

Soon the blinkers of the Astran truck immediately behind flashed impatiently, the cab swung out and accelerated to pass. The Baron sprang to attack position and hung his half-moons through the side window in all their naked glory keeping control with his left hand while preparing an expressive two-fingered salute with his right hand.

But the Astran boys were a bit more fly than that. They suspected the Baron's uncustomary slowness, braked and pulled back behind him letting through a Turkish kamikaze coach driver with a bus full of Turkish guest workers accompanied by wives and families returning home from Germany. The astonished Baron was all but blown out of his cab by the air-horn blasts of outrage from the coach driver and the yells of rage from the passengers.

The Turks are a volatile, touchy race who do not take kindly to insult, particularly if their womenfolk are involved. They tend to hang people who they feel have affronted them, no matter what explanation is offered.

The Baron had to get in front of the coach, which involved some hair-raising motoring, and keep in front until he outpaced and finally lost them.

The Astran pair motored serenely on.

Bratislava, it says, bump, bump, bump, rumble, crash . . . that's a bit better, not good, but an improvement. This is a proper city, once wide and spacious and still with the overtones and shadows of a former provincial magnificence. It must have been a proud and pleasant place to live. Not so now.

Komarno is the border crossing drivers opt for, the smaller of the crossings into Hungary but the easiest. Take a right out of Bratislava,

113

another right on to the secondary road, well, you're used to them by now.

Farewell to Czecho, but not without another bridge, you can not possibly leave without another Czech speciality bridge right across the TIR route. This is a beauty, 3.8 metres on the right hand side going in this way, 4 metres in the middle going out on the other side. Make an acute left as you turn the right hand corner, that's the joy of this one, a right hand 90° corner to negotiate before you make a left to get under—if she'll fit.

Complete your acute left-hander, swing her more acutely right, slew the tilt to go under at 45°, spin the wheel acute left under the bridge, fling her back right, straighten up so she snakes across the road and that low girder just ruffles the top of the tilt tarpaulin on the right hand side. It hasn't torn, marvellous, pull her out—easy: thank you Czechoslovakia, after this, Rubik's Cube is a cinch.

There is a two mile queue of trucks to the customs point, maybe more. The Brits in front have been waiting five hours, they think the border may be closed for the night. A scout is sent out and returns—unscalped— with the good news that the border is staying open and the bad news that we'll all have to pay them overtime for the privilege of going through—£20? £30? Peanuts, it's a pleasure to pay to say goodbye.

On the left is a block of flats and a bus stop. The girls at the bus stop give furtive little waves to the drivers, they make whirling motions with their index fingers and mouth the word: "Tapes?" More mouth motions: "Adam and Ants? Polis?"

Children swarm around the trucks. "Cigarettes? Chewing gum? Chocolate, meester? C'mon, meester, you plenty, you rich."

On the right is the hotel, the centre of local social life. The restaurant has linen tablecloths and silver service with waiters in black ties and monkey jackets. There is a big party on tonight with the hierarchy of the Party attending. There is much handshaking and presenting of wives and the pecking order is marked. The Big Chief Comrade Bosses occupy centre stage, underlings come forward in ordained priorities, spend their allotted time with the Top Brass and retreat. A signal and they march in to dinner following the leaders in strict order of seniority.

It is called the Kaviar Hotel, all right for

some. We open the cab windows wide and give them a decadent blast of Showaddywaddy. To follow Showaddwaddy, a few tracks of Simon and Garfunkel and "Feelin' Groovy"—a song celebrating the joys of uncommitted indolence seemed appropriate to the occasion.

Then the queue moves up with a splutter of engines and a puff of exhaust smokes; it goes in fits and starts until the bridge is reached. The instructions read, "TIR 60m apart". The spaced out crocodile moves its allotted 60 metres, stops and waits until the next group at the head of the queue are signalled to move into the customs bays. The soldiers stamp their feet, smack their hands together and bum fags from every new truck when it comes within their range.

5

KOMARNO is the exit from oblivion. Komarom, the Hungarian side of the border, is the entrance into the pearl of the Communist world, even the visa and stamps in the passport are several classes above those in Czechoslovakia. They are in two colours and there is a touch of style about them, as there is a splendid ring to the words Magyar Republic—Magyar Nepkuztarsas-agba—you could play it on a gypsy violin, but roll it round your epiglottis and get the same sad, passionate sob as a zigeuner fiddler.

The relief is instant the moment you step inside the Hungarian visa office: cheerful people, a hum of activity, pay the girl at the bank, bang, bang and the pretty stamps adorn your passport. And out there, through the barrier, there are roads, real roads, black, smooth asphalt, white lines, lovely signposts, smiling faces in handsome features. A very good-looking race, the Hungarians, a bit manic-depressive when the drink is in, but full of music and laughter.

Ahead is Budapest, a handsome, splendid city with wide, sweeping boulevards, architecture befitting a capital city of a once great empire and great stores with window displays of taste, style and imagination.

But back at Komarom, there is still a drama to be played out. All the familiar and fearsome trappings of Communist country borders are apparent: watch towers, barbed wire, minefields, dogs—all the elements of terror. But this is between friendly Communist republic and friendly Communist country, both are members of the Warsaw Pact, nobody is going to invade or threaten anybody, the fortifications are there to keep the citizenry in its place.

Hungary has prospered through its relationships with the West, it has put itself up to the eyeballs in debt to do so and is paying the price for it, yet a lot has been placed in the way of the comrade in the street—life is better in Hungary. And Hungarians are not a peasant people, they expect more and make their lives tolerable. So their country has become a magnet for their not-so-lucky neighbours and the authorities next door are not happy about it. Basically they detest their own people seeing a better way of life and higher standards of living, so they keep them locked in.

Two young Czech girls, students at a polytechnic, had managed to get exit visas and set off for Budapest to go on a shopping spree. They had collected from their colleagues and were going to buy whatever they could for themselves and their classmates. That was the story—convincingly told—but things are seldom what they seem to be on the surface in this world. They had a lot of money with them and the probability is that they, like everybody else, had been dabbling in the black market. When the black economy becomes more powerful than the official one, who is to blame if the people become involved with it?

Arriving at Komarno they were given a cold reception by border guards, they were searched and stripped of every penny by the officials, everything was confiscated.

Then they were turned out penniless into Hungary. That is the way it works in the awful, all-enveloping bureaucracy of the Marxist world. Paper rules the people's lives, without the right permit you can do nothing. If you have an exit visa, all must be done by the book and *out* you must go before you can return.

They stand, forlorn, tearful and very apprehensive in the area just beyond the actual border. The British and Dutch drivers are chatting just before moving off and the girls approach them. One of them has a fair smattering of English—it is, she says, one of her subjects at the polytechnic. The drivers know there has been trouble at the border and glean the story. The girls are determined to carry on to Budapest and two drivers agree to give them a lift.

"How will you manage when you reach Budapest? How will you live? How will you get money?" They are asked.

"Oh, I suppose we will have to sex our way out of trouble—go with men. If you want favours, that is what you have to do."

Sentimentalists to a man, the drivers immediately organise a whip-round and give the girls £35 to see them through. That, in fact, in hard currency, makes them rich, it will buy them the equivalent of £200 worth of goods in the local currency.

"Watch it, don't be tempted, leave the girls alone," the old hands on the run warn all first-trippers, "VD has reached epidemic proportions in the Commie Bloc and it is a particularly virulent strain. Most people won't risk casual sex even with a French letter."

The incidence of the great social disease soars in wartime and when the fabric of society is crumbling.

The Danube splits Budapest like an inland sea, one half of the city is Buda and the other Pest. It is a mighty, magnificent river and it dominates whole countries, often dividing one from the other—the Blue Danube, once a great European highway, a playground and a romantic dream but now diminished to the status of fortified barrier between "allied" countries. No pleasure boats are to be seen, no sail craft or cruisers, only barges and tug boats followed by police launches. The great waterways of Western Europe are lined with yachts and the skyline is a forest of masts with jingling rigging—the Danube is naked.

The Danube is also a flaming nuisance, you've got to get across it and bridges are remarkably few except in big cities. So study the road map carefully otherwise you can be clocking up kilometres going the wrong way, your destination just across the water but un-reachable, which is guaranteed to raise the blood pressure to an unhealthy level. Travelling directly north there isn't a bridge between Budapest and the Czech border, there's just 60 kilometres of river and a long way to drive back to Budapest to get on the appropriate bank.

There is terrible confusion in the middle of Budapest, the signposting is not all that clear. A swing to the right brings narrow streets with parked private traffic, it doesn't seem feasible that there is enough room to squeeze through but there is no going back, it isn't a question of a few inches room—clearance is measured in millimetres. This takes us to a magnificent square, a place for ceremonial and flamboyant display; another swing to the right and we pass an ornate palace resplendent under the red flag. But the magnificent building isn't a palace, it is the main railway station.

This is a city built for the early 1900s and the days of horse traffic. Admittedly it is a city on a grand pre-war scale. But it grew sideways and spread, it did not grow upwards like Western cities as the price of land has soared. So the station square is a driver's nightmare, being surrounded by low railway bridges bringing the network to that palatial terminus. Wide, beautifully accommodating roads come to a sudden full stop where a low bridge crosses and the great juggernauts are trapped in a maze. Somewhere is that one exit, with a high enough clearance to allow escape to the open road. *Finding* it is the problem. We try every possible road, retreat and attempt the next. It has to be there, people *do* get out—there are no reports of "Flying Dutchmen" trucks condemned to cruise the boulevards of Budapest for eternity. The search takes four hours, we try 11 bridges until she's under, only just, but enough is enough and the map shows that the railway runs west while we are heading north-west, so goodbye, railway bridges.

We leave the busy city, the crowded, noisy bars, the communal exuberance, the splendours of the past, and soon the all-prevailing dilapidation of the socialist system reveals itself again.

To digress from our outward bound journey: the instructions from the agents on the return journey were to take on a load at a factory in Vac, 30 kilometres north of Budapest. This is a big factory making fluorescent tubes and doing an enormous export trade with their products which are priced well below Western rates. Good business for Hungary, a good deal for the Western consumer, though tough, maybe, on the Western worker who is made redundant because of the competition. The inescapable conclusion is that conditions of work in the workers' paradise would not be tolerated for five minutes in a capitalist sweat-shop.

The point about this massive factory is that it was built in pre-war days in an opulent industrial style. Once the best of its kind, it has been allowed to slide into near slum condition, to become uncared for, abused, steeped and marinated in disinterest. The only visible enthusiasm in the work force is to get the hell out of the place. Here stands this great works, an electric light factory of all things, which works in gloom. Where the workshops are ill-lit, the faces are glum and there is an atmosphere of festering despair. We arrive in the early evening, drive into the factory and learn that we have to stay overnight until loading can begin in the morning. We ask for washing facilities and food—if any. A jolly lady in the office wants to take us out for a meal as her guests, but that seems an imposition on her—and we have no local currency so we decline and settle for a shower instead.

Amenities are basic. Lavatories are spartan with sheet metal cubicles, torn newspapers on the floor and makeshift wire pulls on the cisterns. There are showers for the workers built out of zinc sheets, three-sided with no curtains; the overflow from adjoining cubicles and other drains surges up the central drain hole in each individual shower to soak the feet in slimy fluid. These are the sort of standards troops fighting a guerrilla war in the jungle might have settled for.

The offices are better, much better, but still designed and operated in a style circa 1940. But there is no interest, no incentive, no will to work: the same attitudes apply as in a conscript army, a work detail will evaporate the minute the overseer's eyes are turned away. They grin sheepishly at us and signal with a raised finger to the lips to keep quiet and they slip away. The woman overseer spends her time chasing them. Even she, in signs and monosyllabic English, says: "Not good. Too hard work. Little pay. Food much money. Bad times." With a shake of her head she frowns.

But yes, there is something pleasant to

report, like the kindness of the stranger busily sweeping the snow from outside his door who dropped his shovel and broom, leapt into the truck cab and showed us the way through winding streets to the factory gates two miles away with no hope of transport back to his home. There are things like that . . . and the very beautiful women.

As well as beautiful girls Hungary produces big girls. We met one. To get to the customs office at the factory it is necessary to walk along the railway line beside the loading bay, some rail wagons are being loaded there. We are walking along the line when suddenly we hear the clink, clink, clunk of rail wagons being shunted coming from behind us. But this cannot be, there is no engine attached to the wagons at the loading bay. However, the wagons are moving down the line and we have to jump for our lives.

A woman is pushing the wagons along with one hand. She is one of the big girls, built like a brick outhouse, not an ounce of flab on her, it's all muscle. She probably threw discus in the Olympics, lunches on anabolic steroids and eats three husbands for supper every evening.

Back on the road heading south and east the

motoring is good. We pass the impressive main depot of Hungarocamion, the Hungarian state international transport company. We know them well, all international drivers know and like Hungarocamion, they are cracking people. If you break down or hit trouble, no Hungarocamion driver would ever pass you, they are among the best drivers on the road, helpful, kindly and always cheerful. A group by the main gates spots the GB plates and rig, arms are thrown up in greeting, faces split into wide smiles. Give them a friendly blast on the air horn in salutation, we'll see them down the road or on the way back to London, bound to. Hungarocamion drivers once towed a broken down British truck 1,820 miles, repaired him and sent him happily on his way, all for no charge.

It is no fault of theirs that their bosses are among the worst at working "third country loading" dodges. They will "import" a European load for the Middle East into Hungary and instantly "re-export" it to the Middle East without even changing trailers—they just make out new documents from Hungary onwards. It is simple and difficult to detect but it knocks hell out of proper rates for the job.

It is a comfortable spin down to Naglac, the border with Rumania, a fast, easy run. But slap on the anchors, there are three Astrans in the lay-by, going home.

They are not happy. Java John, Bobby Holland and Rick Ellis have all been weighed coming in at Naglac and each found to be overweight on one axle—the cost in fines, £200 a man. The total weight of their trucks is under the maximum allowed but because of uneven distribution the weight over one axle is greater than it should be, so the Hungarians say. They are carrying the autumn crop of satsumas and nuts which they have loaded at Mersin in southern Turkey.

Java John says: "What chance do you stand? What can you do about it? They haven't got weighing machines at Mersin and the Turks just chuck everything they can pack in onto the trailer, they are not the most skilled loaders in the world."

So the happy-go-lucky ways of the Turkish worker have put £600 on the bill before the produce is a third of the way to its destination.

There is a queue at the border, there is

always a queue. All you worry about is the length of the queue, if you haven't the patience to sit in a queue, don't drive the route. The driving is only a restful, relaxing interlude between queues; the art, skill, aptitude and fun of the game is in handling queues and the lunatics who cause them. This queue has all the constituents of a good one.

There are F-Troop in numbers, Wombles, Willi Betz surrogates, Ursella Turks, Freewheeling Turks, a few Poles, Dutch, Germans, Swedes, even Iranians and Iraqis, which is curious, Brits . . . enough to clog up the works for a day and a night.

Alongside the road is a ditch and some sort of communal land working. A man is measuring distances, women lean on long-handled shovels making a few desultory prods at the ground; they talk a lot between themselves and don't do much work. They huddle close together in conspiratorial fashion and break into giggles. The man speaks and one of the women affects enthusiasm in running along the ditch to recover a tool, the rest giggle. Then they all squat and watch the trucks. Not a lot is happening but it is a diversion, something is afoot. The man stands and signals that something ought to be happening, he urges the women to get on with it. They respond by exaggeratedly mimicking him behind his back, then they all laugh and sit down again. The man gives up and walks along the ditch collecting pegs, string and tools, the women light up cigarettes and blow smoke rings. They do not look like manual workers, their shoes are too lightweight and they are wearing what could losely be described as town clothes.

A driver offers cups of tea, three women break from the group, cross the road and accept the proferred mugs. Their companions adopt poses of modesty and reservation. A few words of German are exchanged, a snatch of English. They are office workers and schoolteachers, this is their afternoon for community work; it is all a bit of a giggle. A driver tells them that he knows how they feel, his community work at home is cutting the lawns when his wife insists. They are intrigued. What is a lawn and why have one? Lawns are unproductive and bourgeois—it is more sensible to grow food in your garden.

6

ALL are equal, but some are more equal than others: the awful truths of Orwellian prophecy begin to sink in on the Rumanian side of the Nagylak border. Maybe it's just the fact that it is two o'clock in the morning and umpteen hours after you joined the queue and it is pissing down. But look at them in the border post, they've all got their great coats buttoned up to the neck and every one is the spitting image of a pig.

It is a comfortable border for those who work in it. On the right, seen through glass doors, is the officer's dining room—well laid tables, napkins, candles on the table even, very civilised; and the mess through the other doors is lively and comfortable. They are in smart, impressive uniforms; you are road-stained and crumpled; their shoes have a high polish, yours are dull and muddied; they are exquisitely manicured, your hands are black with grime; they have slept in beds, you have dozed fitfully over a steering wheel between sporadic bursts of movement along the queue. It is an unfair contest from the beginning.

The girl in the bank speaks perfect, fluent English. The best English so far along the route, so you compliment her on a very good English accent. When she asks why you should notice a true English accent, you explain that it is refreshing to hear when the predominant voice of those who have learned English as a second language is nowadays strongly American.

"American," she almost spits the word, "not in this country. You are a politically ignorant man, you should avoid comments on subjects you are not competent to discuss."

Sorry. Is that the clink of the man coming with the keys to the lock-up?

She is, however, quick, shrewd and fair. "Those are Deutschmarks you have there, I can give you a better exchange rate on those today. But it's up to you, if you wish to change sterling it is no problem." She taps her calculator, produces the slip and the difference is quite marked by comparison with the rates of sterling into D-marks that day. So you nod your head in agreement because you are too intimidated to open your mouth again.

The Dutchman comes clattering along in his clogs, big, ungainly and full of smiles. He opens his purse on the bank counter. " 'Allo, sweetheart," he says to the girl, "that's a nice voice you've got, very English sounding . . ."

Across the entrance hall is the customs office and they also speak good English, of all the countries en route the Rumanians are the best linguists. It seems to be a simple procedure: carnet, triptyches, £20 transit tax. The officer takes the cash and produces his stamp, then he flicks through the papers for a second time, pauses and consults a colleague. They confer.

"How many axles?" they ask.

"Four."

"Not five?"

"No."

"Well, sorry, you are overweight."

"No I am not. I haven't been weighed here and I gross exactly what is stated on the carnet, 32,121 kilos."

"Yes, overweight, you must pay a fine."

"Not overweight, the limit is 32,500 and I am 379 kilos under."

"The rules changed last Thursday, now the permitted maximum is 32,000 four axles, 35,000 five axles."

"I know nothing of this change."

"Here are the new regulations."

They are written in Rumanian. I explain that according to the date on the document, the only part which can be understood, the rules changed after the vehicle had left the United Kingdom. If it was, in fact, a change of rules agreed between Rumania and the EEC countries including Britain, no other country had questioned the weight. Nor had it been mentioned in England.

"That does not matter, you must pay."

They operate their calculators and say "Sterling £367, that is the excess fine."

"For 121 kilos! That is ridiculous."

"That is the rate, you must pay."

A second Dutchman is sitting on a chair in the corner. He says: "They are robbers, bandits, they want 900 Deutschmarks from me, I am five axles and less over the top than you. Now I have had to telex Amsterdam for the extra money and I have to wait here until it arrives. They want hard currency, the bank here will not pay out in hard currency, so somebody will have to bring me the money from Germany."

The argument begins. How do they calculate the charge? The answer: on kilos and kilometres to be driven through Rumania. In that case we won't take the long route through, we'll specify our point of exit as Calafat which is less mileage. All right, so we have to pay the ferry charges across the Danube at Calafat, we will do that. Anyway, we haven't got enough money to pay the extra. No, the truck can stay where it is until this matter is sorted out, they are causing the argument, so they are creating the bottleneck. Dig your toes in. There comes a time to say: "To hell with them, enough is enough. They get enough out of Western drivers in the ordinary course of events, their lives are spent thinking up new methods of extortion, they *are* bandits, robbers, legalised thieves in fancy uniforms. If they want the truck moved to clear the road, they can move it themselves, otherwise swallow the keys and let them wait for nature to take its course. We are not running away, none of us is running, we are not escaping, in fact, none of us intends to move an inch, and now that makes half-a-dozen or more Europeans in the same boat. So what the hell are they going to do about it?"

Trevor Long says: "Show them you don't give a monkey's and it is surprising how they cave in, they can't handle it, they are so used to calling the odds that they cannot understand when somebody answers back."

The office window is slammed and the officers retreat to an inner sanctum to confer, it looks like a mini-meeting of the supreme-soviets. They have a way of giving meetings a sinister air, these Socialismus officials, they imbue them with a degree of menace which is so often reflected in socialist dissidents' writings. It is disturbing enough in the pages of a book but through all too brightly lit glass windows it looks worse. This must be what it's like waiting for a jury to pronounce its verdict.

In 10 minutes they return with an attitude of confirmed resolution. There is a pause. Then the window is opened for the spokes-man to announce: "You—£215 sterling. You, Dutchman, 450 Deutschmarks, pay now."

It is extortion but we must weigh the relative costs, further delay could result in penalty clauses for late delivery if there should be, as there probably would be, more hold-ups down the road. The Dutchman is still short of cash, his money is waiting for him at Kapicule where everybody picks up extra cash from the agent, Youngturk. His company is well known on the road so the drivers float him enough to pay and get him through to Turkey. He signs scribbled IOUs. If we don't meet at Kapicule the companies will settle between themselves back at home. It is standard practice which everybody follows just to keep the show on the road.

The customs robbers' hash is settled. It is infuriating, but the stamps are on the documents and trucks and trailers are cleared.

So what the hell is happening now? Soldiers are swarming round the truck, inspection lights are blazing, dogs are out, guns are unslung from shoulders—all hell is being let loose. They are looking at the TIR tape, the vital wire which runs through hoops and eyelets all round the trailer cover and is secured with a customs seal. As long as the wire and seal are intact the load is considered to be exactly as declared. It is vital, however, that both tape and seals should not be "tampered" with. At the back of the trailer a soldier is pulling out the vertical TIR tape like so much spagetti. It is tough, thin high-tensile wire embedded in plastic and it has broken. It could have frayed and rusted, hard to spot under the coating of road film and mud. It could have been snagged by brushing against a tree. It could have been snicked by the night people trying to break into the load—that is just the place they would cut so that they could fold back the flap and lift the cargo out.

The fact is that it is broken and that spells very big trouble.

"Welcome to Rumania", says the placard by the side of the road. Some welcome, a £215 fine—now this.

So, again, the argument begins. "What the hell have you done to my tapes, you clowns? Your idiot bloody soldier has broken that. It was intact coming out of Hungary 200 metres away, now it is broken. That soldier is an oaf, he must have been swinging on it with all his weight."

It has to be a forceable argument and hotly contested every inch of the way—all night long if necessary, so much depends on it. They can legitimately demand that the trailer be unloaded, there, on the spot by the side of the road; all 18½ tons of cargo. And they will stand and watch you do it. Two cases of machinery in there weigh a ton-and-a-half each. How do you manhandle that on to the road?

They can open and examine every package

and the manifest lists 781 packages. First they will look for stowaways, then drugs—there is no answer in legal terms, the cargo TIR has been violated. If they find nothing they will stand and watch while you re-load which cannot be done without a fork-lift truck, which will cost a bomb. And they will charge overtime for each customs officer and soldier who stands by and watches as you sweat.

Worse still, if they discover something wrong with the cargo, something to arouse their suspicion, out will come the crowbars, sledge hammers and axes and those cases that canot be thrown off will be levered off to crash into the road, then they will be smashed open. Already a soldier is inside the tilt scrambling over the cases, prodding into gaps with a metal probe; there isn't much room for him, the tilt is packed so tightly.

Argument and protestation fall on deaf ears at this time, the searchers are too engrossed. There could be people in there, people trying to get in or out of the country, people making a run for Turkey and their freedom. The probes fail so the dogs move in to do their job.

The officer realises that it will be a fruitless

exercise, it is clear that the cargo has not been disturbed and it is too solid for stowaways to squeeze between. Nevertheless, we keep up the barrage of argument and outrage at such an intrusion; demand that the tilt is lashed up again and the tapes repaired. "Damn it, man, your half-trained louts wrecked the thing in the first place."

He is impassive. He barks orders at his platoon, they drop to their bellies and crawl under the trailer, others bring stepladders and climb to the top of the tilt to examine each inch of the fabric. Slowly the officer walks away to the shadow of the guardhouse building. We follow him.

"Problem," he says, "problem, but not a big problem, maybe we can fix." He smiles and adds: "No troubles, maybe we can fix, eh?"

His tone is obvious and his gist is clearer still but the game still has to be played.

"I need that tape fixed and plumbed, urgently."

"Sure, sure . . ."

A rapid assessment and plunge. "One hundred Deutschmarks."

"Two hundred is better . . ."

"OK, but no problems."

"No problems."

He walks rapidly back to the truck and barks commands. His squad re-thread the tape, others wipe the rest of the tape clean, there is another possible break in it. They clip the broken tape with strong wire staples, pierce and thread through customs wire linking both ends of the broken tape and do the same with the suspect area. The precious quarter-inch circular lead pellets are placed on the wires, the officer produces his plier punch, puts the pellets in its jaws and seals them with the offical customs stamp. Now we are virgo intacta again and free to roll.

Not another word is exchanged, the officer calls off his men, turns and hurries back to the warmth of the guardroom.

The rest of the drivers are waiting just beyond the customs area through the barrier.

"OK?"

"Yes."

"You're going Calafat, aren't you? We're going the other way. See you Kapic then, or if not, Istanbul."

The driving, as usual, is the interlude between borders and hassle. Calafat is down in the south-western corner of Rumania so the route misses Bucharest, the capital, and runs through Arad, Timisoara, down to Orsova and Craiova. Which seems simplicity itself, except that the signposts change from the Roman alphabet to a mixture of Russian, Croat, Serbo-Croat, Greek and Turkish spellings, not as bad as in Bulgaria, but enough to confound and confuse. The further off the main road you get, the worse the spelling and the greater the challenge. Along that main road to Bucharest it is comparatively easy to find your way, the TIR route is well marked in readable lettering. Off the beaten track, however, signposts are clearly considered an unnecessary luxury. Why have signposts? Everybody here knows where they are going, they don't get lost, they can even find the way home blind drunk, which is just as well.

There are a couple of other problems en route: one is Arad, the other a little hazard called the Transylvanian Alps. There is no way to avoid either.

First comes the unforgettable town of Arad. What's happening? Surely this must be a playback of Armstrong and Aldrin's landing on the moon. No it cannot be, their landing was smoother, so much smoother; but there are remarkable similarities, like soaring feet into the air at will and, more often than not, when not willed. Ahead are several other trucks, some coming this way, they lunge and plunge tossed as wildly as deep sea trawlers off North Cape in a Force Nine. It cannot possibly be, this is the centre of a big town, marked in black type on the map, an important town, full of civic dignitaries and officials who would not tolerate such conditions.

The truck coming this way gives two flicks of his headlights, a Brit, he is weaving and bucking like the best. He stops, winds down his window, grins and says: "Watch the puddles, mate." He lays heavy stress on the word puddles and laughs, "You going Calafat? It's a good border, no trouble, dead easy, if you can survive this lot. It is *unbelievable*, isn't it? Watch out for the Womble down there, you can see his back, he's in dead trouble, he went in a puddle." He winds up his window, pauses and winds it down again: "By the way, if you think the road's finished and you've gone off the track, it hasn't and you haven't, just keep going."

Such information is vital, keep going, forget the doubts at the back of your mind, press on, if it is not a road, it is a route.

The Womble is stuck. He has plunged

right into a puddle, a 20 by 50 foot lake across the street, but he didn't stop going down, deeper and deeper he went. So he gunned his engine hard, changed rapidly down and moved to blast his way through which he succeeded in doing, lurching out the other side. Then he stopped, dead. He climbed out to find a complete, rusted car engine impaled on his radiator and half his own engine knocked out.

He doesn't want assistance, his colleagues are coming to collect him, but he laughs until the tears roll from his eyes. "An engine, a blutty engine in a pottle. These Rumanians are a big joke. Maybe I repair and polish and sell on the black market."

Telegraph poles lean at acute angles into the roadway and the actual road surface is ridged with three foot bumps and drops. On one of the crazy, leaning poles the TIR sign points to the right. It doesn't look like any kind of road, but the man said follow the signs, have faith. Electric tramlines cut across in a curve. Swing right, move away and jam the brakes on. This is the road but there is a telegraph pole smack in the middle of it. Traffic runs either side of it, you can tell from the tyre tracks, it isn't on an island or anything like that, it is placed in the middle of the road. A tram is approaching so press on.

Left. Stop. Oh, no. It can't be the TIR route, impossible, not this back street. Single storey hovels lean forward and threaten to tumble into the road. Open drains run in front of the houses and out into the roadway where sections of the tarmac have crumbled into the drain.

The headlights reveal deep craters gouged in the surface, deeper than the ones we have already passed. A yellow ochre wall seems to form a dead end but scratched into its crumbling surface is a TIR sign with an arrow pointing left.

Carry on, the man said, he had driven this way. So be it. Have faith, but faith is sorely tested. Julie Sprinkler, a Canadian travelling truck lady at times and a girl of robust character being by profession a nurse and qualified midwife, journeyed along this same road until she said: "Stop, so far, no further, this is it, not another inch. No power in the world will convince me that any major truck route anywhere ever runs through the middle of a farmyard and no trucker ever finds himself stranded in a herd of pigs. You have made a mistake, admit it like a man, turn round and retrace your steps until you find the right and proper route."

It was not until a Volvo Turbo 12 with Dutch markings turned the 90° corner at the opposite end of the farm yard, scattered a flock of geese, air-horned a couple of wandering goats out of the way, gave a friendly flick of the lights and drove past that she conceded the point.

These are peasant countries and have always been so. Progress, if it is progress, has been slow in coming and often resisted. There is no deep understanding of the automobile, no craving for it as in the West, it is not in the East European genetic make-up and no love of it is passed from generation to generation. If a road is good enough for cattle and horses, that is sufficient.

The lack of progress does not inhibit the local people, nor does it make them discontented or unpatriotic. See these countries on May Day and the patriotic feeling is a revelation: no house, animal, farm implement, man, woman or child is without a red emblem, it is absolutely universal and quite emotionally shattering.

However, the lack of mechanical inheritance causes many problems. For people who have not grown up with them, automobiles present difficulties. In this country all traffic moves at a crawl—why rush? This is the pace of life, why hurry it? Their motor vehicles are slow, built to the prevailing pace of life and suit it perfectly.

Where there is no ingrained tradition of driving, every driver is as good as the next, lack of universal experience leads to lack of individual skill.

Ahead there is a mountain, a man-sized mountain with hairpin bends, steep tortuous climbs and wide, panoramic views of plunging valleys, pine forests with the snaking ribbon of road twisting in arcs and curves below. On high days and holidays in the State calendar every Lada, Skoda and Moscovich car in the country comes over the mountain to attend great political rallies.

On that hill, on those days, truckers are embarrassed by the huge crocodiles which form behind them. The cars have not the power to overtake. Truck drivers, contrary to what many private motorists think, detest crocodiles behind them. Their chief aim at such times is to find a lay-by, let the crowd pass, wait for a gap and make some more progress before the next lay-by.

This is a holiday and the following cars are stalling all the way up the mountain road, so the trucks pull off the road into a lay-by to allow a free run. But still they stall, every tenth car or so jerks to a stop and hiccups to a shaky hill start with all the following cars stopping and restarting in a similar way, shaking and shuddering into a forward crawl. All the way up the mountain little clutches of cars are juddering an erratic progress along the road. The drivers cannot handle a hill, it is beyond their average driving experience, they had not got in enough driving time or miles to know what to do. Nor do they have the class of roads to help them learn. Any driver should be obliged to have a certificate of proficiency from the Alpine Club before even being allowed to look at certain sections of the Transylvanian Alps. The predominant feature of these roads is that they are cobblestoned, excessively slippery in dry weather, grease-pan slithery in wet weather, glassy in snow, abominable in mist and fog. And rain, snow, mist and fog are the prevailing climatic conditions. They are also, without exception, built on the wrong camber but, on a clear day, the views are breathtaking.

There are other disadvantages. Eric Barker found a new route to a small, unknown border crossing which had the distinct advantage of not possessing a weigh bridge, so there was no possibility of fines for excess weight. So, to save a possible £200, he left the known route and headed slightly more east into unknown territory. The road began to climb rapidly and kept getting steeper. In a few kilometres it revealed itself to be a really rugged mountain road, flanked by precipitous drops and surrounded by towering pinnacles just visible through gaps in the cloud. The map reading put the height at 8,300 feet which is peanuts compared with the Swiss Alps or the Turkish Taurus mountains, but the shape and configuration of a mountain is what counts and this one possessed every treacherous feature in the book.

The road sloped to the edges of precipices and the truck slid alarmingly. Blind corners presented bottomless pits filled with swirling cloud below. There were miniature crevasses gouged in the road surface by the winter's snow and ice. Worst of all the clinging, opaque mist often blotted out all vision.

Then the light began to go as the mist thickened. Eric stopped at one of the rare places where there was sufficient room and the great loneliness of the place crept up on him. There was absolute isolation, with no habitation or sign of life. Although back along the road he had caught glimpses of castles on mountain peaks which only confirmed the veracity of Bram Stoker's romantic landscape in his Count Dracula stories—the stuff of a thousand horror movies come true.

Now something was wrong, there was a wind moaning and sobbing round the windows of the truck. Fog and a howling wind? That should not be, but the fog was cloud driven by a gale. Over the noise of the wind was the hint of another eerie sound, he strained his ears to listen. Was it just his imagination? No, the sound was definitely there, a baying which echoed and sighed to die away in the valley, sometimes sounding near at hand and other times distant. There are wolves in the area and bears, wild boar and other less homely creatures to meet on a midnight walk. The hairs on the back of his neck and hands began to prickle and his imagination speeded up. Then came another sound, sharper, different and distinctly nearer. By now the myth and legend of vampire and werewolf land had completely filled his mind and would not go away.

Suddenly in the mist he saw a form, an enormous shadow. Then under the windscreen there stood a massive animal, mouth agape and fangs flashing, it snarled at the truck door. The shadow grew more distinct and loomed larger through the distorting mist. A tall figure of a man emerged clad head to ankle in shaggy sheepskin, the wool hanging stringy and dripping. A hat sat on his head like a hairy tea cosy with strands of fur covering the eyes, his open mouth displayed a wide gap of missing front teeth with two yellowing incisors either side. He did not smile or make any sign of recognition but just stared from eyes sunken in brown hollows. It was a shepherd and his dog.

"I know it's daft, but my bottle went completely. I think my eyes popped out of my head and I was shaking all over. I kept telling myself how bloody silly it was but I couldn't stop it. I switched the engine on, slammed in the gear and went out of there like a bat out of hell. I took that mountain faster than a skier on a slalom run and I didn't stop until I reached a village and I was still shaking then.

"All to save £200, I'd have willingly given £500 to be off that weird hill. Even now I go hot and cold when I see a horror movie on the tele."

Loneliness and all its accompanying doubts and fears can arrive at any moment. In the wild deserted regions there is a shortage of friendly little villages and hostelries and the lack of life can get to a man. Feelings from a slight uneasiness to the downright unnerving often easily overtake a solitary man, no matter how self-contained and fearless he may appear.

Guide books are generally rather dismissive of the Transylvanian Alps and the whole Carpathian mountain range. Nowhere does it top 9,000 feet so it is not permanently snow covered, nor does it possess the imposing statistical data of the Swiss Alps. One book records that it has never formed a barrier for human movement, armies have crossed and recrossed the mountains at will and with ease. In cold print they make it read like a Sunday afternoon stroll.

It isn't like that at all. They are the poor relations of the mighty Alps in every way.

Nobody has spent money on these Rumanian mountains in the way it has been lavished on their Central European counterparts. So the mountains have become mean and spiteful; they can produce more impassable roads in a 100 square miles than the posh Alps to the north can produce in 10,000.

At about mid-morning Timisoara comes up on the signposts and rolls under the wheels in a slightly more civilised manner than Arad; the roads are at least negotiable and do not play at being motor-cross circuits. There are cars in abundance, hundreds of them, it looks as if every car in Rumania has come to Timisoara for an automobile celebration. Not moving cars, however, but cars in a queue strung along the side of the road in lines five or six miles long, parked nose to nose. Their owners stand by the side of their vehicles chatting on by their open boots picnicking and drinking. They have been there a long time obviously, because they have settled into a routine and share each others' vehicles as social centres; the waiting has become as much a social event as an ordeal. They are waiting for petrol and it is apparent that this has become an accepted chore, something which must be endured and made the best of.

And this is in a country with its own oil wells and petroleum industry.

As they wait another queue materialises alongside. One moment there is nothing, the next a rapidly expanding line of people growing like dividing cells on a slide under a microscope. A meat delivery van has arrived outside an empty butcher's shop and that is the signal for an instant queue to form.

The meat arrives not in fine sides of beef, lamb or pork, to be hung in display on the hooks around the shop, but in trays about three feet square and nine inches deep. They are filled with a predominance of white bone with flecks of red flesh attached. It looks, at best, good soup-making stock but hardly worth the attention of a butcher. No matter, it is eagerly awaited and, to the fortunate ones who happened to be on the spot, it is a bonus.

The inescapable fact is that throughout this great chunk of Europe, from the Baltic Sea in the north down to the borders of Turkey, Communism has come to the crunch. A saddening, terrifying crunch with nothing in the kitty, nothing in the larder, nothing in the shops and nothing in the fuel tank. Here, in the 1980s, is the evidence of the collapse of a system, which might bring bitter joy to the hearts of the hawks in the Pentagon and other Cold War strongholds but which can only bring fear and misgiving to more generously minded people living in immeasurably better conditions.

For, in these backwoods of Communism, far from the permitted beaten track of the tourist and the visiting VIP, the failure strikes at the roots of society, every society. The system is decaying and with it morals, honesty and hope. Corruption is the rule, the Black Economy dictates life and the simple fact of being able to live. Everybody is sucked in, bad breeds worse and it cannot do any good to the affluent West that poverty should be winning hands down in the midst of potential plenty. This is the classic imbalance that leads to wars.

So Western truck drivers, working men from a capitalist society and therefore, according to the ruling philosophy of these countries, oppressed and exploited human beings, can look upon the scenes they are privileged to witness with compassion and sad wonderment in their hearts. It affects them all without exception. They are too aware of the woefully ironic fact that this remaining fabric of society, such as it is, is supported only by the despised profits from a detested, so called decadent, society. Without massive loans from the West, hell would have broken out years ago.

The debts of the Comecon countries to the West in 1972 totalled a mere 6 billion dollars, in the 1980s it had risen to 80 billions.

Truckers do not philosophise or moralise publicly, theirs is a pragmatic trade so they play the bends and twists of the system like they drive a bad road, eyes wide open and with considerable care. They see very clearly, say nowt and turn it to their advantage. But it takes two to play.

The normal rules do not apply to truckers, they ride in kingly fashion through the regulations, encouraged and assisted, pushed and coerced in fact, by the local population who want a share of that hard currency in their purses. They stimulate the black market. No eyes are raised nor protest voiced when a truck pulls to the front of a queue and stops by the diesel pumps. Police do not interfere and the army is compliant, the only excitement is the press of private individuals from the queue all wanting to complete their private deals and gesticulating for anything from tyres to food or cassettes. This is not a quick, furtive, undercover transaction. The pumps are old-fashioned and it takes half-an-hour to pump 1,750 litres of fuel into the side and belly tanks of a juggernaut. The black market price of the fuel is known to everybody, the negotiation is a haggle round minimal percentages either in the price of fuel or exchange rates of varying currencies.

The price works out between 44p and 62p a gallon compared with between £1.50 and £1.70 in the West. A good deal. It will not show in the filling station manager's records because he buys his supplies with coupons paid for in local currency; the more coupons he buys, the more fuel in his tanks. The profit he will make on the currency puts him into the best part of a 1,000 per cent profit, so he is not worried and there is plenty left for a share-out all round. But everybody is in on the fiddle from the refinery to the filling station pump—loaders, checkers, drivers, inspectors and law enforcement personnel.

Time has changed little in this landscape. There is a folksy gaiety about the villages with houses decorated with ornate tiled designs on the outside worked in the most intricate of patterns. Each house is graced by its own garden wall shaped to its owner's individual taste and with shutters to shield the windows. The whole house is tiled from roof to foundations and no two houses in a street are the same. It looks all very pretty in the sunshine as if the streets were clad in Fair Isle pullovers, bright, warm and snug.

The women still work the fields and trundle home on the oxen and donkey carts. The whole village moves out to work in the fields in the morning returning en masse at the end of the day's labours, the men and women keeping to their own separate groups. It is a countryside of horse, ox, donkey and manual labour with primitive tools, the same as it has been for centuries with no visible signs of change except for an occasional tractor. Nothing has touched these people and their way of life in hundreds of years; there has been no fundamental change. The great juggernauts roaring through their lives have no real meaning for them, they come from a world they know nothing of and which they cannot begin to imagine, let alone understand. The peasant mentality has defeated the ambitions of oppressors and politicians from time immemorial.

The Shell Map of Europe doesn't bear any resemblance to the Rumanian touring map, not a single road matches but Calafat is 56 kilometres away if the latter is to be believed. We treat it as a mystery tour. It is a hairy run in but much softened by the knowledge that the ferry is just round the corner, or the next corner, or the one after that. When it does come it is a surprise but, in contradictory terms, a familiar surprise. The mud-obliterated arse-end of a stationary truck is parked by the side of the road and, just as we are preparing to overtake, we spot the dozen more trucks ahead.

7

THE Danube lies in wait round every major corner for European travellers: a conceited bitch of a river which demands not to be crossed once, like any goodhearted waterway, but a dozen or more times in the course of a journey. It has the same persistence as a dog at feeding time which shoves itself between master and feeding bowl before the job can be neatly accomplished.

The river has come a heck of a distance and taken a long time doing it since it has risen in the far western corner of Germany in the triangle formed with France and Switzerland and within walking distance, figuratively, of that upstart brook, the Rhine. It has crossed the width of Germany, Austria, Hungary, and Yugoslavia, flowed through great capital cities, segregated millions from other millions and dictated the tide of history, and here it is in front of us about to dissect the Balkans. An influential river which is about to cost us £46 to get across for the last time, which seems trivial homage to pay to so mighty a creation of nature.

A philosophical driver who considers such things says: "Think about this, the Danube rises the other side of France and comes all this bleedin' way. Now, water don't flow uphill, right? So from France to 'ere has gotta be downhill, right? So why have I been floggin' up and down these bloody ridiculous mountains all the time?"

The drop to the ferry landing is steep and the road goes through a 360° turn to run back on itself at a lower level. Trailers bottom and scrape the ramps and the rig is rested at an acute downward facing angle. The landing is the usual collection of unsophisticated buildings not matching the natural drama of the setting. Bored, dishevelled soldiers mooch, smile sheepishly, ask for cigarettes, shift from one foot to the other and lean against the buildings first on one shoulder then the next. The ferry closes for the night.

We are half way down the approach road, which is good for a quick getaway in the morning but not so good for sleeping since we are tilted at so acute an angle.

The river slides by in the moonlight, so smooth, so flat, so still and quiet that it is difficult to see why movement becomes so noticeable. It is more a sense of movement than an observation of it. By night the distant bank has merged with the horizon so that the whole world through the window seems to be sliding away softly from right to left. There is not a sound, not a light, not a movement.

But aproaching dawn reveals swirls and eddies on the changing face of the river, the far bank begins to etch in blacker on the canvas and trees mould out of the half-light. Dawn comes in a desultory manner, doors open, weary soldiers shamble out, blink and immediately lean against the walls. There is movement on the jetty. Unexpectedly, without warning, the ferry appears.

It is as good a way as any of entering Bulgaria, very easy, unfussed and quick by the standards of borders. The Bulgarians clearly do not believe in personality cults and prove it in the customs hall. The walls over the counter grills are lined with portraits of the whole Bulgarian leadership, all identically sized five by four feet photographs, all taken from the same angle and all with the artificial, metallic gloss of airbrush treatment. And all, men and women alike, with the mandatory expression of serious intensity: a square-faced, square-jawed group of solid citizenry they look. Who would dare to come through here with a Micky Mouse permit when such an auspicious body scrutinises the proceedings?

Bulgaria is a very curious place and not for the nervous or weak-minded. There are two Bulgarias; the countryside which, in common with Comecon neighbours, they run like a graveyard, and the city which they run like a lunatic asylum.

They have a chequered and explosive history which is liable to break out again at any time. In the beginning Bulgarians "lived by and from war" according to authoritative historians; most of them look as if they still could and probably do. One thing is sure, they are a nation of rugged individualists no matter what political system they live under. Always treat a Bulgarian on his merits and be careful of his sensibilities, otherwise he might turn sour.

In January 1982 the Bulgarian Communist hierarchy announced a return to a more "flexible" economic structure which would allow a degree of private enterprise and profit "along the Hungarian lines of economic development", which is an instance of politics belatedly catching up with the facts of life. Ever since the collectivisation of the farms in 1950 antagonised three-quarters of the population, three-quarters of farm production has gone "private enterprise" and official production has declined so that State targets have never been met. So all that the Party pronouncement did was to regularise an existing situation along the lines of "if you can't beat 'em, join 'em".

But notwithstanding their individualistic and entrepreneurial inclinations, Bulgarians are remarkably gregarious. Sofia is one big swinging city with all the social attributes such as large department stores, restaurants, bars and crowds. Saturday in Sofia is get-together day, get-drunk-and-be-happy day, let-your-hair-down and sod-the-system day.

It is also one-way traffic day and the longest-meal-in-history day. The crowds foregather in the main square and walk, all going in the same direction, in a solid phalanx filling the width of the pavements, nose to the back of the head in front, in a continuous all day perambulation, round and round the square with lots of chat, ribaldry, flirtations, intrigues and laughter.

There is no chance of walking the other

way, it is a physical impossibility. People leave the crush only to stoke up energy for the next stint of walkabout with quantities of the local brandy and vodka. The static queues the observer sees are not for chiropodists but to gain entrance to eating houses which are packed all day long. Plan your meals well in advance, begin thinking about supper shortly after a late lunch—it is bound to be a late lunch because nobody has warned you about the queues.

Free enterprise entrepreneurs are in abundance with every known commodity for sale, suede coats, booze, foreign currency. There is the vibrant atmosphere of a gala day on Blackpool's Golden Mile. And a foreigner finds it difficult to buy a drink, it is bought for him, or rather drinks come up in a never-ending stream. But, if you do hand over money, do not expect change, it all goes into the universal kitty.

Bulgarians are phenomenal breeders, they have had a birthrate of 39 per 1,000 and doubled the population during the first half of the century. They are still trying hard. It could have a lot to do with the Sofia Saturday Walkabout which is a splendid thing for meeting people and making friends—close friends.

They take their friendliness with them wherever they go and Wombles, like Hungarians, are good mates on the road. They will not pass by any trucker in trouble or leave him stranded.

Drivers of other nationalities naturally reciprocate. At the borders going into Bulgaria, customs give the closest scrutiny to their own nationals from the Bulgarian International Transport fleet. They are prime suspects to the officials and their trucks are often stripped, bunks, linings, panels are ripped out and every nook and cranny probed. Other drivers take through whatever goodies the Wombles have purchased during their wanderings abroad and meet up with them a few kilometres along the road inside the country.

A favourite pull-up lies on the road to Sofia—a "modernised" café in 1950's ex-presso style—veneered panels, plastic table-tops, plastic chairs and multi-coloured Venetian blinds. This is a popular drinking place both with drivers and locals and, being a central night spot, it has its quota of racketeers—professionals as opposed to the ubiquitous happy amateurs.

It is a fun place, good for giggles. The waiters wear dinner jackets and floppy bow ties, their shirts and jackets are spotted with beer and grease stains, but the dress makes the staff easily distinguishable from the customers. The waiters tend to have a faraway look in their eyes and an abstracted air about them, which could come from the fact that they serve drinks on the basis of one for the customer, one for the staff. Party time in this illustrious establishment is a truly democratic affair with staff, customers and party-givers all joining in the high jinks.

A failing is that the heating often breaks down and the kitchen staff also allow the cooking ranges to go cold and serve white French fries from a tepid frier and "biffstek" with the middle still chilled from the ice box. But customers still flock in.

The spivs are busy pressing their demands to drivers. Tyres are the big deal tonight. Good money for all types of tyres, spot cash. They pester and harangue until one experienced driver says: "I've got a funny feeling that this is a set up. They don't usually go on like this for so long and there are too many of them about. I don't like it."

A German driver comes hurriedly back into the dining room from the truck park to say: "My cab's just been done, they've smashed the window and cleaned it out. They're all over the place out there, flitting behind every truck."

It's a fit up. There's only one way to handle it—mob-handed. There are several factors in favour of the visiting team. These yobbos are not out for mindless violence just for kicks, most of all they want loot to sell. Violence can put them in the hands of their own police, a quarter where they may not be too popular already. On top of that, they know that in tangling with truckers they might get badly hurt themselves. They are quite capable of picking off a trucker by himself but not too keen on tackling several at once.

So, mob-handed let it be and watch each others' backs. Then let's all shove off, who needs aggravation? We'll square the German up later and get him through to Turkey. There's no use complaining about the robbery, nothing will result from it—except a lot of lost time.

It is quiet in the truck park but when the headlights are switched on there are a lot of legs showing under trailer chassis where legs ought not to be. Thieves never seem to realise that you can see legs under a chassis in the glare of headlights and legs will throw an elongated shadow on the ground on the other side of a truck when spotlights and Cebies are switched on. Behind the trailers there is no hiding place. There is a lot of aggro about, and a bad feel to the place tonight. Never mind, let's not hang about. It will be chilly for the German who now has to drive without a side window, but he'll put his heater on and lash it up when we stop later down the road. We'll find another gaff.

"Early start tomorrow, eh? We can wrap up Bulgy in half a day, down to Kapic, I mean. Kapic, Oh God, bloody Kapic, I try not to think about Kapic until it's under my nose. A bloke up the road was telling me that there was a five day queue there when he came through yesterday."

Kapicule is a nightmare.

8

MOST of the great crossroads of the world are known to every schoolboy and have become household names: London, New York, San Francisco, Sydney, Tokyo, Singapore, Istanbul, places to go to and come back from, to pass through while going somewhere else. They are all great ports, airports and commercial centres, vital links in the international chain of trade, finance, travel and communications. Over the years they have been refined to relatively smooth-running, efficient centres of interchange between nations with docks, cranes, runways, marbled halls, pavements, asphalted roads, and a semblance of order, comfort and help for the poor traveller. And the wandering public, from package holiday-maker to executive businessman expect it to be so. Yet there is one great vital crossroad which, thankfully and blessedly, the bulk of travelling humanity has never heard of, and pray God, never will experience.

It is called Kapicule.

Kapicule. It is a name to bring a particular expression to the face of a driver, a look both of an Indian mystic who has received a revelation and a nun who has seen a vision—but he of something frightful round the corner and she of the wrong fellow. The look will never leave him for he is a man whose soul has been stamped with an indelible experience. In its horror Kapicule is as much a spiritual encounter as a physical happening.

On the physical side it is the commercial reincarnation of the Somme battlefield: the trenches, the clawing, sucking mud, the shattered flora and fauna, the blasted buildings. Here humanity is under extreme stress, ensnared in impassable ground, frightened, angry and fed up. Humanity, in fact, is at the end of the line and at the end of its tether.

On the spiritual side Kapicule is living proof that old Rudyard Kipling knew a thing or two: "Oh, East is East, and West is West, and never the twain shall meet, Till Earth and Sky stand presently at God's great Judgement Seat."

This great crossroads is not marked on the map, not even on a large scale map, and yet it is the gateway between the West and the

East, between Christianity and Islam. It is the teeming, clogged people-jammed capital city of Bedlam but so small that its telephone numbers are listed only in single and double figures, there are not enough telephones in the place to reach triple figures.

Kapicule stands on the overgrown cart track between the Bulgarian village of Svilengrad and the Turkish town of Edirne. The world has never heard of it. Until a decade ago it had never heard of itself and was a hamlet which could barely support a crumbling hovel and tumbledown shack, its children ran ragged-trousered and bare-arsed across the one mud road—there is still only one mud road but now it is covered with a coating of asphalt—while their fathers squatted, drawing deep upon their hookah pipes and their mothers baked unleavened bread.

Then three things happened almost simultaneously: engineers in Europe put real power under the bonnets of heavy trucks and the juggernaut was created, Arabia exploded into vast wealth from its oil resources and the smiling, affable Bob Paul proved that it was feasible to drive overland from Europe to the East.

Soon Bob Paul's infrequent visits, on his way out and on his way back which so relieved the tedium for locals handling peasant traffic between two impoverished countries, became less of a world shattering event for them as a gentle trickle of trucks began to arrive regularly. The locals had never had it so good, the foreign drivers carried untold wealth in their purses and spent liberally, or so it seemed to a native population living at subsistence level. They were rich on the loose change from a driver's pocket when he bought food, baubles and trinkets.

Before the natives could catch their breath this trickle, as trickles have a habit of doing, turned in quick succession into a stream, a deluge, a torrent, a flood and everybody became stinking rich because nobody has a quicker eye to a profit or a fiercer dedication to turning a quick buck than a Turk. In time they came to realise their unique advantage in this particular geographical situation and turned the extraction of quick bucks from passing drivers into an art form, the subtleties of which could confound the finer brains of Wall Street and the London School of Economics.

A quick reference to the atlas shows their strategic advantage. All overland traffic to Asia and the Orient has to go through Turkey, down to Istanbul and across that magical, historic strip of deep water you could spit across on a good day with the wind behind you, the Bosporus—the dividing line between Europe and Asia. There are only two ways into Turkey, through Greece, which involves a considerable detour, or through Kapicule. So all traffic from the continent of Europe to the continents and sub-continents of Asia, Asia Minor, Arabia and the mysterious Orient had, of necessity, to converge on this sleepy, inadequate hamlet.

The sap flowed the way the sap of a mighty, spreading oak tree does when it retreats from the highest and furthermost twigs into the branches and down through the trunk to rest in the roots during winter. And it returned like rising sap in springtime. It travelled ten thousand roads to meet and coagulate on this oxen-cart highway and the names emblazoned on the trucks read like a gazatteer of the Northern Hemisphere: Aberdeen, Glasgow, Kristiansund, Bergen, Helsinki, Stockholm, Oslo, Malmo, Liverpool, Carlisle, Ipswich, London, Hamburg,

Groningen, Rotterdam, Gottenburg, Lille, Frankfurt, Graz, Innsbruck, Warszawa, Budapest, Bucaresi, Sofia. The northern world, from the icy outposts of the Arctic to the troubled Balkans was flocking south and east through the eye of a needle in northern Turkey.

The numbers became staggering, 2,000 trucks a day, which meant a daily 68 miles of snorting, pulsating machinery fighting to get in and get out. A continuous, nose-to-tail three-mile-long queue at any given time choking and polluting those remote Bulgarian and Turkish villages but bringing a rare sparkle to those dark, sad, faraway Turkish eyes of peasants, officials and policemen alike. A Turk loves and glories in his money. So does his government but it has to be pretty slick and quick-witted to prise it out of Turkish citizens' pockets. There is a running battle between government and subjects as to who gets the lion's share of the take, and the government is on a loser from the start.

The money which changes hands in Kapicule adds up to a lot even in official taxes on the value of goods and produce going through—an average of two million sterling a day. But that is only the tip of the iceberg.

If the true value could ever be discovered it would certainly come to much more. But it cannot, Turkish and European agents are skilful at concealing the true value of goods and thus avoiding tax on them.

For example: a cargo of gold-plated cigarette lighters was valued for European insurance at £1.3 million, the agents winced stricken by sudden acute financial pain. A tax of two-and-a-half per cent or even five per cent of the value of such a load comes to far too much money to give the government on a platter. The papers were doctored to show a value of £130,000 and an arrangement made to split the saving between parties concerned. The cargo arrived safely.

Whichever way it is approached Kapicule is Fun City, Asia Minor, for dedicated masochists, but by far the most bizarre approach is from the Bulgarian side. Questions approaching drivers ask are: does the queue begin this side or the other side of the village Svilengrad? Is the border open or closed? Is traffic moving through or stuck?

The answers do not matter a damn except to get you into a suitable state of mind for the unavoidable wait. One side of the village is just as boring as the other and just as unrewarding. The villagers, understandably, grew bloody-minded at their village being permanently dissected by an iron curtain of juggernauts parked for hours and days outside their front doors so now the village is kept clear.

On the side of Svilengrad furthest from the border is one of the most confusing sights in Communism. It is a café and discotheque, hopelessly, noisily out of context in the drab social scene. It is so garish, flashy and loud that it would never be tolerated in the sleeziest quarter of any capitalist city. But here in this village its lights blaze all night and it thunders decibels of din without interruption into the streets and across the fields, day and night. The bar inside is stocked with whisky, gin, and vodka all on open display. The disco equipment is the latest Western hi-fi and the tapes come from the current Top Twenty. Inside the noise is excruciating.

The scene, the pool of brilliant light, the music, the frantic comings and goings, the shrieks of drunken laughter, has an air of unreality about it. At any minute you think the police will arrive to arrest everybody and restore peace and quiet and Socialist sobriety. But nobody comes, the revelry continues unabated.

More confusing still are the people. They are as seedy a collection as ever assembled outside the pages of Damon Runyon or James Hadley Chase, dressed for the part and dressed to kill. They wear a lot of leather, long coats, Chelsea boots, leather jackets with Davy Crockett fringes. Sleep is something they have never heard of, they drink and lounge all night; work is clearly abhorrent to them. The girls wear slit skirts, high heels, a lot of make-up liberally applied, and they are available, very available, but never far away from their leather-clad minders.

The girls are prostitutes, the men are ponces. They are gangsters. Gangsters with a fearsome reputation along the road. Violent, nasty men as evil as any Mafia godfather. Drivers have been maimed and mutilated by them. The least harm to befall a driver who crosses them is to be beaten up and robbed.

So this is an inherent risk of the road which happens wherever hard-drinking, fighting men forgather to let their hair down and look for sex. But in most places it is kept underground and the violence is covert—

pimps, ponces and minders keep in the background and do not make themselves obvious, they mingle with the crowd. Here they *are* the crowd, there is nobody else about.

Yet this is a Communist country, subjugated, controlled at the point of the gun, ordered and directed by an all-powerful State organisation. And nobody interferes. Moreover, if you complained about the gangsters, officials would look at you with unseeing eyes, look right through you, in fact, and tell you: "There are no gangsters. This is a People's Socialist Republic and we do not have gangsters. Gangsters are a product only of decadent Western imperialism and the dupes of that society. What you are saying is an insult to the Socialist State, you are acting as a Western reactionary troublemaker, you are a subversive element. Have you connections with the CIA?"

So careful men keep the cab door locked and the windows closed. Especially when the Socialist gangsters are touting their women along the line of trucks or suggesting currency deals, or offering deals to buy anything there is to sell such as porn magazines or CB radio equipment. Most of the drivers who know the run never deal with them because there is always the awful danger that the one you choose to bargain with is also a man from KAT, the ubiquitous State Police.

"Tricky bloody monkeys, this lot, tell 'em to fuck off," says a happy driver from Blackburn, Lancashire, and continues to munch his bacon buttie. "D'y'want a bite?" he asks, "I've got 'alf left, go on, it's Wall's best back bacon, luv'ly."

Quick, back in the cab, move up. Now we are in the village, something has gone wrong with the system, we are stopped dead in the middle of the village. Off we go again, no we don't, all the engines are running but we are not moving, some clown has switched on his engine to warm his cab, the rest have followed suit thinking we are about to go ahead. One by one the engines die. Still, we made a whole kilometre and it is only a night and half a day so far—good progress.

The village is quiet. There is a children's playground on the right, brightly painted and quite adventurous. "Funny thing," says Gavin Waugh, "in all the years I've been coming here, I've never seen a kid playing in it."

"You're right," other drivers agree. A

quick poll among the drivers and nobody has ever seen a child playing there.

This time the engines roar and we do move, a heck of a way, a good one-and-a-half kliks. "Might get through tonight," is the optimistic consensus. A flock of geese waddles down the road and under the trucks, they find nothing interesting on that side, so they waddle back; an old man prods a donkey along the side of the road. There is a shed there with open sides, it must be a cattle market of sorts, it looks as if it is used by livestock. We have been here a whole day now and seen eight people, nobody has come out of or gone into the houses. What do they do all day?

Evening brings the chill so switch on the engine and heater; all the way down the line behind engines roar into life, and lights come on. It is time really to put the night heater on. The lads without night heaters run their engines when it gets too cold to sleep in the cab without heating. It is an expensive way of keeping warm, the engine will burn fifteen gallons idling during the night, £25 to stop freezing, you could stay in a good hotel for that, if there was one. A night heater pays for itself in a couple of trips.

The noise that we hear now is a meaningful roar as engines are started. We are in business, jump out of the bunk in your underpants, we're moving. What is the time? Seven o'clock, ah well, we got a night's kip.

Stop. Now the actual border is in sight, just over the treetops are the watch-towers, little boxes with sloping roofs and windows all round mounted on four spindly legs with a ladder running up one side. A couple of silhouetted figures move around in them, they must have been a bloody sight colder than we were during the night, God help them.

The guard must just have changed, a group of soldiers is scurrying up the road, they walk semi-crouched and huddled, collars turned up and hands deep in pockets. They are too cold, tired and hungry even to think about bumming cigarettes.

They are kids. Just how young they are shows on the NCO's face, he is about 20 and after a night's duty he has a five-o'clock shadow growth of beard on his face. The others haven't a whisper of a whisker between them, smooth faces pinched by the cold, tiredness in their eyes; 17-, 16-, possibly 15-year-olds. A straggler is in the rear, he is having trouble with his bootlaces and kneels outside the cab to fasten them. We are all in the cab sipping the early morning brew of hot, steaming Maxwell House, well laced with Bailey's Irish Whiskey. Offer him a Jacob's Club chocolate biscuit and a mug of coffee, he hitches his AK-47 automatic tighter into his shoulder, his eyes light up and he smiles a wide, spontaneous smile grasping the mug in both hands. He gets the aroma of the Bailey's, nods and says: "Gud," laughing when he has clearly got the word right.

He looks like a schoolboy. The ex-Paratroop Regiment sergeant sitting in the cab says: "Poor little sod, he looks as battle-ready and as tough as a Boy Scout patrol leader, he's a whiff of a kid."

Give him a couple of packets of Rothmans International and his cup brims to overflowing, he is as happy as Christmas, except that they don't have Christmas in these parts.

We gain another 500 metres. The chain of watch-towers is clearly visible now, on either side of the road are still, quiet tree plantations. The happy man from Blackburn sings: "If you go down in the woods today, you're sure of a big surprise—CRRUMPPP!"

This is the end of the line, the end of a 2,000 mile long barbed-wire, land-mined, searchlighted, watch-towered, Communist cage enclosing two-thirds of a continent. Through that gate and across that no-man's-land is freedom. Well, not quite, the army is running that country too.

The view from the driver's seat in a truck is remarkably different from that in a car in many aspects. Physically the driver's feet are above the roofs of passing private cars. He looks forward and above everything other than another juggernaut. He looks straight down at the road below his feet. He sits above, sometimes in front, of his wheels and his mirrors which are possibly 10 times the size of car wing-mirrors and give a panoramic view behind greatly enhanced by their height above the road. His posture is different from that of a car driver since he sits upright in a dining chair position rather than an armchair slump. His steering wheel is flat in front of him inclined only at the angle of a school desk and his view is unimpeded.

Which is why such features as watch-towers and fortified frontiers become so marked in his vision—from road level they are scarcely visible through hedges and fencing.

His view is conditioned even more by the

other factors: he is there for a different purpose than the car driver so he thinks about the situation from a different standpoint. For the private motorist to travel from England to Bulgaria is an adventure, for the trucker it is distance, time and work. His involvement colours his views; distances rolling under his wheels colour his views; time overrides countries and people; borders are commercial hazards and a nuisance, they are not political.

Familiarity never fully removes the adventure but it does change his viewpoint, it removes the consciousness of differing nationalities. There are just people you meet and know en route. And the route becomes a long, continuous road in a long, continuous world.

Enforced waiting in an enclosed cab is an ideal environment for the amateur philosopher and the driver in a tartan cap with a bobble on top says: "I'll tell you what amazes me about this run, and that is how abrupt the human race is as a species. It doesn't do things gradually, there's no gentle change. The countryside changes gradually most of the time, you don't run out of lush, green meadows straight into burning desert, it changes gradually. Yet you go across what is shown as a thin line on a map and every-thing changes completely. People look different, they speak different languages, they do different things, they think differently. If they'd been born 200 yards the other way, they'd have turned out completely different people. I mean, these bloody barbed-wire borders haven't been here for ever, they must have been able to walk across in the old days and mix a bit, somebody must have had a bike, you'd think they'd be a lot more like each other along the border, but they aren't, they change immediately you go across. Watch 'em, half the buggers at one end of the border crossing can't speak to the other half at the opposite end, they don't talk the same lingo. We get on better than they do. I mean, less than half a mile from where we're sitting there's a completely different race. You tell a Turk that you mistook him for a Bulgarian and he'll stick a knife in you."

Action! A flash of headlight down the road on the opposite side is followed by a roar as trucks begin to rush by in the opposite direction. They pass with a snarling of gears bounding, like Labrador pups let off the leash. If they are coming out, the chances are that we will be going in.

It is a good run this time, maybe four minutes, it feels like 400 miles before we stop. A driver comes back along the line seeking water. "Tomorrow morning," he says, "they've still got a couple of hundred in the customs area and they've filled up the park. Get another night's kip tonight."

Not bad, two days, might be clear in three with luck, a man without patience is a non-starter in this tortoise race.

"Two-and-a-half days. Two-and-a-half bloody days." "So what? I was stuck here for a week." "I can beat that, I've been stuck here for nearly a month." "Yes, but not in the queue, waiting for documents or something. My best was five days." "I went through in four hours, once. It's better now the military have taken over." "Yes, but you can't fiddle like you used to. Christ, can you imagine it at Dover?" "Listen, mate, I've had as bad at Dover. Worse."

Harry Robinson is one of the Carlisle drivers, with the cool eyes and quiet disposition of a high country man, a Zapata moustache to add a touch of melancholy to his face. He knows the journey and its vagaries better than most and he asks: "What right have we to criticise them, either the

Bulgies or the Turks? Just look at the shambles out there. Nobody back home could believe it because nobody could imagine what happens. It is beyond anything we know about in Britain or in the rest of Europe for that matter. Nothing like it happens anywhere else."

In every direction there are trucks, they fill the vision and overwhelm the senses. There are trucks in lines, trucks shunting, jostling and buffeting for position, trucks at angles to the traffic flow, trucks sliding and slipping in the mud, trucks with wheels spinning fruitlessly in the slime, trucks which have fitted their snow chains in a desperate effort to claw a way through, trucks attempting to pull out others which have stuck, trucks moving, trucks stationary, charging trucks rushing from all angles to fill a gap which has appeared.

Behind high fences are other trucks in massive compounds segregated from the rest and parked at crazy, lunatic angles. There are unattended trucks, trucks with their curtains drawn when the driver has temporarily given up and gone to bed, trucks which rolled shining and sleek off production lines a month ago, trucks with patchwork quilts of repair work all over them. But new and old alike they are all reduced to the same state of frustration by the turmoil.

In the middle of the pandemonium are the diminutive figures of the soldiers, checkers and officials who shepherd this snarling flock.

Harry surveys the scene. Standing with a group of drivers, he adds: "Nowhere anywhere else is there an organisation which could deal with this, there is not a single country which could absorb such traffic and the work it makes at any of their borders, these people work miracles with nothing to help them. They didn't ask us to come here, we are not invited guests, we invited ourselves. We all suddenly arrived because it suited us and we kept on arriving and as we rolled up they kept on coping. Anywhere else there would have been a public outcry, letters of protest in the papers, demonstrations and questions in parliament. It would have been banned."

Which is probably true. Other borders are busy, others are hectic, chaotic and jammed, but this is the big one.

There is one unpredictable hazard, the Bulgarians may be drunk. They are often drunk and no social stigma attaches to it in their own society. Drink is a national occupation with them as it is with the Russians, Poles and other such aligned countries—it is a national pestilence. Your progress may depend upon how the drink has taken them that day, sometimes it brings happiness and the way is clear, at other times it goes sour on them and life becomes problematic for those with whom they deal . . . so tread carefully and handle affairs circumspectly.

Do not blame them, they live in a perpetual madness which you have helped to create and are exacerbating by being there.

The "Golden Gateway", the actual crossing point into Turkey and thus into the marvels of Asia, is a series of tumbledown shacks which would hardly grace a dossers' encampment on a derelict building site. Somehow it works, the documents get stamped, passports franked "exit", trailers checked and cabs examined, the barrier lifts and Bulgaria, for the time being, is a thing of the past with no claim or lien upon the driver.

Across the wasteland the Turks have set aside a vast tract of flat land where trucks may park in preparation for the entry into the seat of the once great Ottoman Empire. It is a mile or more long, at a critical distance from the entrance a deep trench has been bulldozed along the length to stop the spread of vehicles laterally but with a bridge of solid earth to allow a crossover into an overspill area. Turned from the blade of the bulldozer the clay has been left to be tempered, moulded and crumbled by the weather and crushed by wheels straying a fraction beyond the defined limits.

Because it forms a natural trap, the litter of years has accumulated in the cut: cans, boxes, food containers, paper, plastic, broken mechanical parts, bumpers, radiator grills— all the dross of the age of the automobile lies rusting and decaying in the dust.

But the litter spreads beyond the trench to cover the whole area, pressed and trodden into the muds of winters, ground and embedded into the baked surface and dust layer of summers. Nothing is ever cleared, so rubbish lies accumulating in layers like the debris of an archaeological site over centuries. A wheel moves squeezing the mud in a curling foil from its tread and extrudes a crumpled tin from deep below the surface.

The problem is insuperable because nothing is ever still, there is movement all the time for 24 hours a day. And litter is a way of life to the Turks, so nobody cares.

Getting into that immense truck park is the first test of nerve: plunge into the maelstrom on the given signal, ride the buffeting turbulence under the wheels, suffer the shuddering shocks of hidden rocks under the surface, roll out of the trough of unseen swells concealed by the flying spume of mud.

Watch with an eagle eye the wheels of the trucks in front. If they are riding rim-high on a breaker of rolling ooze, follow them, they are on firm ground underneath. Push and shove, fling her about like a dodgem car to make that firm ground, let the rest sink axle-deep or up to the cab door in the slime. Wide lakes dissect the approach to the park entrance, they used to be water, now they have the consistency of workhouse gruel, grey-brown and so heavy that they can only splash in slow-motion.

Amidst the uproar of screaming engines and hissing airbrakes stand the Turkish soldiers attempting to impose some discipline and order. Improbable young men, they flinch not an inch when great mechanical

192

monsters bear down on them. In practice, an inch is a good clearance, by sheer nerve the soldiers impose their wills on this seemingly ungovernable mob.

Every male Turk has a moustache, there is not a man to be seen without one. Very few grow beards but the moustache is de rigueur: a thick, luxuriant, black growth sculpted and trimmed to a half-moon ending at the level of the lower lip, a three-quarters Zapata. No Turk ever visibly shaves and the accepted appearance is a thick, black moustache on the upper lip and a heavy, five days' growth of stubble on face and neck; it applies to all classes and categories. Nobody has discovered how they manage to keep it that way but a moustache and five days' growth is as much a macho symbol to a Turk as a fat wife and 10 kids is to a Brazilian peasant.

So the soldiers stand, holding their ground in the maelstrom, unshaven desperadoes from cap to neck and splattered with mud from feet to waist; a villainous crew they look. The armament has changed from AK-47 and Kalashnikov to NATO FN and Thomson sub-machine gun, but that does not make them appear any friendlier, except that technically they are on our side and we hope that somebody has told them so.

Only fools argue with Turkish soldiers and press the argument to its limits. That remarkable sea-change of character the philosophical driver had noted at borders is nowhere more clearly evidenced than entering Turkey. The mind changes, the ethos is wholly different. A Turk will argue for the love of argument to the furthest ends of reason until complete impasse is reached. Then, if honour requires it, he will produce a weapon to enforce his point. This is no idle threat on his part and unless his views prevail he will use it.

"That's a little fact it's worth knowing, saves a lot of bother, like having your body flown home," comments Bobby Brown.

The sergeant in charge, exercising his hard won right to sit holding court in the café all day, accepting gifts and drinking chi, creases his eyes and flashes his white teeth to explain: "I throw my new recruits into the mud up to their necks, after a week they come back to me battle-hardened warriors without ever firing a bullet. Every day is a tank battle for them. With this experience, no tank could ever catch my infantry, they could outdodge and outrun them every time."

He laughs delightedly at the thought, takes the whole packet when offered a Marlboro, adding as an afterthought: "I have worked for a long time with Yankees here in Turkey, my men are thinner and harder. Turkish soldiers live very hard."

The park is an objective and reaching it, to be actually in line jammed on either side by close-packed trucks, induces a "high", a feeling of elation and achievement. It is a false emotion, a delusion, a sensation equivalent to Everest mountaineers reaching South Col or round-the-world yachtsmen sailing into Mar del Plata, fantastic—except that the best, or worst, is yet to come.

At the Turkish border everything changes, certainly Asia is still officially 300 or more kilometres away across the Bosporus, but Islam and the Islamic mind and code begin here. This is the East. Western civilisation, whose influence has been dwindling for several hundred kilometres, stops at this point. A whole new set of rules begin to apply, a new morality as well as a new religion. The package deal papers of the European TIR carnet, under the Paris agreement, begin to lose face, they do not pull the weight they should or that they do in Europe. Though technically they should carry truck, trailer and cargo through to the borders of Arabia, this does not take into account what every experienced driver knows full well. The Turks will make up new rules as they go along, on the spot reserving the right to change them within 10 minutes and not prejudicing the right of the next man along to amend the new rules as he feels fit, with the final right to change the lot at the discretion of "the chef"—the almighty, unquestionable, infallible "chef".

The dreaded phrase is "see chef", a ubiquitous phrase which translates into every European language as "this is going to cost you money".

Thus the euphoria of being in the line soon wears off and the dread anticipation of what is to come replaces it. Confirmation of these misgivings is quick to arrive when all the drivers who are "stuck for paperwork or money" wander down lines seeking compatriots for a chin-wag and cuppa. There are never less than a dozen.

Time is beginning to take its toll as inevitably it must, living at top tension for prolonged spells of concentration shows around the eyes and features. The drivers from Furth-im-Wald have all made it in about the same time and look a little frayed around the edges as they stand in unofficial conference, faces unshaven, hands stained from chores along the road. Lack of sleep has left its pallid imprint on their features, their clothes are soiled and crumpled, their shoes . . . but who can see shoes in this mud?

Leo Smith describes his love for the work like this: "For anyone who is prepared to get a bit dirty, go without a proper wash for days on end, feel scruffy and down at heel, work hard when all he wants to do is sleep, this is the job. The reward in freedom is worth it, that's why it gets into your blood."

Bobby Brown, on the other hand, says: "I make a special point at every border to have a good scrub, even in cold water. I shave, clean my teeth and put on a polished pair of shoes so I can breeze about looking fresh and alert and deal with them on my terms. They wonder where the hell I've come from."

This is a job where there is no time off. The routine must run: drive, eat, sleep, drive until a suitable spot is reached to park and relax. If a queue at a border lasts two days and two nights and the following day, then that is the working day—72 hours—there is no other way.

From here, relaxation is a short 300 kilometres down the road in Istanbul. But first, the rest of Kapicule: Kapicule proper. It is here at the end of the line, every Hollywood B-movie Western director's vision of a deserted, hick, Wild West shanty town falling apart at the seams after the miners have quit and left it to the coyotes— but with minarets.

The nub of the affair is an unprepossessing single-storey, breeze block building entirely surrounded by unintentional lakes forming natural hazards to protect the entrances in winter and clouds of aggressive mosquitoes in summer. It is an unsuitable piece of architecture to welcome you to the land of the Sultans and the wonder is that the same people who constructed the Blue Mosque and the other miracles of Istanbul could actually contrive this one. Yet it has one remarkable attribute: the ability to absorb and retain people in numbers entirely out of its range and scope. They go in by the hundreds, all the time, and stay in so that inside there is just one large compressed block of humanity.

To enter, first negotiate the lakes, the chances are that you won't and will spend the rest of the day wet to the knees with soggy trousers clinging to the lower leg. Open the door then push boldly, the natural elasticity of the place will guarantee entry, but there is no guarantee of exit. That will depend upon the black-moustachioed men with hooded eyes sitting at the tables or in ramshackle offices each surrounded by his own personal mob.

The mobs never diminish nor do they ever relapse into silence. The jabbering and yelling goes on all the time. This is the initiation into the Turkish—the Islamic—way of doing things, the art of conducting business, Eastern style. It is the method which will prevail from this point on.

Queue and line are not words which are in the Turkish vocabulary. Or maybe they just mean something else, for instance, a struggling, heaving, squirming mob in a circle round any available official. If there is a wall between you and the said official, form a similar crush in a half-circle round the hatch through which he will talk to you. Perhaps body-contact to the point of personal injury is an essential element of Islamic queues. With luck you can be in an Islamic queue with your feet off the ground for the whole time until your document is delivered into your hands, then you are eased out to land lightly on your toes on the perimeter.

That is the scene within this beaten-up building and it all takes place in a curiously dim, blue-yellow light created by a haze of tobacco smoke. The sun filters through darkly stained windows on which the dust and filth is slowly creeping from the frames to the centre so that eventually the glass will become opaque.

Bare electric light bulbs glow like street lamps in a London fog, they hang from wires whose bared metal cores have been twisted together without insulation, the flexes themselves emerge through jagged holes in ceilings festooned with wires running every-whichway and dripping cobwebs and dust.

Every triplicated, quintuplicated document in creation seems to have found its way on to rudimentary desks and there is no lack of industry. Flying hands, writing at great speed from right to left, inscribe the papers in a non-stop rush of scribble. The officials write interminably throughout the day, occasionally leaning back in their chairs to stretch and ease the cramp in a hand, then back to it in a flurry of whirling ball-points. The ubiquitous, essential rubber stamps pound the desks, initials are hurriedly scratched. Flick, flick, documents are slotted into relevant passports and the package flung at the window to be sucked into the seething crowd.

It is a frenetic scene which, suitably dressed and polished, could fit well on the floor of any major stock exchange or money market where, out of similar bedlam, comes order and profit. But all is not as it seems in this outpost of high finance.

There is a little something called baksheesh.

The *Oxford English Dictionary* defines the word concisely: it is Oriental for a "tip", *Chambers's Dictionary*, being of Scottish origin, devotes a little more space to it: "a gift or present of money in the East, a gratuity or tip."

Neither, you note, refers to a bribe.

A tiny, flimsy sheet of paper, unsigned and unstamped, can halt all progress; it can place in jeopardy driver, truck, trailer and all its contents; it can result in the total, irrecoverable loss of everything. A touch of baksheesh can instantly rectify the gravest of errors, solve the most intractable problem, speed the slowest of processes. Kapicule has thrived and grown rich on baksheesh and the opportunity to extract it on such a grand scale has greatly refined its techniques; the rest of the East are but clumsy novices in the art compared with the inhabitants of Kapicule. A dedicated student could obtain the Islamic equivalent of a Ph.D. in baksheesh by working in this unglamorous customs post. To the devil with posh postings like Istanbul International Airport, send me where the money is: Kapicule.

Methods of extraction are varied. The vital stamp is poised in the "chef's" hand while he is flicking through the papers, ten seconds and all will be clear, then the telephone rings, down goes the stamp back on its inkpad again. His wife is calling to say that his kebabs are going cold in the oven and she has wasted all morning preparing a beautiful dinner which she doesn't intend to have ruined while he spends his time talking to idiot foreigners, most of them infidels, anyway, and he ought to know better, so if he doesn't come home she will give them to the dog.

The ruin of domestic harmony can cost a tidy bit of baksheesh.

And it costs relatively more if the "chef" is in the middle of his afternoon siesta and has to be wakened to scribble his initials over a stamp.

Best and most costly of all is when some clown back in the office at home thousands of miles away has committed a genuine error in formulating the documents. Best, that is, for the lucky Turk into whose hands the faulty document falls: this is his summer holiday, a new sheepskin coat for his favourite mistress. Allah has been bountiful and it warrants the full treatment: a lengthy pause, the gravest of expressions, a slow shaking of the downcast head, a light drumming on the desk with the fingers, the funereal tones which utter: "Mucho proplem, mucho, mucho, mucho proplem . . ."

"That's a couple of thousand liras for starters," mutters the Old Middle East Hand, "probably more, count a thousand liras for every mucho, and you've had four already."

"Mucho, mucho, proplem. I see chef."

"That's six thousand so far, now double that for the chef," the OMEH sagely adds.

There is no meanspiritedness in the Turk,

if he is in luck so are his relatives and friends. He spreads his joy around. So the "chef", by now fully equated in breakneck, machine-gun fire Turkish with the nature of the "proplem", says solemnly: "I haf gud friend who will help with thees problem, no trubbles. I weel call heem and say you weel call on heem, then he weel help you." The longer you take assessing the required amount of baksheesh necessary, the more friends will become involved and you will find yourself with a standing committee of advisers and all will expect to be made happy. You will part on the best of terms with half of Kapicule but lighter in the pocket for it.

So pay up and to assuage conscience remember that the authority invested in the *Oxford English Dictionary* baulks at calling it so mean and dishonourable a thing as a bribe.

If a smouldering sense of injustice should prompt you to protest to higher authority, it may allow you to give vent to your anger but will be to no practical avail since all that happens is that higher authority costs more. Save your money and leave smiling.

For those who protest or refuse to comply with Turkish etiquette in these matters, or simply do not have the money to pay, there lies another fate, it is behind those high wire compounds. The defaulter's goods are forfeit.

The compounds stretch for acres on both sides of the road. They are filled with every known type of vehicle and cargo which has been seized, impounded and cannibalised: skeletons of trucks, and trailers, seized cargoes, new Mercedes cars minus their wheels and interiors, caravans, mobile homes, coaches, tipper trucks, earth movers, tractors, even a 65 foot motor yacht are piled in an untidy mass. Any unauthorised person going into the compound is shot.

There is no hesitation about this, stealing from the government is as heinous a crime in Turkey as raping your grandmother and this is government property. It is a sore temptation to pick up that odd spare part you might urgently need at the moment since it is lying there rusting away on a vehicle which will never see the road again, but venture into that compound and, bang, a warning shot— the next one for real.

Turkish authorities are very touchy about the compounds and will not allow inspection. A company of London insurance loss adjustors, alarmed at the claims being made against insurance companies and the difficulties and expense of recovering stranded cargoes, sent along a senior inspector travelling incognito to assess the situation.

He saw the compounds at Kapicule and said: "I gave up counting when I reached £70 million in vehicle and estimated cargo values." Slowly he repeated: "Seventy million pounds sterling, that's what I put it at. Not by any means all on the London insurance market, but the value of impounded stock in those compounds is by any scale enormous."

It is only by relating it to this estimate that the value of Ewe Ploog's work becomes startlingly apparent.

There is one sure way of minimising the hassle and cost of Kapicule, and he goes under the name of Youngturk. He uses that name because the drivers in the early days would tell each other: "Get the young Turk to do the paperwork, he speaks the language and knows them all."

Youngturk was one of the original ragged-trousered, bare-arsed children besieging the first trucks when the began to arrive. The children are still there and active and clamber over every newly arrived truck asking for "Papers, papers, take my uncle, my uncle verr gud agent, see you through quick quick." Quickly they scurry along the line of trucks, find a customer then dart, skip and hop back to the village. The work is done as they promised it would be, they take their cut and whatever else they can persuade the driver to part with.

Turkish children go into business from the ages of nine or 10, and it is real business, they can argue a deal and deliver the goods, it is their education. One young tycoon of 12 years of age fell into trouble with the police and during the investigation into his misdemeanours it was discovered that he had accumulated the sum of £12,000 in cash, in hard currency, from his energetic private enterprise hustling the trucks and changing money. Then he was in trouble with the tax authorities. With a philosophical shrug he said: "I'll pay."

They do not come any sharper than that young fellow, he had read about the financial world and made great friends with a Swiss driver whom he had persuaded to open a Swiss bank account for him to lodge his spare cash.

"When they call me for the army," he said, "I will go and live abroad for a few years, one of my friends the drivers will take me out."

From these sort of beginnings Youngturk built a formidably successful business and became the most famous man in the transport worlds of two continents: the name echoes along the route, everybody knows and deals with Youngturk, everybody collects cash at his offices.

His real name is Suleyman Sirri Aksu, his address is Petrol Ofisi Sitesi Kapicule, he has three day telephones, two night phones, the busiest telex machine in Turkey and the unique distinction that he shaves all around his black moustache. Success has come to him not least because of his undoubted charm which is the typical, quiet, unhurried, smiling charm of the relaxed, cultivated Turk, an asset they can use to quite devastating effect. An interview with a Turkish businessman can be as beneficial as two expensive hours on a psychiatrist's couch, hurry and tension are to be avoided at all cost, everything will come right, God willing, and tomorrow is soon enough, my friend, the world will still be here and you and I will be older, wiser men, so I have ordered chi for us while we contemplate.

So Suleymen smiles his gentle smile and says: "Tomorrow, all will be right."

But, as a good Turkish businessman whom Allah has graced with his smiles, he takes the responsibility of the business Allah has entrusted to him with great personal seriousness. He is known to advance money to very dubious risks who are stuck for cash at Kapicule and when asked why he replies: "I know it is foolish, but it is my duty to help, the trucks have made me a rich man and it would be wrong if my friends all over the world should hear that Youngturk would not help, they would be ashamed and shame would sit on my house. The risk is as nothing to the loss of a good name with my friends. Insh'allah, all will be right."

His runners stand in a specially allocated corner at the far left hand of the frantic customs house, they have become a central pivot of the whole operation. "Leave it to Youngturk," the knowing drivers say, "let's go for a kebab."

Allah is well known for working in mysterious ways and pulling the rug from under those nicely ensconced in paradise and on September 12, 1979 he gave the elaborate, hand-woven Oriental carpets in Kapicule a sharp, nasty tug. The instruments of his displeasure were a group of gold-embossed Turkish Generals in Ankara who, growing weary of the excessive baksheesh being universally demanded and the squabbles of politicians and 300 political and sectarian murders a week, seized power and applied Martial Law.

A dark shadow in the shape of the FN rifle appeared over Kapicule: the army doesn't like baksheesh and stamps it out whenever discovered nor will it indulge in it itself, except, perhaps, in taking a full pack of Marlboro when one has been proffered, but that could be a simple mistake.

"There has to be discretion, my friend," say the Turks who desperately wish to be helpful and expedite matters to your satisfaction. So be discreet.

Actually, it costs a lot less with the army in the offing.

Walk through the striped barrier and meet life. Life! Teeming, bubbling, effervescent life all around; the bazaar is crowded, the stall-holders follow prospective customers down the street, the children tug at sleeves to drag a client towards a stall. Slippers, coats, brasswork, trinkets and baubles glitter and tinkle in the breeze. Egbek, hot unleavened bread and hot, crusty rolls scent the evening air. Chickens turn on the spit and kebabs sizzle on charcoal braziers. "Coke, Pepsi, Seven-Up," the vendors yell. Shoeshine boys grab at stationary legs and a shoe is half cleaned before a protest can be uttered. There is noise, hubbub, vibrant activity. And this is half-a-mile from Bulgaria. An entirely different world even under the gun.

The day looks immeasurably brighter in this lively society. But there is a snag, the papers have not gone through, true to form a new rule has been invented so it is no-go until the silly little "problem" is resolved. At the top of the document, following accepted practice of 10 years, the destination is marked, in this case "Kuwait/Riyadh". Now the official requires this to be repeated at the very bottom of the document in a place where it has never been necessary before. And, anyway, it doesn't matter, that form is finished now, another document has taken over for the remaining journey to Arabia.

"It must be marked," the man is adamant. Youngturk shakes his head resignedly.

It cannot be simply typed in because that

would invalidate the whole document by making it wrongly altered. Procedures must be followed, the document must be taken to the Chamber of Trade in Edirne, 20 kilometres away. There it must be typed in by the official, and sworn and stamped with the official stamp before it is returned to the customs here. If the customs man is to be denied his fair and proper share of baksheesh, he'll show them all, so there. In no circumstances will he stamp the rest of the papers and release the truck from customs until this is completed.

Take a taxi to Edirne, pay £20 stamp duty, taxi back, a tiny present to the official is still needed in case he finds another equally trivial snag—he could. Transit taxes are paid, passports stamped, police driving permit obtained and stamped, insurance cover paid. Youngturk settled. Now move into the customs area for examination. Open the tilt, turn back the covers, tell the checker that she's ready.

The customs officers go about their duties with a gang of helpers who carry curious axes with a blade set at right angles to the shaft, slightly curved toward the hand, a lethal weapon. They are dealing with a German truck loaded with wooden packing cases labelled "Fragile—Glass—This Way Up". It is high quality packaging, beautifully done and substantial. The axe swings and crashes into the side of the case, it splinters but doesn't open. The axe swings again with greater momentum, and again, then two join in, they swing alternative until a jagged, gaping hole is punched into the splintered side. The officer jabs a probe inside but with, apparently, no satisfaction so he sticks in a hand to shake, twist and pull an object from the inside. He looks at it, shrugs his shoulders, and stuffs it back again. They all laugh at some private joke.

Case by case they go through the contents of the whole trailer, the ground is littered with splinters and strips of broken packing case until, tiring of the sport, casually the officer signals the driver to string up and secure the tilt.

Next in line is the fridge from Liverpool. The bolts on the doors are unclipped and the doors swing open in a small cloud of evaporation. The helpers clamber up, turn and let out a cry of pleasure; other officers and their helpers gather round in an excited group. The axe sinks into a cardboard container, is jerked to rip open the side, and cartons of chocolate Mars and Snicker bars shower to the ground followed by packets of Treets. There is a mad scramble to gather them, rip off the thinner cartons, tear the wrapping paper and suddenly everybody is chewing chocolate bars.

It is of no use to protest. The driver climbs up to protect the rest of his cargo. He shakes an admonitory finger and says: "No more, that's it." The officer shrugs, smiles and says: "Samples."

He is within his rights, he is entitled to take samples, not to plunder the cargo, but to take a fair sample. No protest would be sustained. For the next few hours the staple diet of Kapicule is Mars bars.

The officer is well pleased with his day's work, he signals the following trucks clear without a look, still munching and smiling. Cab control is a smiling formality, more a request for a cigarette than an examination.

As Eartha Kitt sang so evocatively: "Oh, those crazy Turks."

A feeling of delicious anticlimax settles in: an open road, the whole stretch of glorious Turkey ahead, three-and-a-half hours to

Istanbul . . . food, baths, beer and a lot of fun
and more fun to follow that. Just sitting in
comfort will be a lot of fun.

9

WHEN Bob Paul first trundled down this road it was cobblestones all the way to Istanbul, and decrepit ones at that, which dictated the course the truck took as much as the steering wheel. Even that ride was a luxury, once across the Bosporus ferry and out of the city on the Asian side there were no roads of any sort, only cart tracks.

In the short intervening years, Turkey has worked miracles. For instance, she has become the poorest country in the Western Alliance, gone bust several times, gone to war and incurred the wrath of the world, subverted democratic governments, run up the biggest debts ever with the World Bank until Poland began to hog that scene, come close to anarchy and civil war with 300 political murders a week, suppressed with the gun pitched battles between Sunni and Shi'ite Muslims, imprisoned Prime Ministers, disenfranchised huge sections of her population, kicked the United Nations in the

216

teeth repeatedly and caused an emergency meeting of international finance ministers to save her from finally disappearing down the fiscal plug-hole.

Amid this blackest of black economic horror scripts she has contrived to build very good roads including splendid, brilliantly engineered motorways across the most rugged country in Europe, constructed an engineering triumph in the bridge across the Bosporus, built hotels, houses, kept food and goods in the shops, stayed well fed, drunk better, smoked tolerable cigarettes, and, most of the time for most people stayed happy.

There are, to be sure, areas of bleak, crippling poverty with peasants living below subsistence level, as there have ever been in Turkey. There are Kurds in the mountains, ungovernable and at war with the world. There are bitter and disillusioned politicians and minorities. How the rest of the population can thrive and even prosper in the turmoil is the real miracle.

This is a big country, in size, history, tradition, culture and spirit. A country of shocks and surprises. Turkey springs surprises immediately upon coming within her borders. With the innocent coquetry of a

217

Victorian maiden lifting her long skirt to allow a flash of provocative ankle, she reveals beyond the corner of a mundane provincial street, hung with a tangle of electric and telephone wires, between rows of mean houses—the stunning magnificence of the great mosque at Edirne. A cascade of broad steps, a massive dome and towering minarets dominate the town crouched round its railings. The shock is the greater for having travelled so many hundreds of miles in a landscape devoid of architecture on the grand scale.

This, almost contemptuously thrown away, is Turkey's tempting overture to the splendours she has in store.

The road runs sweetly, expectantly, under the wheels and the curious ad-mix of modern Turkey becomes increasingly obvious. Ancient crones with toothless mahogany faces, grizzled grey men in traditional baggy trousers with the crutch hanging to the knees, oxen, mules and donkeys pull grossly overladen carts, bent-backed women toil in the fields, a peasant guides a one-share wooden plough which has not changed in shape, design or function since biblical times, while modern Turks, snappily dressed with elegant womenfolk in company, flash by in their Mercedes cars.

The Turks and their Mercs: it is a standing joke and nightmare along the road, beware the Turk and his Merc. Over the last couple of decades a multitude of Turks have left home to do the dirty work in the post-war German economic miracle, never less than a million of them in any one year. They are there as official *gastarbeiters* working for high German wages and entitled to all the benefits of West German social law—many now draw a German State Pension. When they return to Turkey they are rich men and every returning Turk, as a measure of his affluence, buys a Mercedes which he exports from Germany under Z-plates, German export registration number plates, then he re-registers the car once he is home.

So the Turks and their Mercs are known as Zoomies to be watched with an eagle eye and kept well clear of, because the sad fact is that one-third of all Z-plate cars which leave Germany never reach home. They lie in ditches and car dumps all the way along the road, which is a testament to the Turk's driving abilities and temperament. The figures are quoted from official government returns.

The Turk's rules of the road state: there shall never be anything in front of me and everything coming in the opposite direction must give way, the accelerator foot must always be on the floor and brakes are only for the weaklings . . . oh, where *are* the brakes?

The result of this is that half Turkey goes at walking pace and the other half moves at the speed of lightning.

Another mandatory Turkish rule is that no vehicle shall be driven except by a committee. So every Turkish truck and car carries its committee with it, three to five in the front of a truck, five to seven in a saloon car. They pile out when the vehicle stops for any reason and hold an instant meeting to decide such questions as what work shall be done, what food eaten or which road should be taken. Then they all pile back again into the vehicle in order of seniority, the most senior sitting next to the driver and, in the case of trucks, the youngest hanging on to the back grinning at passing traffic. They take the description family car literally and keep the family in it.

There is one other vital rule which the un-initiated should be made aware of: a Turkish truck is not overloaded until the weight on the back axle is such that it has compressed the springs so much that the wheels are trapped against the chassis and will not turn. Then it is permissible to take off a few tons. This means that the axles will snap clean in half at the least expected moment, so give Turkish trucks a clear berth, if they will let you.

Knowing the nature of the beast is half the battle so you can motor along with quiet confidence through the upland, rolling landscape until the road from the plateau begins to drop toward the coast. From now on it will run along the northern shores of the Sea of Marmara. Soon the holiday apartments of the Istanbul middle classes will begin to appear, they face the sea a gentle stroll from high water mark and the road runs past their back doors. Now the atmosphere changes, a bustle of activity brings a suppressed excitement into the air and suddenly a sign reads: "Istanbul, nufus 1,870,000". They tell you how many people there are in all Turkish towns.

From Kapicule to Istanbul is only a mere snippet of Turkey, this peninsula is a dog's ear pinned on the rest even though it houses the bulk of the greatest city of the East. It is easy to see why Kemal Atatürk, notwithstanding Istanbul's greatness, made Ankara the capital city, Ankara is at the heart of the country while Istanbul is an appendage to it.

Like all great cities, Istanbul sends out its tentacles far beyond its city walls. The style of housing changes, a multitude of new trades appear by the roadsides, shops multiply, traffic thickens and the type of traffic changes—a service industry of vans, bread vans, laundry vans, small trader's pick-ups, delivery vans, tricycles, plumbers, electricians, builders, and refuse vans are all under the wheels without warning and milling in every direction. The people are now city dwellers, cosmopolitan creatures who know where they are going and must get there quickly. You need to adjust after days in the darkness, time to shake off the feeling of being the man from outer space.

The first stop is Londra Mocamp. Notorious Londra where the fun runs fast and furious and the fights break out, monumental fights which go into the annals of fisti-cuff fury and have involved the polisi, the army, embassies and governments. "Classic punch-ups," say the one-time hard men like

John and Chris, with a wistful smile at the memory. There is a lot of muscle among these driving men and they drink enormous quantities of the potent Efes lager to relieve the high tensions of the testing road. Mix up a dozen or more nationalities all drinking heavily, throw in a handful of women and a few insults and you have the perfect recipe for trouble.

Trouble follows a simple, elementary pattern: somebody feels insulted, either by nationality or personally, it doesn't matter which, or maybe somebody smiled at the girl the other fellow had been buying beer for all day, or it could be that somebody just did not feel like paying the bill, so a scuffle starts at that table. The dining-room cum beer-hall is so packed that, inevitably, the strugglers crash into an adjoining table, that table crashes over and the rest follow like pieces in the Tokyo domino tumbling championships. Everybody is on his feet, the women dive for cover and God-awful mayhem breaks out.

Somebody sends for the police and the army comes along too as back-up and for battle practice, a good punch-up is meat and drink to Turkish policemen and soldiers. They love it.

At this point the international fraternity of truckers feels that their privacy has been invaded and that these uniformed buffoons have no place in a domestic squabble which is going along very nicely, thank you. As a man they turn upon the combined forces of law and order. Then the hall is filled with whirling batons, rifle butts, broken chair legs and monkey-wrenches which have appeared from down the drivers' legs. Efes beer bottles, brown and heavy, fly through the air, chairs follow, heavy tables are hoiked and dropped on struggling combatants, blood splashes the walls and pools on the floor. The sound of shattering glass, the solid crash of plate glass windows and the crunch of beer bottles fills the ears. Some scurry for shelter and escape, others come running from all directions to hurl themselves into the fray.

As quickly as it begins, it finishes. There's no given signal, the fracas just subsides spontaneously. The opposing factions group themselves at either end of the arena and hurl the occasional abuse in each other's direction, casualties are lifted away and walking wounded escorted to ambulances. Mocamp staff sweep up, righting the surviving tables and preparing for business.

Few arrests can be made because, as in all riotous occasions, nobody actually knows who hit who or what with and it is going to be a hell of a job to prove anything, even under Turkish law. Apart from that, any attempt to arrest a driver will meet with stiff opposition and probably lead to an instant replay of the action and the police could then be held as instigators. So the forces of law and order retreat to their transportation muttering dire imprecations and issuing colourful threats. The drivers curse the police in turn and rush to make up lost drinking time.

It grew so bad at one stage that the Turkish Government complained to the embassies. As a result the British Consul in Istanbul telexed British transport companies with an urgent plea: "Please make Londra Mocamp off bounds for your drivers and forbid its use while in Istanbul. The British embassy can accept no further responsibility for the consequences of drivers staying at Mocamp and will in future be unable to offer assistance."

Naturally, the immediate response to such a request from so exalted a quarter was that drivers who did not usually use Mocamp felt deprived and rushed there to find out what was happening. Mocamp became even more popular.

Its full designation is Londra Mocamp Camping or, to those of a more lyrical turn of mind, "the last great water 'ole" which, as the hairy Mancunian driver explains succinctly, means: "the last place for a decent piss-up, a real good drink, before you get down among the rag-'eads, or up among the Commies coming back". It was the inspiration of a distinguished, silver-haired Turkish gentleman called Mehmet Dogme and his sons Mustafa and Huseyin. They opened it up as a tourist spot but the tourists didn't come, not a great many do, in fact, since certain aspects of Turkey are a little too rugged for the average package-deal rubbernecker (like the loos, it takes a brave man to handle the average Turkish loo—constipation is a treat compared with the rigours of a fully-fledged, matured Turkish squatter). Brooding on the problem outside their front door, as Turks do for most of the summer, the Dogmes noted the number of juggernauts cruising past and the idea sprang from that.

Now it is a 10 million dollar complex with parking for 1,000 trucks in security compounds patrolled by 15 guards, a 90 room hotel, a shop, a leather factory to take drivers' orders on the way out and have the goods ready by their return, a swimming pool, a service station for trucks, a truck wash imported from Europe and a spares shop. On average 200 trucks arrive daily.

Apart from making them exceedingly rich, Mocamp has brought other benefits to the Dogme family. Their car broke down in Yugoslavia when they were going on holiday and that is not the best of places for service. But every trucker on the road knows the Dogmes. Trucks roll along that busy road day and night and it was only minutes before they were being towed off the road by truck drivers who recognised them. They enjoyed a home cooked meal in the cab while the car was dismantled, repaired and put back on the road better than new. The silver-haired old patriarch said with a self-effacing charm: "It was then I learned that it really does pay to have friends. I could not believe that they remembered me so and would take so much trouble over an old man like me. I consider them truly gentlemen of the road."

However, they are not always gentlemen. Across the road from Mocamp there used to be a place which sported the name "West

Berlin". It was the fruitiest non-stop brothel in the town, a classic of its kind providing a 24 hour service in the bar downstairs and from the girls upstairs. And good-looking girls too.

The routine was to take a lot of drink downstairs then go upstairs to enjoy the girls, down for more drink, bawdy talk and laughter and up again to compare the charms of a second lady with those of the first. And so on through the day, up and down, down and up as a test of both capacity and stamina. A peak of excitement would occur when someone came downstairs to announce: "They've all changed, a new lot have come on duty."

Turkish bills are unclear at the best of times and worse at times such as these. There were cash presents for the girls but nobody could make out whether the house charged as well . . . 11 Efs lagers, 420 ls, Soraya, 1,150 ls, 11 Efes lagers, 640 ls, Yasmin, 2,250 ls . . . Another difficulty is that Turkish numbers differ from Roman ones and what is taken to be a zero is a 10 and what looks like a decimal point or full stop is 50. It leads to misunderstandings and confusion.

The Swede—known as the Swede even to

all the other Swedish drivers on the run because he is, in a way, the definitive Swede—was by common consent a big man. Chris described him as "a big lad," John confirmed that view with, "bloody enormous," others added, "massive", "huge", "a man mountain". A certain authority was added to this assessment because every one of those talking was over six foot one except John who made up for lack of height by a 54 inch chest and 22 stone.

"Was iss ziss?" roared the Swede on receiving his account, and without waiting for an answer he bellowed, "ziss I am not paying, yunk, now, now, now. Not paying." His eyes glazed and he looked formidable. Turkish bouncers rushed to their hidey-holes and came out with an assortment of weaponry—pickaxe handles and such.

Now, in a situation like this there has to be a first. Someone has to move in and strike a blow for honour, profit and to get the bloody money. One Turk moved forward, measured the distance and swung his handle in a great arc. The Swede stood up. The handle struck him across the shoulders and bounced off as if it had hit a pneumatic tyre. The club flew from the Turk's hands and he stumbled as the impetus of the blow carried him forward to within range. With the slightest inclination of his head and no visible movement of his body, the Swede jabbed his right arm and hit the Turk in the face. The Turk rose in the air in a gentle arc and landed on the polished counter of the bar.

In the finest Hollywood Western tradition the Turk slid along the counter top for its full length ploughing through glasses, fruit, carafes and general bar impedimentia until he sped off the other end to crash to the floor. He did not fall in a crumpled heap but lay full length as if stretched out for a burial. A Turk from behind the bar slapped his face and threw water on him. There was no reaction, he was comatose. A fearful silence fell into the bar room.

Anger blazed in the Turks' eyes. They stood in a menacing group, clutching their weapons, but nobody moved. Somebody now had to be the next and, even in a combined rush attack, a second, third, fourth or fifth could easily suffer a similar fate to the luckless first Turk before the Swede was overpowered by numbers. And that without the intervention of his friends, who were not exactly midgets.

At the end of the bar the floored Turk had not moved.

The Swede now decided it was time to go but, for reasons nobody felt inclined to question, he considered the best way out to be straight ahead despite the fact that the table was in his way. He placed the first two fingers of his right hand under the lip of the tabletop and flicked it over. Those who were leaning with their elbows on the tabletop on the right hand side fell forward in a heap on the floor, those on the left crashed backwards, but all were instantly on their feet. It does not do to be on the floor when tension is running so high.

The route to the door was clear so the Swede's companions made for it in a hurry, nobody wanted to be last through. But the Swede ambled along half turning to face the Turks every few paces. They inched behind him in a compact group stopping dead whenever he did.

Whatever his failings, the Swede was fair. He usually paid his dues promptly. Taking a big bundle of Turkish notes from his pocket, he flung it at the West Berlin management. He had no way of knowing that because of inflation it amounted at most to £10.

The procession made its halting way across the road with the Swede controlling the pace in the middle. Finally it reached the doors of Mocamp where the groups stood glaring at each other from a safe distance.

A driver said: "Anyone fancy a quick spin down Ankara tonight? These buggers will be hanging about all night long, there could be a few throats slit by morning."

"Good idea," a number of others murmured in assent.

"Not for me," said the Swede, "I will sleep in my cab tonight, not the hotel. The hotel beds are children's beds."

He slept like a baby with his door unlocked and his windows open, surrounded all night long by a semi-circle of Turkish waiters. They were still there in the bright light of day. The Turk in the bar did not come round for three days.

The telex machine has greatly raised the status of Mocamp and enhanced its importance. The messages never stop all day long: Truck driver Willum, Heinrich, Klaus, Harry, Mocamp, Istanbul, notify ETA, advise route, back load Mersin, Teheran, Kabul, Constansa, Cluj, Budapest, ongo

Greece, Yugoslavia, Baluchistan, regards, bibi . . .

It may be a week, a month before the driver arrives but his telex will be there waiting for him. No message is ever tampered or interfered with. In its own way this curious, rowdy, beer-soaked institution has become one of the world's major commercial exchanges greatly facilitating world trade. So we pick up the telexes. A back load Mersin, Dec. 3. Please notify if can do. No chance, not even half way there yet. There is a quieter, more relaxing stop-over across the Bosporus which is our destination. But this is rush hour in Istanbul and the Bosporus Bridge tolls are excessive at this time of day, so we drink a few beers with the boys and cross over later.

We forsake Mocamp, we are aiming for a quieter, more relaxing stop-over across the Bosporus—the Harem Hotel. This establishment is not what its name suggests, it simply lies in the Harem district of the city. It sits atop a steep cliff directly over the Bosporus, with panoramic views across the water to the Blue Mosque, Suleiman's mosque, Topkapi Palace and the teeming hills and crowded inlets. At the foot of the steep hill below us is the ferry jetty where inshore fishing boats berth to unload their catches. The fishermen bake piquant fish slices on braziers and serve them wrapped in heavy paper napkins to the ferry passengers. The quay is a centre of life; the chi shop is buzzing from five o'clock in the morning; vendors of crisp-baked delicacies flit and dart among the swarms of people flocking to and from the boats. They are solid institutions, these fine ferry boats with crossed golden anchors painted on the funnel and mahogany panelled saloons. A trip on one of these is a voyage spent in a hubbub of activity; agile chi-vendors expertly balance trays loaded with slim glasses full of the brown, glutinous liquid; shoe-shine men clamour for business; a dozen pedlars of different baubles and commodities press their wares; a stranger is considered a lucky omen and so is asked by his travelling neighbour to select a ticket from the lottery seller on his behalf.

From the vantage point of the Harem Hotel Istanbul is seen as from the dress circle and is altogether too theatrical. Those facing hills are too sharp, too steep and it should not be possible to pile so many dwelling houses roof to basement, cheek to jowl, one upon the other. And no city should have an inter-national seaway running like a main street through its very centre. Massive super-tankers, cargo vessels with derricks fore and aft and funnels midships, new bulk carriers like grossly inflated canal longboats, sleek motor yachts with acutely raked masts flying the hammer and sickle flag, all these progress in a continuous procession day and night. And there is the Bosporus Bridge, a miracle of engineering slung between two continents as if suspended on gossamer thread.

Here is a random mix of life and experience, intermingled and seldom segre-gated. Behind the hotel the yellowstone mass of the Selimiye Barracks stands next to the dome and soaring minarets of the Selimiye Mosque, symbols both of spiritual and temporal power. Under the walls of the barracks, in an island between two roads, lies the international truck park which holds several hundred vehicles. Just to the left, in the Bosporus channel but close inshore, lies the imposing blackened hulk of a huge supertanker which caught fire and blazed from stem to stern for days under the Bosporus Bridge. It threatened to blow the whole city apart until some astonishingly courageous tug boat captains flung lines aboard the incandescent menace. They towed her past the homes of the residential districts of Abdullaha, Uskudar, Salacak, across the mouth of the Golden Horn, in front of populous Harem and Selimiye to where the city ends on the seaward side, out to the beginning of the Sea of Marmara. There the 300,000 ton time bomb, unpredictable as a Roman Candle and glowing red-hot with danger, exploded and sank. She had been dragged with breath-taking bravery from the very heart of the city. And now the hulk remains as a permanent reminder of such deeds and a monument to heroism.

Now assembled in the hotel bar is a group of people almost unrecognisable from the ones we know: truckers and their women, bathed, groomed, scented and dressed to relax. The stresses, tensions and residual grime of the road have been washed away and they are as clean as miners fresh from the pit-head showers. This is half-way house and everybody is aware of it. Yesterday was Europe, tomorrow is Asia, next week will be Arabia or the Orient, but today is half-way house and a time for talk, food, drink and reminiscence. Time too for banter with head waiter Remsi and barman Friday who are an integral part of the enjoyment of the Harem Hotel. Turkish businesses do not suffer from the turnover of staff which has come to be accepted in other, more advanced, parts of the world; here, old and expected faces are usually there to greet and reassure.

Remsi Tas, the man with a keyboard ivory smile in which the black notes are solid gold, *is* the Harem to most drivers. He is known from the Tropic of Cancer to the Arctic Circle, which is a pretty far flung fame. "He is the most fortunate man in Istanbul," says an old jeweller in the Grand Bazaar whose services are much used by the drivers, "he has no need to want for anything in these times of great austerity, he has friends who will bring him anything he wants from the ends of the earth, what man can be more fortunate?"

This is true. When Remsi's wife was pregnant she longed for the refinements of Johnson's baby merchandise which is much superior to the coarse, local products but unobtainable because of Turkey's intractable international exchange problems. Says the smiling Remsi: "My friends the drivers brought me enough Johnson's products to open a drug store, I have creamed and powdered more babies' bottoms in Istanbul than any man in history."

At first he spoke little English but he was quickly taught by the truckers so his conversation tended to be rather more colourful than grammatical—it was also highly spiced. When the hotel's first bone fide tourists were expected he was desperate to make a good impression so the drivers helped him with special instruction. His first guests were members of an Australian and New Zealand church women's association, wives and descendants of the soldiers who died storming the beaches at Gallipoli in the Great War. They were elderly gentleladies, accompanied mostly by daughters and nieces who had come half way across the world to visit the faraway graves of their loved ones. They were also a very good and jolly crowd.

Remsi greeted them with enthusiasm when they arrived from the airport for lunch: "Good morning, you old cows, welcome wankers, I wish you fucking wonderful stay in Turkey. Have no worries, I speak well English my friend the truck drivers have teached me. For lunch we have bloody marvellous loop the loop for starters, Kelly's eye and plenty of crap Turkish dishes to follow . . ."

Anzac ladies are made of stern stuff and gifted with insight, there could be no mistaking the warmth of the greeting nor the sincerity of the beaming, gold-flecked smile of welcome. The leader of the party, a tall, angular, hawk-faced lady of formidable demeanour, said: "Be seated, ladies, I'm sure everything will work out just fine, let's enjoy our meal."

The luncheon was a success and at the end the hawk-faced lady asked: "Who are these truck drivers you said taught you to speak English so well, Mr. Remsi?"

"English truck drivers, all go Middle East, very far," replied Remsi, "good friends, some are upstairs in the bar."

"Poms!" snapped the hawk-faced leader, "take us to see them, Mr. Remsi, I and some of my committee ladies would like a word with these Pom truck drivers."

By the time they climbed the short staircase and reached the bar at the top, there was not a rugged truck driver left in sight. Half empty glasses of beer and partially eaten sandwiches stood on the bar tables. And barman Friday said: "They all left big rush when they hear you coming."

An innocent ambling the fascinating streets of Istanbul can soon find himself in the situation of a spectator at an important auction who gets caught up in the excitement and finds himself outbidding the field for a priceless Ming vase. In similar circumstances, Scottie drummed his fingers on a table one breakfast time as he battled to introduce some cogent thought into his throbbing, battle-scarred head. He screwed his eyes at the intensity of the effort and presented a distraught figure to his companions—a picture of suffering humanity recovering from the after effects of raki and Efes lager.

"What's the matter, Sco'ie?" asked his travelling companion.

"I cann'ie remember where I put the truck, I cann'ie find it in yon park."

There was an impatient silence until his travelling companion, who was also his cousin, said: "Och, mon, ye sold it to yon Turk in Topkapi last night, yew've got a sootcase full o' money in m'cab, it's all stashed away, yew're comin' back wi' me in m'cab, remember?"

"Oh," said Scottie.

Then a thought crept into his tortured mind. "Wha'll we tell the boss?" he asked naively.

"We're not exactly goin' to tell him anything, we're not go'in a go to him and say, 'We flogged y'truck in Istanbul, Jamie,' I dinn'a think he'd like that. We'll tell him that we rolled the truck and a Turk was killed in the accident and the Turks wanted £75,000 cash for the deed man's widow, so we skipped. That'll frighten him, he won't ask too many questions."

Scottie's expression eased from one of acute mental anguish to one of puzzlement. "How did a come to sell the truck? It's no verra clear in my mind, I dinna exactly remember."

"Och, go back in y're coma, Sco'ie, how do we know how yews sold the truck, yews just come along and said, 'I've got a great deal, I've sold the truck to this Turk . . .' "

Drink is the curse of the driving classes when they are not driving. Most of them are good drinkers at any time but being in Istanbul and far from home introduces a competitive element into the boozing. It has become accepted as a tradition that Istanbul is the place for a booze-up and it has led to complex problems. So round the bar or sitting under the trellissed vines by the swimming pool on a warm sunlit summer evening is the time when the drink brings out travellers' tales. And every trucker has as many tales to tell as he has miles under his bonnet.

Burley John Martin, whose 20 stone frame gives him considerable capacity in the boozing stakes, tells the story of how he first became involved with the Middle East.

He says: "Getting pissed was responsible for me coming out here. Not me getting pissed but Broomstick and Chris Bedder. They were stuck at Kapicule because of some duff paperwork so they took a trip to Istanbul to try and get it sorted out. And they got on the beer.

"They'd been drinking all day and probably all the day before that while they waited for the papers to be ready. Then in the early morning, Broomstick got maudlin and homesick. He looked at the date on his watch and said, 'It's nearly bloody Christmas.' "

It seems that the more they drank, the more maudlin they became until the attractions of Turkish whores, raki and Efes beer seemed infinitely less desirable than a fairy on the Christmas tree and a turkey dinner at home. The rest of the time was blank in their minds until they were shaken awake on an aircraft. In an alcoholic haze Broomstick asked: "Where are we?"

"Bloody London, mate," said Chris in astonishment, looking out on the tarmac and grey skies of Heathrow.

They had been taking a cargo for Ron Prankerd for delivery to the Oman Defence Department, it was at the time of the Oman—Yemen War, and Mr. Prankerd was surprised, not to say unhappy that his two drivers were back in England while his trucks and their consignments were stranded at Kapicule.

"Jesus," the transport manager had exclaimed on learning that the trucks had been abandoned, "Holy Hell, there won't be a thing left of them, you'll be lucky to find a stub-axle."

There was slight comfort in the fact that they had been left on the Bulgarian side of the border where chances of survival were minimally higher. However, Turks can pick a truck clean down to the skeleton quicker than a waiter in a fish restaurant can fillet a sole.

John picks up the story, "I'd seen Prankerd back in June about a Middle East job but when he rang on December 28th I couldn't remember who he was. Anyway we got it sorted out and he said, 'Get your jabs and your passport and be at London Airport at ten o'clock in the morning on January the first.' So that put paid to the rest of my Christmas.

"When I'd seen him I'd spun a great yarn about how well I knew the Middle East, and how I'd worked in Saudi and knew how to deal with Arabs all of which I'd boned up on from mates who had worked there. In fact the nearest I'd ever been to the Middle East was reading the Arabian Nights in my kids' picture books and my desert experience was strictly limited to climbing out of bunkers on Clacton golf course. But, there we were, Chris Bedder and me on our way to Istanbul, the blind leading the blind because he was just as green as I was at the time.

"When I saw Kapicule I nearly turned round and went back home. It was then that I realised that Chris Bedder hadn't been lying or pulling my leg. There was all the hassle of getting a visa to go a 100 yards into Bulgaria to pick up the trucks and getting another visa to get out again and into Turkey. With a lot of backhanders all round we managed to get out of Kapicule with the trucks intact. It was only then that I asked Chris where we were going, I'd never thought to ask before. He told me it was Doha. I asked him where that was and he said in Qatar, I asked where Qatar was and he replied, 'I'm buggered if I know, we'll have to buy a map.' So we stopped at a Petrol Ofisi garage and bought a map. When I opened it I gasped and said, 'This bloody thing's in Turkish.' Well, it would be, wouldn't it? We got another English map in Istanbul and I went over with a fine toothcombe and then I said to Chris, 'There's no such place as Doha, Prankerd's having us on.' Then a bloke in the Londra pointed it out to me on the map and it was spelled Al Dhawha. At the same time he pointed out H4, the Jordanian desert fort, and the salt desert between Qatar and the United Arab Emirates and told me that there were no roads at all there and that you would need a compass and, for the salt desert, bedouin guides and a sand tractor. I thought, charming, it takes me all my time to read a wristwatch let alone a compass. I visualised myself ending up in the desert with a hand sticking out of the sand like the bloke who was buried in *The Desert Song*.

"It was a brilliant start on the whole. We had no idea what we were doing. We had been told that when we got to Bab al Awa, Syria, we should look up the agent, Mr. Howard. I spent half a day looking for a Mr. Howard with no success until it dawned on me that it was Mustafa Awad. We were as green as that."

Not that it is unusual to be so green at the beginning, they arrive wet behind the ears on every trip and a lot do not survive, the death rate along the road is frightening as we will see.

Turkey is synonymous with fraud and fraud has been the utter damnation of transport companies and drivers running to the Middle East. The pickings used to be so easy and, for the dishonest, so foolproof that every villain with an eye to a quick, dishonest penny jumped on the bandwagon. They were the deliberate swindlers but a great number of people were involuntarily involved: these were the ones who committed fraud by incompetence, by over optimism, by coercion, or out of sheer desperation.

246

The root of the problem was then, as it still is today, the lack of sufficient funds to see the journey through to the end. There is a serious doubt as to whether many agents and shippers ever intended to see the job through, the evidence suggests that they just wanted to grab their money and run. If the activities of these swindlers were to be condemned out of hand, and nothing can condone them, so too were the attitudes of many major British companies—companies which are household names—who handled their own export cargoes with what can only be called culpable irresponsibility. Without checks, references, guarantees or knowledge of whom they were dealing with they handed over cargoes valued from £66,000 to £1 million and made no effort to ensure that they were delivered.

The drivers get on their high horses—with justification—about the casual way export business is conducted. The cargoes above are but two out of thousands—literally thousands—which have been dumped, wrecked, impounded by customs for default, or simply stolen. The remains of these can be seen to this day by the roadside, in mountain ravines and customs compounds.

These hideous losses couldn't be allowed to

continue unabated. But, serious though it was, in the way of most things on this journey, it managed to produce its own grim humour in the following way.

One evening a terrible silence fell in Londra Mocamp. It was all things a silence could ever be: pregnant, menacing, uneasy, one that could be cut with a knife. It was also deafening. A strange phenomenon in so rowdy an environment. Its cause was the presence of four strangers at the reception desk. They were strangers to Mocamp but not to a number of British drivers who recognised them as Scotland Yard officers.

Scotland Yard detectives registering at Mocamp! It was unbelievable. The shock to some members of the British trucking fraternity resident in the hotel was such that they paid their bills and quit instantly.

Others were less precipitate but they were uneasy and the Scotland Yard men were not made to feel immediately welcome. In fact, they could have had good reason to believe themselves ostracised such was the general lack of enthusiasm for their company.

Ned the Nutter, so called not because of his mental state but because he used his forehead as much as his fists in a fight, put it succinctly: "That's fucked the jollity, that's put the skids under the fun and kyboshed the merrymaking for a few days." He was heard to add: "The fuzz in Istanbul . . . in-cred-ible! It just proves that pigs can fly."

The Scotland Yard men had come in response to the mountain of complaints from insurers and exporters being lodged in London. The fact that they had sought and received the co-operation of the Turkish police was what intimidated the drivers the most. The sophisticated skills of Scotland Yard combined with Turkish police techniques would be formidable!

The foreign drivers were quite in sympathy, their hearts went out to their British colleagues in distress. Sympathy went so far that they even loaned money to the more agitated to pay the bills and recover their passports so that these worried men could sleep in their cabs until their funds arrived.

The Scotland Yard men eventually returned to London with the impression that Londra Mocamp was one of the more discreet, orderly and refined hostelries of Turkey, a place quite suitable to send your maiden aunt on holiday—such was their effect on the clientele.

One type of fraud the Yard men were trying to investigate involved the Turkish "mafia"—a menacing fraternity. Its agents studied the truck park, noting the length of stay of each vehicle. It soon became apparent which drivers were in financial difficulties because their trucks remained for more than a couple of days.

The mafia then sought out the drivers who were stranded. The deal was simplicity itself: the driver could not leave Turkey while his truck was intact, because it was entered in his passport—he could leave only if the vehicle was wrecked. The mafia would buy the cargo from him and he would deliver it to their warehouse. Then they would take the truck into the mountains, set fire to it and roll it into a ravine.

There is nothing unusual about that, at least a dozen trucks a week, often more, go that way in the natural order of things. It is difficult staying on that road at the best of times. Accidents are so frequent that they are commonplace and too often they are fatal. The wrecks are so inaccessible that a proper forensic examination is impossible and, apart from that, the Turkish police are not all that well equipped to conduct forensic researches.

The driver, as required by law, would report his "accident" to the police. He would say he felt his brakes going and jumped clear, which is the usual and proper thing to do. Many drivers faked a jump to show bruises and torn clothing.

The driver's documents would be cleared by police and customs; the accident would be reported to his company and their insurers. All too often the insurers were relieved that there was no loss of Turkish life because when that happens the costs are frightening. And the driver would return home with his ill-gotten gains.

That was how it happened—it was absolutely foolproof, nothing could be proved, no guilt could be apportioned. For the professional swindlers it was too good to be true and they cashed in heavily. Nothing appeals to a crook more than a foolproof fraud. London insurers were swindled out of millions over the years. Scotland Yard faced an impossible task and if anything ever came out of their enquiries, nobody heard much about it. They were not alone in their investigations, insurers sent out private investigators and Willhire, the international vehicle leasing company, had a team trying to discover what had happened to trucks and trailers they had out on lease and which had disappeared without trace.

That was fraud and thieving on a grand scale but the Turks are adept at either end of the larceny scale. John Martin was asleep in a Turkish lay-by when he thought he heard "night people" on the prowl, but all went quiet and he decided he was mistaken, so he dozed off again. He woke for a second time a little later and, though hearing nothing alarming, could not get rid of the feeling that something was going on. He thought it would be wise to move. Starting the engine, he switched on the lights. Instead of the flood of dazzling light he expected just one single beam shone at a crazy, cockeyed angle into the night sky. He glanced instinctively in his wing mirrors to check the trailer lights— there was nothing, just a blank darkness, the mirors had gone. So had five of his battery of six expensive Cibie lights, airhorns, badges and sun visor. The remaining Cibie was pointing into the sky, its thread had jammed and the thieves had not had time to saw through the bolt. In the garage it takes a considerable effort of muscle to turn the nuts on those fittings, it usually requires a sharp rap with a hammer or spanner to accomplish the task. John had not heard or felt a thing. Too late. Nothing could be done so he went back to bed; a certain resignation overcomes Middle East drivers.

All great cities have secret centres where the cognoscenti gather, obscure places which present unpretentious faces to the rest of the world but are widely known to those who need to know them. The Pudding Shop is in no guide book to Istanbul yet it is known to the travelling youth of the whole world. Even Japanese arrive at the Pudding Shop.

It is a seedy double-fronted shop directly facing the Suleymaniye Mosque, the windows are curtained in ragged drapes and the name is hardly discernible. Inside on the right is a self-service food counter with an array of cafeteria foods which look as if they could have been there since last week. The fried eggs on the savoury mince have set solid, turned pale yellow and withered at the edges; they were like that yesterday and do not seem to have been touched. The tables are plastic topped, covered with red check

253

table cloths. Efes beer bottles, Coke cans, fruit and drink cans and cigarette packets clutter their surfaces.

The clientele is young and talkative; the men with beards and floppy-brimmed "digger" hats, the girls with long, free-flowing hair. Smoke and chatter fill the air; they sit all day long drinking Coke, beer and chi. Upstairs is another bar/dining room but more in the style of a club. The youngsters look like all the youngsters the world complains about—unkempt, uncaring, defiant. In a word, drop-outs. Then you talk to them and discover that they are the kids next door doing their thing. And, under the bravado, they are slightly awed and diffident. From all corners of the world they come to the Pudding Shop to find their way around the rest of the world. A lot of them have travelled remarkable distances and done astonishing things, pushing back frontiers and visiting countries which, only a few short years ago, were the preserve of professional travellers. Nepal is now commonplace, some have been to Tibet, nearly all have traversed the length and breadth of the subcontinent of India; they have taken in Indo-China, the islands of Oceania, Asia and Europe—all on a few pennies and a lot of ingenuity. Mostly they have managed to look after themselves very well and stay clear of trouble.

"They *all* look like hippies and drop-outs and a load of teenage trouble," comments one trucker, a man in his forties, "then you talk to them and discover that they are really nice kids. Honestly, I admire them, they've had the guts to get up and go and do something for themselves, they've seized and made opportunities for themselves and packed in more in a couple of years than most of their parents have done in a lifetime. I do everything I can to help them."

He adds: "Mind you, I don't know whether my wife would be over the top to know that I was ferrying a nubile 18-year-old around in the truck."

That is the crux of the Pudding Shop's importance to the teenage globe-trotters. By the food bar there is a noticeboard which, particularly in the high summer travelling season, carries dozens of messages.

"Hidlegard, Joanna, German, require lift to Essen, guaranteed no trouble."

"Jackie, Australian nurse, good sport, wants lift to England with nice, friendly driver."

"Anyone going Denmark??? Zelda, 19, good fun and co-operative, leave Thurs, Fri, Sat, Belgium/Holland will do. Ring Mocamp."

"TWO, TWO, TWO Dutch girl students going Amsterdam, good time guaranteed."

"I will go East as far as you are—anywhere, Afghanistan, Pakistan, India. Will pay own way, good company."

"Two English roses to be plucked here in Istanbul. Take us anywhere nice in Europe."

They throw their sex around a bit in the 1980s fashion and in a way which would shock their grandmothers, but they get around. And travelling with the truckers, they are pretty safe, they will not come to much harm. The girls are wise, they will be well protected through some situations which otherwise could be very hairy indeed.

A tall, blonde girl from Blackpool walked into Williams and Glynn's Bank in Quetta, Pakistan, smiled and said, "Oh, you're English. What's going on? What's all the fuss about. I've just come from Afghanistan and there are soldiers everywhere."

Bound for India to sit at the feet of a guru, she had hitch-kiked through the Russian invasion and never noticed a thing.

10

FIVE o'clock in the morning is the time to leave Istanbul. At this hour the myriad close-packed lights on the hillsides have died, leaving the hills in darkness. The road scythes through the city nearest the Bosporus but shrinks to a double-tracker in the outer suburbs. It is clear save for an occasional car or van, with or without lights. Lights, signal and brake lights, are considered to be optional extras by Turkish private motorists and a bit effeminate at that. On the other hand, Turkish truck drivers consider a truck unroadworthy unless it is festooned with coloured fairy lights so that it resembles a fairground carousel. It is not unusual to see a bank of bright red, rear-light looking lights driving towards you—which can be confusing. Rear windows are also considered to be an offensive intrusion into privacy by Turkish motorists. They cover them in pretty, frilly, elaborate drapes like those hanging from the proscenium arch of a

Victorian theatre. This naturally obliterates all rear vision.

But at five in the morning such hazards are greatly reduced in the city and the road runs toward the mountains clear, dark and untrammelled. Though not for long, the Turks are early risers and soon a string of soft lights begins to appear at the roadside as the chi shops and stalls open. Shadowy groups of men huddle round the tables, their collars turned up, one free hand deep in pocket as they sip the day's first enlivening glass before the work and haggling gets under way.

On the right is the velvety black Sea of Marmara, its tall seaside apartments outlined against a near-black sky. On the far shore the grouped lights of villages reflect in the softness of the inky water. The map states that this is Asia and it feels and looks like Asia. The sun, when it comes, is measurably bigger, the evening and morning stars so much the brighter; day and night arrive dramatically. Here, on the shores of the Sea of Marmara, dawn comes through the windscreen in a diffused rose-red glow. The sea turns a rich burgundy and the surrounding hills a deep port colour, lights in the roadside shops burn yellow and the sun, an incandescent, hazy orange, rolls up the side of a mountain. Its right-hand bottom segment is flattened against the hillside until it bursts free to flood the landscape with daytime greens and browns and reveal the buildings in their ochre, fawn and multi-shaded white.

It also reveals the blue-green uniforms of the traffic polisi signalling us to pull in. They are arranged in the style of a military ambush with scouts strung along both sides of the road. The outlying scout signals the approach of a potential victim, a second flags down the victim with his reflective lollipop, a third directs the victim to stop besides the chef's car. Only those who look as if they have the potential to pay are stopped. European trucks are the first choice.

Turkish police have been known as legalised bandits ever since foreigners first turned a wheel on Turkish soil. Each one wears dark glasses, day and night; his cap is tilted forward so that the peak touches the bridge of his sun-glasses. The effect is intentionally evil-looking and macho so that nobody need be unnecessarily surprised by what follows.

"Tachograph."

The tachograph is not part of Turkish law

and is not legally enforceable but the police insist on its use since they think it gives them additional authority—as if they ever needed any. It is a delicate nicety which helps add to the convolutions of their individualistic enforcement of the law. The officer holds the tachograph disc upside-down and peruses it. He can't read English so the details written in the centre of the disc at the commencement of each journey mean nothing to him. A tachograph presents a complete visual record of a vehicle's journey down to every change of speed.

The officer takes the tachograph to the chef's car and returns to say: "T'ree t'ousant liras." This amounts to about £20.

"What for?"

"Sshpeedink."

"Nix speeding, tachograph say nix speeding, nix over 60 kilometres. Nix pay."

He takes the disc back to the chef and returns again to say: "Speshul leemits thees road, sshpeedink. T'ree t'ousand lira vit fatura, two t'ousand lira, nix fatura."

That is £20 with an official receipt, under £10 without a receipt.

We look dumb, shrug the shoulders, take 1,500 liras from our pockets, pull out the empty pockets to show him and say: "Nix 2,000, 1,500 . . . all I got until banko, nix more."

The chef, listening intently in the car alongside, gives a curt nod. The officer pockets the 1,500 and with a peremptory wave signals the truck to move as he calls up the next customer.

Turkish traffic polisi live well, they suffer no shame or embarrassment at what they do and, providing they get the money, can be friendly and hospitable.

One night, sleeping in a Turkish lay-by, there came a hammering on the cab door. Outside, lights were blazing and flashers flashing, these were obviously not "night people". Through the opened window a polisi, still wearing his sun-glasses, commanded: "Get out, you see chef."

In the back seat of the police car, the chef peered at the passports through his dark glasses, rested them on his enormously fat stomach, flicked the pages and pronounced: "Inglisi, hmm, Inglisi, s'gud, Inglisi verr gud. You know Scotland Yard?"

"Yes, we know Scotland Yard."

"Scotland Yard verr gud, OK?"

"Oh, yes, Scotland Yard is very good."

"Me," he jabbed a fat forefinger into his chest, "Me go London, Scotland Yard, speshhul traininK." And a flashing smile revealed glints of gold. From a voluminous Gladstone bag by his side he produced a tie-box with a Scotland Yard tie inside and a letter of fraternal greeting from the Metropolitan Police to their visiting Turkish colleagues. With a vehemence which indicated that he would stand no contradiction he said: "Scotland Yard, verr, verr gud. Scotland Yard my verr gud frents."

So we agreed, what else can you do?

His tone altered: "Fife t'ousand liras vit fatura, for you, two t'ousand lira nix fatura."

"What for?"

"Sshpeedink."

"Speeding? We were in kip, how could we be speeding?"

"All'a TIRs sshpeedink, all'a time, sshpeedink, sshpeedink all'a time."

We paid the man quickly—there is no use in argument, you will have to pay eventually.

He stuffed the money into a purse and protested: "My frents, do not get out, we will drink Scotland Yard, my gud frents."

Out came a bottle and glasses and the toasts were drunk to Scotland Yard, the FBI,

Interpol and the Turkish constabulary. He asked: "You go mountains? Mucho bad men in mountains. My cousin ees chef of polis in mountains. You see my cousin, I weel tell heem you come. He weel protect you in mountains. You haf bottle whisky in cab? All'a TIRs haf bottle whisky in cab, mucho bottles, I come collect bottle, you my gud frents. My cousin weel protect you gud in mountains."

"Thank you, chef, but if your cousin is anything like you, we can use him like a hole in the head."

Down the road from the first police ambush is an official army TIR check point. Stop, hand in the papers to show that you are keeping to your prescribed route. Collect the necessary stamp and motor on. Miss the check point and they will send you back from the next one along the road which could be 50 or 400 kilometres away. Without the stamp, there is no way through.

There is no love lost between the soldiers and the police. If a military patrol arrives at a spot where the police are running one of their happy little ambushes, the police leap into their cars like wanted men and roar away down the road. Sometimes the soldiers have caught their police colleagues red-handed and made them pay back the money.

The world rages at the imposition of martial law but a lot of Turkish citizens love the army because they have cut down on extortion, brutality and robbery at gun point. Military rule is not nice but it is considerably more comfortable than anarchy.

We are now approaching the mountains. The sign reads Bolu, this is the first big climb, a strenuous grind to 8,000 feet. It is a wicked mountain, not with the reputation for evil of Tarsus mountain, yet it must be treated with respect as the wrecks alongside the road will testify.

Now is the time to watch the sky for ominous grey clouds and scrutinise oncoming traffic for tel-tale signs of snow. We also ponder whether it might be worthwhile investing £300 in a set of snow chains, we can always sell them later. But maybe the snow tyres will suffice. We must keep a sharp look out and make the decision in time. It will be too late on the mountain with the wheels spinning uselessly and the tilt sliding out of control.

So far it doesn't look bad. We flash the approaching Brit and stop. "Well, there's a bit of snow about, not enough to worry you, I got through."

Here minarets dominate each hamlet, the people wear Asian clothes and look distinctly Asiatic, stalls loaded with fruit, pumpkins, gourds and edible delicacies stand in niches by the road. Wherever there is a settlement the women are in the fields or grouped together waiting for transport. The ancient now ousts the modern. Europe is a little finger's width away on the map but has ceased to exist. Those Turks in Western dress driving cars between Ankara and Istanbul would be as much out of place in this rural Turkey as the truck drivers are.

Inevitably, a Turkish truck has broken down by the side of the road, its rear end has been jacked up and its occupants are arranged round it in committees of 12. At night they would have put the blown tyre (for that is the most probable cause of the breakdown) 50 yards behind the truck with another old tyre 50 yards in front and set fire to them both to blaze as a beacon warning to approaching traffic.

A jacked-up truck with a squatting figure beside it—there is no more common sight in Turkey. If the average person spends a third of his life in bed, a third at work and a third at play, the Turk spends half his life mending punctures and repairing vehicles.

Turks see their vehicles as stages on which to act out their lives, and as such they decorate them like stage sets. A Turkish truck is known among drivers as a Tonka because of its similarity to the child's toy truck; it has the same angular construction. Every inch of the rear and side walls of these trucks are decorated with paintings of paradise. The most popular picture is of green meadows under blue skies, a stream winds through the meadows and beneath an arched bridge a cottage nestles under orange and olive trees, there are geese in the garden and ducks on the water—it is an idyllic setting. There are nearly a dozen similarly evocative scenes on each truck, not an inch is left undecorated with romantic mountains, waterfalls, horses, sloe-eyed Turkish girls, elegant leopards, majestic lions and dancing bears.

We are not to be distracted by prettiness, however, for this is Bolu. And the word is: beware of Bolu. It is a rough area peopled by wild men and only a fool forgets it. Beyond Ismit, between the villages of Golcock and Mankoy, is an official roadside park by the side of a lake. In the park is a café and a fountain that has been known to run with blood.

Glynn Francis, a 33-year-old father of two, from Crynant, Glamorgan, pulled in here to prepare his evening meal. With no second thought, Glynn went to the fountain to fill his kettle, a group of men appeared from the shadows and demanded money. He laughed it off and told them: "Nix money, sorry." He turned to climb back into his cab and they shot him in the head at point blank range. When his bloodied body hit the ground they ransacked his pockets, trampled over his corpse, stripped the cab clean and disappeared into the night. The sound of the shot reverberated through the park. Not a light came on, not a person stirred. In the morning the café staff showed no reaction or interest. They had heard nothing and seen nothing despite pressure from the British Embassy. The murder remains unsolved.

A great danger in this region is to have an external gas bottle, with which many trucks are equipped on the theory that it is safer to keep the gas outside the cab. Somebody once noticed that two Dutch trucks had been parked for a number of days, and the drivers had not been seen. A passing driver said: "Let's give them a knock, see if they are all right."

The cab doors were open, it was clear that the locks had been forced. Inside the Dutchmen were dead in their bunks, gassed. The robbers had disconnected the hoses from the gas cylinders at the back of the cab and fed them through the air intakes into the sealed interior. When the gas had done its work they had brazenly set about the gruesome business of demolishing the cab interiors and taking watches, chains, rings and money from the bodies of their victims. The incident warranted a shrug of the shoulders from the locals.

Some years ago the area hit the headlines in Britain at the time Liverpool Football Club played a European Cup match at Giresun, on the Black Sea. When the local club scored, the Liverpool players and British press were astonished to see the local supporters shoot live ammunition into the air. The incident caused a minor shock at home, it didn't raise an eyebrow in Turkey. Guns and killing are part of life in this remote district.

This is not to suggest that you meet violence and danger every day. You may never see it at all if you work the route properly and experienced drivers do just that; trucking companies and owner-drivers are looking for profits, not heroics. The old hands at the run have plenty of advice to offer first-timers.

If you've any sense, you don't go looking for trouble. But you've got to realise the dangers that exist. Ask the British consulate in Istanbul, or drop in the embassy in Ankara and get chatting there. Ask how many Brits have been topped in the last ten years—in accidents as well. You'll get a shock. These people here are not playing at being evil bastards, they are doing it for real, and you keep out of their way.

Bobby Brown says: "Often we have to go up in the mountains to back load for Europe, and up there you see things you've only ever read about in comics. There are still old boys who wrestle bears—in the village square. They cover themselves with thick grease and do a bit of wild wrestling with each other then they throw in a bear to liven it up. If someone gets topped it's all part of the fun. I watched it happening a couple of months ago, they think it's hilarious when someone gets ripped apart. The point is that once you've seen it, you realise that life here is very different and very primitive."

Another experienced driver adds: "You haven't met the Kurds yet. They are the other side of Ankara and they are supposed to be the real wild bunch, not this lot."

Don't talk to Trevor Long about the Kurds. On his first trip he was involved in an incident in a Kurdish village in eastern Turkey. A child was killed. It was not Trevor's fault, and, by the grace of God, a young Turkish soldier had witnessed the incident. Trevor had given him a lift to the village. The Kurds went mad with anger and grief over the death of the child. Their simple approach to justice—and it is the *official* attitude throughout Islamic countries—is that if the foreigner had not been there, there could not have been an accident. The very fact that he was there, uninvited, was the cause of the accident, therefore, in the eyes of Allah, his very presence must make him guilty.

Without ceremony, the Kurds dragged Trevor from his cab and strung him up from a branch of a tree in the village square. The dead child's parents and relatives stood witness to Allah's justice.

At this point the young soldier whose protests had been ignored opened fire with his sub-machine gun over the heads of the crowd. Then he fired at their feet. When he aimed directly at them and declared that he would open fire on the count of five, the mob suddenly dispersed. They knew that a Turkish threat issued in such circumstances would be carried out without fail. The soldier cut Trevor down and waited by his prostrated, half-strangled body until military and medical aid arrived. For months the livid bruise and burn marks from the hangman's rope remained on Trevor's neck. Traces of them can still be detected seven years after the horrific ordeal.

"Why the hell are you still coming down then?" Trevor is asked.

"At first it was because I thought that I wouldn't let them beat me," he replies. "Then it got into the blood. You can get hooked on the trip and you just can't stay away."

Today Bolu is benign, the warm sun is shining and the high country has an exhilarating freshness about it. Bolu, however, can change climates a dozen times a day and swing from sub-arctic to the sub-tropical in a matter of minutes.

John Martin and two mates once drove from Ankara on a brilliant sun-splashed morning when the air was filled with bird-song and the peasants were lazily tilling the fields and tending the sheep. All was well with the world until, in mid-morning, it went dark. Snow was in the air, glinting in the headlights. The convoy of three trucks stopped and fitted snow chains. To say, "fit the snow chains" is much like saying "paint the Forth Bridge". Chains for those big wheels are heavy and very tricky indeed to manipulate on to the wheels, then fix and tighten. If you make a mistake it is easy to lose a finger or incur other injuries. Inevitably, because of their purpose they have to be fitted in appalling conditions. And as soon as the snow clears the chains must be removed or they are smashed and the road surface is cut up.

John and his team clunked along, the chains rapping the thin covering of snow on the road surface. Gradually the clunking stopped as the snow settled deeper. The darkness turned into a sheet of reflective light and the wipers began to rasp as snow accumulated on them. Through the windscreen it was impossible to differentiate between road and weather, it was all one. Through the side window, the snow could be seen surging over the wheel hubs. They stopped. The rotating wheels could push the truck no further.

With the inevitability of a rising tide the snow crept up the sides of the trucks until they sat afloat in a sea of white. It lay feet deep on the roofs of the tilts and covered the fifth wheel so the trailers appeared detached from the tractor units. Since the first fleck of white dust had appeared in the headlight beam it had taken just one hour for them to become totally marooned. One problem is uppermost in the mind in such a situation: how do you stay alive until help arrives or a thaw comes. The solution is not so simple, it calls for guts, ingenuity, imagination and some extreme measures if needs must. How extreme? Well, if the cargo is inflammable you might have to burn it, but that is the last resort. It *can* become that serious. The first thing is to keep the engine running as long as possible and keep the warmth flowing. However, the diesel and radiator can freeze solid in the temperatures that occur on these mountains and you must assume that they will freeze at some time. You are going to need fire, which means that the most vital assets are lighters and matches.

To be stranded in a convoy—as John and his friends were—is obviously preferable to being stuck on your own. It means triple supplies of the vitals—gas, food, flame and active bodies. However, to get from the leading cab to the rear one requires supreme physical effort, a battle for at least 150 feet through deep snow drifts, often in the face of a blizzard.

If and when the engine stops and things become desperate, you can rip open the tilt and smash the wooden retaining side boards for fuel. The trailer floor and side walls are metal and a number of metal frames form the height and shape of the tilt, these have metal boxes, eight inches high, two inches wide and an inch deep welded to them, they are open at the top and on one side; the wooden retaining slats are slotted into them to stop the cargo sliding out of the sides of the tilt. Each trailer has a hundred or so of these wooden slats which means a plentiful supply of firewood in dire emergency.

You clear a space and light a bonfire under

the diesel tank, and, if necessary, under the radiator. The idea horrifies Department of Transport Inspectors and Safety Officers but they are safe in bed at home and not about to freeze to death on a Turkish mountain top. It is nowhere near as dangerous as it sounds because diesel is not as volatile as petrol and explodes under compression not by ignition. You wrap the nozzles of the gas bottles in cloth, they too can easily freeze, so you must keep them as warm as yourself. Then you sit and wait.

A mountain wind lifts the surface snow and suspends it in a swirling white froth. The grey of day merges with the black of night and, when the wind drops, the stillness accentuates the sound of your own breathing and heartbeats. Cramp from sitting aches the bones. You sleep and sit and wait again . . . and again . . . and again. If you are liable to panic, annoyance, temper or suffer a lack of patience, then it is your own fault, you should not have been here anyway. But do not let your impatience get the better of you now because it will kill you.

Eight days, six hours after John and his companions ground to a shuddering stop, the first grader and snow plough reached them.

Emerging out of the murky evening gloom their headlights were not visible until they were on top of the convoy. On the way through they had dug out private cars with the occupants frozen solid inside. The damage was insignificant, only one trailer side of slats had been burnt. They lit bonfires under the other two trucks, started up with hardly any trouble and motored on.

Dropping down into Ankara is the testing part of Bolu, it involves a series of vicious, twisting, tortuous Z-bends and hairpins on a narrow road with hidden inclines. The drivers call it Happy Valley. In the ravine below the most deceptive bend are the wrecks of scores of vehicles whose drivers lost concentration and ran out of road. It was their last mistake, they did not live to tell the tale or reflect upon their errors. Nobody ever does.

All the way along, wrecks advertise the dangers for the ill-prepared or careless. There is no need to plaster the road with warning signs, the skeletons of trucks are warning enough. There is not a driver who does not instinctively check and double check his safety factors, touch his exhauster to see that it hasn't blown in the last couple of kilometres, touch the brakes to test response, get into the right gear and come down to a crawl.

Somehow it doesn't seem quite right, this procession of juggernauts, spaced well out, and moving at less than snail's pace. They appear to be stationary, suspended in limbo over the precipices and clinging like flies to a wall, while, on the other side of the road, their counterparts are roaring at three times the speed in the other direction.

The road appears to level out, yet the trucks crawl on. They do not accelerate but crawl slower and slower. The tension in the cab mounts, there is a feeling of being suspended on an elastic band which is about to snap, the engine is revving to a point of protest and the hands on your watch face seem to have stopped moving. But the fruity roar of the exhauster brake is reassuring in the ears.

Lift a toe off the brake—slam it back on again. The instant the brake is released, the mountain exerts its grip and tries to propel truck, trailer, driver and all in a headlong, uncontrollable charge down that snaking road and into the ravine. So, left foot on the exhauster brake, right foot on the air-brake pedal and keep the forces in balance. In every driver's mind is the thought of that awful, mushy, useless feeling underfoot when the brakes have over-heated and gone. He imagines the hopelessness of excessive revs throwing out the gear lever as he tries to change down, and in his ears he hears the shriek of tyres and tearing metal. It makes the adrenalin pump and the heart beat quicker, it heightens the senses and quickens the reactions: the whole of his mind and body is attuned to the feelings transmitted through his toes.

For reassurance you think: nothing can go wrong if I don't let it, these machines are built to handle this and more, we are well within the designed tolerances, she can handle it with ease. Only I can cock it up, and I don't intend to. Patience.

God! The Womble in front is cutting it close, his outer right-side tyres are off the road and over the edge. His wheels are actually suspended over the precipice, they keep swinging out: whenever he passes an approaching truck, he hangs them out into thin air. However he seems to be sitting in the right position on the road, he's tucked in close to the centre, he's keeping a good line, there *is* no extra space between him and approaching trucks. He's sitting dead right and I am following him in a true line: that means that my back outers are hanging in air as well!

I don't want to think about that.

Now the boys down below, on the bends lower down the mountain, are beginning to space out, they are breaking away from the continuous stream of trucks like water droplets from a stalactite and speeding down the hill. This must be the bottom, the end of the mountain. But steady on. Simmer down. This is the danger point where you can relax and lose your grip. This, in fact is the most dangerous part, just look at the wrecks down there to prove the point. This is where it is essential to keep your bottle and not do anything silly—keep her crawling, you can see where you are going, so what's the hurry?

About 11 kilometres outside Ankara comes the parting of the ways. To the right lies our route—Iraq, Syria, Jordan and the Gulf via Tarsus mountain, a real swine but it has got to be driven over. That's what the job is all about and what you are so highly paid for. To the left lies the road to Iran, Afghanistan and Pakistan over Tahir.

The road over Tahir can, in fact, be the worst of all. Since it is so high and remote the weather settles on it with an arctic ferocity producing temperatures below those near the North Pole, accompanied by white-outs which last for days and drifts which obliterate everything. Many drivers think it worse, much worse, than Bolu or Tarsus.

A yet worse disadvantage is that up there is deep into Kurd country, and the deeper you get in, the fiercer and more independent the Kurds become. The simple fact is that it is well nigh impossible to control guerillas and dissidents in remote, rugged mountain country; no government has ever yet succeeded. Marshall Tito kept at bay the German Army during World War II in the mountains of Yugoslavia. The whole might of the Russian army of occupation in Afghanistan has failed to root out the Pathan Mujahedin though they are only equipped with skimpy and antiquated arms. And the Kurds have ruled this region since time immemorial.

That is a problem when carrying a high security load. And the load carried in 1971 by John Martin, Georgie White and Peter Byrne in their three 40 feet metal containers was the bulk of the new Pakistan currency to be delivered to Karachi. This had been printed by the Royal Mint in England and Wales and its value was inestimable . . . 10,000 cubic feet of every denomination of currency note with the odd few tons of coin thrown in for good measure. In Europe, these were just bundles of pretty print hardly worth the paper they were printed on. But the nearer to Pakistan the load travelled, the greater its value became. And in tribal country, it was even more valuable. Security arrangements demanded that a tight time schedule had to be kept. So Tahir was taken in less than favourable conditions which, in other circumstances, would have legitimately held up the convoy. As happens, fortune smiled on the brave . . . or the foolhardy, and Teheran, Iran, was reached without mishap. Then the route lay through Esfahan, Yazd and Kerman, where there appear on the map three significant designations: one reads "Great Sand Desert", another is a little triangle marked ▲4419, a mountain 14,497 feet high, and the third is where the black line of the road leading to the Iran-Afghanistan-Pakistan border through Zahedan (Duzdab) becomes a faint dotted line. Says John: "That means that it's the way people go, but there ain't necessarily a road, not what you'd call a road."

This is the region of Baluchistan where the Baluchi warriors live and it crosses the national borders. The Baluchis, like the Kurds, have been at war with successive governments for evermore.

On the official border, at Mirjaveh, the North West Frontier of fabled British Raj adventure stories, there begins the remote and desolate mountain country inhabited by wild men and their wilder sons who are out to prove that no matter how barbaric dad can be, they can outdo him. The border arrived and with it a strong detachment of the super efficient Pakistani army. Suddenly the load became worth unaccountable millions, a great chunk of the country's wealth stowed in just three trucks.

All around were Baluchi and Pathan tribesmen in their mountain strongholds. Today they are revered as Majuhedin "Freedom Fighters" resisting an oppressive Russian invader. For centuries the British had regarded them as unruly brigands suitable to shoot at and make films about. By profession, Pathans and Baluchis are fighting men who, when they have no common adversary to shoot at and harass, run blood feuds among themselves to keep their hands in.

For the last three decades their pet enemy has been the Pakistan army which they hate with such an intensity that it makes their previous reaction to the British seem almost benevolent. So the army detachment was on alert to the point of trigger-happy sharpness. Fortunately they were a drilled, disciplined, professional fighting unit of considerable skill.

The logistics of a trip like this are formidable. John says: "There aren't exactly an abundance of filling stations and Safeway stores about, so you carry hundreds of gallons of extra fuel in drums stacked on the truck. And you carry all your grub and water. You pack the food locker under the trailer until it is bulging because you never know how long you will be held up on the way."

The convoy parked for the night on a wild mountain pass, selected as a defensible position by the Sandhurst trained officer in command. Machine guns were sited, guards posted, patrols despatched, orders were given and trucks and escorts, all secured with lights shaded, settled to refresh themselves and wait for dawn.

After a quiet kip and a splash wash in the truck, John thought: "Right, a quick pee, get some grub from the locker, a bit of a fry up, a cuppa coffee, then a good night's sleep. It's marvellous having all these soldiers around, there's no need to worry about the trucks." In his underpants and nothing else, he climbed from the cab, walked to Georgie's truck, hammered on the cab door and waited for Georgie to climb down. He was in his underpants too. They turned to walk and give Paddy a shout. In the darkness there were ominous clicks, a dimmed flashlight was switched on, they could make out a circle of metallic rings surrounding them—the muzzles of rifles. They were encircled by the army. In vain they pointed to the trucks, but every move they made towards the cabs was met by raised rifles and sharp jabs from the business ends. There was no means of communication, there was a complete language barrier.

The orders had been given: nobody gets in or out of the trucks, nobody moves. If anybody resists, open fire. So John and Georgie sat out that bitter night in underpants and flip-flops with only an army blanket against the cold until the grey dawn came over the mountain peaks and the commanding officer made his morning rounds.

Whatever excesses Mocamp Istanbul can perpetrate, Mocamp Ankara can outdo—especially in winter. Winter is mayhem time at Mocamp Ankara because of the mountains, the Taurus Range which is the dominant physical feature of Turkey. However it is the habit of the drivers to talk about mountains by the name of the nearest town, so you get Bolu, Tahir and Tarsus; the two latter ones are the more formidable on paper, though, in practice, Bolu can be just as testing. It depends upon how and when you meet them and the weather conditions at the time.

With Tahir and Tarsus we are talking about real mountains which compare with any range in the world. The peaks and passes get progressively higher from west to east beginning at 12,300 feet near Tarsus and rising to 17,000 feet at Mount Ararat, on the Iranian border. This is a couple of thousand feet higher than Mont Blanc in the Alps and should give an indication of the problems they present to travellers. Add to the height and the weather conditions the fact that the roads are really only tracks, until recently they were mud tracks and nothing else, and it is possible to appreciate why drivers regard them with great circumspection. To those daunting prospects also add the fact that many of those travelling over the high passes are Turkish drivers and the wonder is that anybody ever summons up the nerve and courage to turn a wheel on a mountain while they are there.

The awful tensions at Ankara Mocamp build up when the snows are about and the drivers are working out whether the time is ripe to attempt the crossing. Is the road clear? Is anybody stuck up there? Will the weather turn good or bad? Are the borders open or closed? Has anybody come down from the mountains in the last couple of hours/days/weeks?

There are so many factors to be considered that the strain of making a final decision needs a lot of beer to oil the think-box.

Then comes a high, clear dawn with the sun in a cloudless sky and westbound drivers come rolling in to say that the roads and borders are clear. The grizzled road men have done another marvellous job with snow plough and grader, traffic is moving and the weather forecast is good.

"Great, let's go."

But there are always a couple of drivers who remain glum despite the cheering news. "You go, mate, I can't come yet, I seem to have done my money, can't think where it has gone. I swear I'll never stay at this place again, everytime I stop here I do my money. I'll have to telex for some more, see you down the road."

Ankara Mocamp is poison to the well-intentioned but weak-willed. It is also a very good place for a ruckus: some of the best ruckuses recorded have broken out at Ankara, ruckuses to live in the memory as vividly as a Rocky Marciano title fight. Many bear the scars to prove it. It is viewed with nostalgic affection by professional fighting men like the Turkish infantry and riot police as being the place where they come nearest to real action in the whole of their military careers. A bemedalled army major stopped there one day and somebody asked what his medals could be for. A droll trucker replied: "The one on the extreme right is Cyprus, 1974, the one next to it is Mocamp, 1975."

Ankara Mocamp isn't, of course, just cakes

and ale and high jinks; there is a deeply serious reason for hanging about there. The good driver must be absolutely sure that the way ahead is clear in every way, both from the point of view of the weather—and the political situation.

Which adds yet another hat to the collection a seasoned Middle East driver must wear—political analyst. Politics take place on the streets in these parts and he is in the middle of it. That can be a costly and dangerous situation which is best illustrated by the state of affairs following the Ayatollah Khomeni's return to Iran.

Albert Evans and Peter Boalch, driving for John Evans Transport, of Newport, Gwent, passed through Turkish customs into Iran on Boxing Day, 1978. On January 29, 1979, the London *Daily Mail* and the BBC reported the plight of two British drivers, Evans and Boalch, who had been stranded on the Iranian border for five weeks because the border was closed during the disturbances in Iran resulting from the Ayatollah's return and the Shah's overthrow. On February 1, the Transport and General Workers Union pleaded with the British Government to intervene and try to rescue 1,000 British drivers stranded on the Turkish-Iranian border because of the troubles in Iran. That was possibly an overstatement of the crisis because there aren't 1,000 drivers on the run, but certainly hundreds were stuck in the 500 yards of no-man's-land between Turkey and Iran. They were unable to go on or come back. Going out of Turkey their exit visas had been stamped and the Turkish authorities would not allow them to re-enter Turkey until they also had an Iranian exit stamp in their passports. It sounds stupid, but that is the local law and that is the Islamic mind—nothing, not even war, civil strife or natural disaster will move it.

The British Foreign Office was, as it so often is, hamstrung by events and issued two statements. The first said: "The Foreign Office cannot interfere in an internal Iranian matter but hopes to persuade Turkey to re-admit the drivers." The second had the ring of desperation: "This is a continuing and recurring problem, but there is absolutely nothing we can do about it."

While the diplomatic and trade union wires were running hot and futile, the drivers were virtually imprisoned in that dreary, comfortless tract of desert land, running out of food and supplies and completely out of touch with the world . . . stateless men with nowhere to go.

Iran was in turmoil and Turkey, though with less international publicity, was also in a state of acute unrest verging on civil war—a situation in which they did not want too many inquisitive foreigners nosing around. In Kahraman Maras, near Adana, a reported 2,000 Sunni Muslims had been massacred by their Shi'ite brethren and everybody was trigger-happy. So the Turks wanted, for the time being, to keep an eye on each other rather than on foreign truckers. They were not over-anxious to rush to the aid of the stranded host in no-man's land. On the very day the Welsh pair, Evans and Boalch, had driven out, Turkey had declared a State of Martial Law to quell the rumblings of Islamic revolution and the trap snapped shut.

Peter Boalch arrived back in London on February 14 but declined to tell reporters how he had managed it since he was still officially not allowed back into Turkey . . .

From Mocamp into Ankara, the capital city, is a furiously fast-moving stock-car race on the public highway, no holds or moves are barred, shunts and scrapes all count as part of the fun.

As a salutary reminder of the state of affairs in this politically troubled country, on the right of the road the aircraft of the Turkish Air Force stand on the tarmac of the military airfield. This looks like a well-ordered aircraft museum: lines of ancient Dakotas, an old Britannia—and are those even older Avro Ansons? But as the road skirts the perimeter fence it presents a vignette of Turkish life: inside the fence there is immaculate military order, neatness and cleanliness, outside, high-speed chaos and a free for all. Impassive sentries view the scene from high vantage points guarding the airfield.

On the surface, the two systems work together compatibly. The public with whom visiting drivers come into contact—and there are no restrictions on social intercourse—speak well of the military. But drivers do not get much opportunity to speak to critics of the regime whose social intercourse is restricted by prison walls. Being pragmatic, the drivers say: "It's good, since the army took over, the cost of running through Turkey has been slashed by 200 per cent in the baksheesh you save. You are not pulled in by the legalised-bandit-police round every corner and officials on the borders keep their sticky fingers out of your wallet while the army is watching."

The army is watching on every street corner in every city and town, mingling with crowds on the streets, its helmets, rifles and military armbands are an accepted part of the scene. It sits observing in its glass-fronted control posts. It is a big army and it is omnipresent.

Which introduces another salutary thought for drivers pulling into an army check-point to report. Three-quarters of the world we travel in our daily work, from Czechoslovakia to the borders of China and India in the East and the shores of the Red Sea and Persian Gulf in the South, live under the rule of the gun. And living with a rifle muzzle in your neck is not a comfortable feeling.

An even more uncomfortable feeling on a Turkish road is having a Kamikaze coach in sight, whether it is ahead and travelling in the same direction, approaching from the opposite direction or looming in the rear-view mirrors. A Kamikaze raises the hair on the back of the neck and makes the nerves tingle;

Kamikazes are as unpredictable as jumping-jack fireworks.

A wave of shock swept over the Western European press when Turkish Kamikaze coaches began to run cheap, unlicensed tourist travel services from Britain, Holland, France and Germany. There was horror at the age and condition of the coaches themselves and even greater panic at the standard of driving and the hours the drivers worked. Without equivocation, Kamikaze coaches are deathtraps—murder vehicles. They kill an extraordinary number of people every year and form a good percentage of the wrecks strewn along Turkish roads—and the roads approaching Turkey. No experienced Middle East truck driver who, by the nature of his occupation has come to know a bit about driving on the continents, would set foot in or allow his loved ones within a mile of a Kamikaze coach.

Maybe prospective passengers should talk to Errol Flynn (his real name), a driver for Daysons of Carlisle, who was hit by a Kamikaze and, by a miracle, survived with minor injuries—unlike the eleven passengers in the coach whose mangled corpses were dragged from the tangled wreck. The coach driver simply turned out of a stream of traffic and drove on the wrong side of the road accelerating all the time, head on at the Dayson truck. This is standard practice for a Kamikaze who drives in the blind faith that Allah will provide a gap for him to squeeze into.

Errol flung his fully laden Volvo truck off the road into the ditch but the Kamikaze hit his side at full speed. The side of the coach was completely ripped out, the bodywork was tangled like spagetti, bodies were scattered for yards. Apart from the dead, many of the horrendously maimed will never recover. Errol was completely exonerated by the Turkish police. At grave risk to his own life he had done everything he could to avoid the crash. The experience has marked him for life and he is just one of the many drivers who have been seared by Kamikazes. Some have been crippled and some have been killed. Kamikaze coach driving is a national lunacy of Turkey, a mass hysteria culminating in idiot displays of bravado and criminally dangerous road behaviour from a nation of chronically bad drivers. Remember, one in three of the new cars bought by newly rich

Turkish gastarbeiters in Germany fails to complete the journey home.

The Kamikazes are carving up the Ankara traffic but the great relief of reaching Ankara is that after this city the traffic will thin out. The heavy traffic in Turkey is between Istanbul and Ankara, running on a two-way road which is too narrow to handle it adequately. Going east, the two-way road just about copes, not well, but well enough.

Yet Turkey deserves high praise for its efforts to improve its roads. The pauper of Europe, in a state of perpetual bankruptcy, it has managed to lay roads where there were none 10 years ago, to carpet the old cobblestones and mud tracks with a passable surface, to construct splendid new motorways and to continue building them even though economic disaster has crippled the country. Turkey is a big country with a small income, it is a great hunk of inhospitable land where roads have to go for a long, long way between centres of habitation. And the climate is disastrous to roadworks—bitter ice-bound winters and burning summers. With pick, shovel, muscle-power and limited mechanical aids, Turkish road men could teach their counterparts in the sophisticated, developed countries a great deal about keeping the highways open in the foulest of conditions. They work on the highest passes, in weather that could kill a polar bear, and somehow beat the most appalling odds to clear the routes.

Ankara's five-storey barrack block apartments, red-roofed, with their ochre and grey facings enlivened by strings of washing on each balcony, thin out and the foothills of the Taurus mountains rise around us.

We are about to motor a 300 horse-power testament to twentieth century technology into the heart of an 8,000-year-old civilisation. The antiquity of our surroundings is revealed in the guide book, on the map and on the signposts. To the left, the Kingdom of the Hittites, 200 BC; to the right, the road to Yassihöyük which, the signpost explains, was formerly Gordion where King Midas of the Phrygians, of the legend of the Golden Touch, lies buried in his great earth tumulus—the same place where Alexander the Great cut the Gordian knot which gave him the key to Asia. A little further along is Konya, the home of the Whirling Dervishes, and where they still whirl every December to celebrate the festival of the thirteenth century mystic and founder of the sect, Mevlana

Celaleddin Rumi. Straight ahead lies Tarsus, the direct road to Arabia, and the birthplace of Saint Paul. Much has remained unchanged since the days Saint Paul rode these hills. The peasant still rides his donkey, goatherds and shepherds tend their flocks, the one-bladed plough is pulled by the ass through the stony ground, the women weep and the men toil. Twenty years of motorised infidel intrusion and 10 years or less of metalled road have brought more changes to this ancient land than the previous 20 centuries.

The truck purrs contentedly along an undulating road across the high plateau under a wide sky and an over-sized sun. This is the first of the great, empty, one-step marathon runs which will roll up the kilometres and cut back the time deficit caused by the queues at borders: 581 kilometres, city to city, 400 miles, a suitable distance for a big Scania to get to grips with. Knock off 76 kilometres from that distance, a vital 76 kilometres which is Tarsus Mountain from first rise to final level: it is a heck of a lot of mountain. At the moment it is an innocuous, irregular, blue strip along the horizon bordering a slightly disconcerting landscape with a ghost-like quality about it.

The 80 kilometres of the Tuz salt lake shimmers in the sunshine and its mists shroud the horizons. It stretches to a distant emptiness to melt with the sky, their hazy blues an exact match, the reeds and bull-rushes ringing the shore suggest a fringe to the sky itself, so similar is the colour. Away, far away, in the distance is a moving black speck appearing and fading in the mist, it is an approaching juggernaut. We are riding along on a cloud in a dream.

A peasant trundles along the road on a cart of traditional local design where the cart is slung on suspension made from trees grown to the correct shape. The shaped tree trunks form a sort of cradle which holds and supports the load-carrying platform. The design looks as old as creation itself. The Royal Navy used to grow plantations of oaks in the same way, each individual tree grown to the shape of a ship's bulwark. Somewhere in Turkey and Eastern Europe they must still be growing trees in the same way to make their farm carts, for this design is seen from Rumania onwards.

There is little metal used in construction here, which is surprising because the Turks are the finest back-street metal workers and engineers to be found. In every village are rows of open-fronted shack workshops, every one its own scrap yard. The machinery appears primitive, they hammer metal on anvils like an old-fashioned English blacksmith; the smith hammering the hot metal while a young boy blows the bellows. Yet they perform quite incredible feats of skilled, intricate engineering.

A Dutchman blew the half-shaft of his DAF truck along this road. He anticipated a lot of trouble to get a replacement since he was not carrying a spare. The Turks, travelling en famille as usual, stopped to help him. They held a conference round the stranded truck, removed the shattered half-shaft, took it and him to their village where they hammered and milled all night and day. Two days later they had made a new one and fitted it. Four years later it was still working perfectly. Have no worries about breakdowns in Turkey, the Turks will be thrilled to repair or substitute any part, the tougher it is the greater their enthusiasm.

We pass several peasants. It seems that they come from nowhere and go nowhere for there are no signs of habitation near them along the road. How and why they appear is a mystery.

They pay no attention as we pass; their eyes remain fixed in a downwards stare at the road, they act like automatons and show no reaction when rocked in the truck's slipstream.

The truck is as impassive as the peasants we pass. She murmurs along with never a change in engine note, the needle steady on 90 km, working well within herself, half asleep and waiting for a flick of the accelerator to kick some life into her. She will cruise like this all day and night and all the next day. She sets up her own motion rhythms and gently, softly rolls out the irregularities of the road. The sound and feel of perfect mechanical contentment steadily pulls the gathering night towards us and leaves the day behind.

It is time for coffee and self-satisfied appreciation. We're motoring well.

11

IT turned out to be a bad night on Tarsus. A terrible night. There was no apparent reason for it, the weather was good and, although there was no moon, the visibility was clear. A few rain squalls were blowing about but they were no hindrance and helped to clean the windscreen; nor was there a wind to speak of. The traffic was steady, but not excessive, in both directions. In fact, there could not have been a better night for a crossing.

In the beginning, all was well with the world. The coffee and curry had tasted particularly good after twelve hours without eating. Two drivers whom we had left behind in Rumania had made up time and pulled into the lay-by to ask: "How did you get on in Rumania and Bulgaria? We left three hours after you and we hit a blizzard, they closed the mountain and wouldn't let anybody through. They held us up for a day. How on earth did you miss it?"

It is gratifying to know that the luck, for

once, has been with you. But that is the way it goes, one trip you run the whole way in a lucky time-slot and never have a moment's trouble, yet those following half-a-day later hit all the hassles possible.

A contingent from Blackburn, running three-handed to Saudi Arabia, had been resting in the lay-by before making the mountain climb. Two of them had been seen about before, the third was a newcomer. "Who's your mate?" we asked.

"John Thompson, from Blackburn, he's a good lad, he'll be all right. It's his first trip, but he's OK."

They explained that John had been unemployed for two years because driving jobs were so thin on the ground in Lancashire during the recession. This was the first job he had been offered all the time he had been on the dole.

It was agreed that everybody would stop on the mountain top to take up the slack in brakes and check tyres. "Whoever gets up first, puts the kettle on, eh? Boil enough water to do the lot of us, saves a bit of time." That is standard procedure, both the brakes and the kettle. The latter because butane takes longer to boil a kettle than does

302

domestic household gas; the former because it is only a 10 minute job but worth six hours in peace of mind on that drop down to Tarsus and Adana. The brakes are OK, no problem. But it is good not to have a niggle of doubt in your mind as those inclines and bends unroll.

Tarsus begins abruptly, suddenly your nose is up, your tail is down and you are climbing. The road narrows to inches-to-spare width as it hugs tight to the steep mountain side.

Along the side of the road the cruel facts of life are stated in graphic little drawings stuck on poles: they show a car slipping off the flat and level into nothing—suitably illustrated with explosive exclamation marks. The drawings mean that the road ends exactly where you can see it ending, beyond that point to the right is a drop. It can be three, 30 or 300 feet down, makes no difference, you can roll down three feet just as lethally as 300, not so dramatically maybe, but enough to get crushed in the cab.

Now the grinding climb is underway and two chains of vehicles crawl past each other, it looks like a quarry lift only with trucks instead of buckets being hauled slowly up on a cable and lowered at the same speed. There is the same precise spacing, the same gentle rocking and swaying, with little bits of loose loads spilling from truck sides. It seems as if some unknown operator in a hidden control box could suddenly pull a switch and the two lines of traffic would instantly stop.

A left hand bend is coming up so the line of lights is broken where the road turns behind a rock face, then it continues at a higher level on the other side of what must be an intervening ravine. A stream of red on the right and white on the left. In front of the red lights is a glow of white from unseen headlights.

The bend is 50 metres away when sheer terror strikes. It comes in a searing, scorching flash from round the bend to land with the force of a Gurkha's kukri smashed horizontally across the bridge of the nose. The raindrops and specks of mud on the windscreen explode into a million, minute starshells. Light floods the cab's interior and throws sharply angled shadows from wires and protruding knobs never usually noticed. The windscreen turns as opaque as frosted glass through which two blinding orbs of light are defracted in brilliant, concentric circles.

The orbs of light loom like lamps in a third-degree interrogation forcing the head back to the metal of the seat rest. No matter how we twist, turn, squirm in our seats we cannot escape their blinding intensity. They are rushing head on at the cab. There is nothing left in the world but light and complete disorientation; no way of telling which way the truck is moving, no visual point of reference to see where we are.

The dazzle swings off the left hitting the side of our faces with a whiplash of eye-watering glare. The windscreen has cleared and through it, fixed seemingly as permanently as an image in a photograph, we see the interior of a coach. The driver sits hunched forward gripping his wheel, his white face relieved by a black moustache. Behind him rows of passengers with magazines, chocolates and knitting in their laps, look up through their windows in mild surprise at the monster truck towering above them. All are apparently frozen in their seats.

The coach seems to fill the whole road sideways on. Instinctively Trevor spins the steering wheel.

Then we begin to roll in slow motion. All seven driveside wheels on the left come off the road. They peel unstuck like a suction pad being pulled off a flat, plastic surface. For a moment they feel as if they are reluctant to relinquish their hold, then they swing free. The truck wavers on a tight rope, lurching to the right, recovering, lurching again.

Underneath, the rumble starts, a shuddering, grinding, rasping noise which sounds as if the tyres have come off and she is running on her rims. Then come thumps and stunning shocks, a noise of spinning, screeching rubber flinging a hailstorm of pebbles and rubble against metal. The truck wallows like a foundering ship. Above the rumble and clatter we hear a sharper, strident metallic clanging, like the sound of a dustbin lid blowing down a street in a gale. Something has fallen off. An ominously bigger lurch follows the clanging. The world tilts to the right and stays tilted.

The cab swings involuntarily and its new position reveals faces, anxious, alarmed faces, on the left, screwing their eyes against the light from our headlights. They are the drivers of the approaching traffic seen from an extraordinary angle. The truck is crabbing with the tractor unit at an angle to the trailer and the cab feels as if it is much higher than the load.

A Godalmighty thump stops the rumbling. Silence. Silence which seems to last an age—the whole back is off the ground. In one-thousandth-of-a-split-second the mind perceives that how she comes down means everything and in that same suspended fraction of time the thought comes in banal words—life or death. Either she lands on the road or she's over the side and us with her . . .

It takes 10 times as long to think about as it takes to happen. The shock of landing makes her shudder and prance, she has to be ridden like a bucking bronco. But she's on firm ground and rolling. The load has shifted, 18 tons tossed about, dizzy as chaff in a windstorm. We are listing, limping like a peg-legged sailor and that list is pulling us right all the time. The bulge can be seen in the right-hand mirror, hanging wide of the trailer base, the slats have probably broken. The mirror also shows flashing lights and confusion behind, this disappears into blackness as we swing left round the corner and the mirror reflects the empty void over the ravine.

The clamour now is the sound of our own

heartbeats pounding in our ears. Anger wells and surges in uncontrollable waves, shaking the muscles.

A Kamikaze, a damnable, lunatic Kamikaze! If only we could stop the traffic, swing the truck round and thunder after him like the hounds of hell. Catch and beat him senseless with a jack bar, break his legs, smash his hands, blind the bastard—just make sure that he never drives again before he kills you and a dozen others. A Kamikaze on a road like this! Nobody will do a thing about it. The anger will not subside.

We cannot stop, even to examine for damage. The load is pulling us right all the time which is bad, it will pull us over on some of these awful left-handers. If there is ice further up she'll slide off and nothing can stop her. We need a sharp right-hander quickly, it is the only thing. We see one coming and hit it like madmen. Fling her right and brake. That should shift the load back a bit, bound to. It does. The move is made in ice-cold realisation of the danger it involves, but it has to be done. It is curiously simple and the whole operation is done in total detachment—as if you are sitting outside the cab, watching what happens.

The grind upwards goes on and so does the shock, physical shock grips the face like the numbness of a dentist's injection. Perhaps the pain will come when the anaesthetic wears off, we will see.

It is a subdued meeting at the top of the mountain. The Blackburn drivers pull in and the older one says: "What a bloody shambles down there. Did you see it? Two trucks going down have come off, a stupid bloody Kamikaze carved them up, they've gone down the bank on the inside. And there are two other fellows coming up who've gone off, they've not gone right over, just the right hand side wheels over the edge, it will take hours to right them, it'll need a crane. But a bit higher up the road's in a hell of a mess, all the posts are smashed, it looks as if somebody's gone right over and down, poor sod."

"That was us."

"Jesus. It must have been close. The Kamikaze ripped one of his bumpers off, it's lying in the road. His back must have hit you, there's a dent in your front. That load doesn't look too healthy. Do you think you'll be able to shove it right back when you're off the mountain? I don't know what I'd do if one came at me. I've often thought I'd just close my eyes and let him hit me and hope I was a bit tougher than him."

It does not do to brood or even remember. Forget it, dismiss the incident from your mind.

"Let's have a coffee," said the Blackburn man, "tomorrow it's the sunshine, think about that. Lovely, hot sunshine all day and every day. Time to get your desert-wellies out and your shorts on."

Desert-wellies are sandals and the Tarsus mountains mark the beginning of desert-wellies and shorts weather in the winter. The mountains form a natural barrier between European and tropical climates, a sort of weathershed keeping the cold air of Europe out of the Middle Eastern lands. The bottom of Tarsus mountain on the eastern side is always 20° warmer than the bottom on the western and northern side. This is where the great desert sun-trap begins and every day's driving puts at least 10° on the thermometer.

We take up the slack in the brakes which involves lying on our backs under the trailer, checking the play in the brake arms and tightening the cable so that the brake responds instantly to a touch on the pedal.

The plan is to get down the mountain and

to the Oryx garage the other side of Adana. This used to be an Oryx Freightliner station until it went out of business some years ago. Mickey Fitzel used to run it in partnership with an Arab from Qatar. They made a lot of money until the Arab got greedy—or something like that. Micky and his other European partner quit and the business went bust. Every European business partnership with Arabs seems destined to go bust. No matter how much an Arab has he always wants more until he kills the Golden Goose, and that applies to oil sheikhs and kings as much as to small business-men. So Oryx died but the garage lives on as a good pull-up for truckers.

Going down—this brings into play a whole new set of factors and applies infinitely greater strains. Going up, the force of gravity is on your side. It is a powerful asset, holding and restraining the truck all the time and correcting any errors of speed. Going down, gravity is the enemy fighting against the truck. The machine is on its own, holding and containing all those malignant forces of nature working in opposition to it and trying to break it free from its enforced crawl. The engine is now working to hold back the vehicle and its weight instead of propelling it forward. The air in the compressor keeps tight reign on those wheels itching to be away and running free. The asbestos-composite pads inside the brake drums exert their friction to keep it slow and begin to burn red hot under the constant pressure. This is the time when the mechanics of the machine combine fully to keep control. The driver simply oversees the operation and makes minor adjustments to keep it all in balance— skilful adjustments backed by expert judgement.

From above the view is phenomenal, even at night. Looking down from the roof of the world, the darkness lightens appreciably so that the outlines of rock faces and mountains are visible. The road can be traced from the glint of its metallic surface and the bands of light from moving trucks which faintly mark its course. The truck lights are widely spaced giving the appearance of a dotted line stretching to infinity. In the mid-foreground the headlights of a stream of oncoming traffic negotiating a hairpin bend way below flash morse signals across the intervening valleys and ravines—flash, flash, darkness, flash. The flash comes at the moment they swing through the arc of the crucial turn.

Lights appear to be coming straight towards us, then they lead off to the right, to the left and right again until the watchers' eyes move like those of a spectator at Wimbledon. The slopes below disclose a multitude of bends zig-zagging upwards each traced out in a tell-tale string of red and white fairy lights. It is a heck of a road, a heck of a mountain. A glance at the watch shows that we must spend another two hours on it—at least.

Hold a line close to the centre of the road and do not waver from it. There is no room whatsoever to spare on the right, so space on the left is vital. The driver approaching knows the problem so he will hold his line and the wing mirrors will all but brush together. It is as close a shave as Sweeny Todd's razor but unavoidable.

The driving is made the more difficult because of an unpredictable hazard on the road itself—rocks. They shine white in the headlights against the black road surface, mini-boulders of the indigenous stone strewn deliberately on the highway.

The drivers call them Turkish handbrakes. When a Turk breaks down, his sidekicks leap from the cab and push the rocks under his wheels to hold him on the incline. In the case of a bad breakdown they will lay rocks as profusely as plastic bollards on the M1. When the job is finished, they leave the rocks for the roadman to move when he gets round to it. Subsequent traffic picks a delicate path through them. Occasionally a heavy truck tyre will clip a rock and shoot it like a cannonball across the path of an approaching vehicle.

Brake. The line is slowing, glowing red brake lights are coming on—and staying on. We are stopping and nobody likes the idea at all. Now we have definitely stopped. The cab door of the Turk in front flies open and figures pile out to stash rocks under his wheels. He is obviously not happy about his handbrake.

We cannot see what the hold-up is, all that is visible is a descending string of red brake lights curving to the right then breaking acutely left. This is a notorious left-hander, swinging through 120°, with a lay-by of sorts on the right. It forms an extrusion of rock and gravel in the shape of a triangle with the road the curved third side as it eases round the part-hairpin. Beyond the road is a sheer drop.

It is a nasty corner. Maybe somebody has stalled or an oncoming truck has taken the bend too wide and so blocked the road. It will sort itself out.

Now there are flashing lights on the bend, traffic polisi. It is remarkable that they are about, but lucky—they'll soon get things moving.

A Womble is hurrying along the lines of trucks peering into each cab. We have seen him along the road and know him.

He puts on a spurt past the Turk and calls: "Inglisi, Inglisi. Where other Inglisis? Colleaga, colleaga, over the cliff. Not you, other Inglisis."

He scuttles along. The polisi shout: "Get back, back." They forcibly direct dismounting drivers back into their cabs while furiously waving their powerful torchlights to keep traffic in the other lane moving. The Blackburn men come hurrying past, running with the escorting police. The Womble stops at the cab door: "Colleaga, Inglisi colleaga, run off mountain." He gesticulates to indicate a rendering crash.

"What the hell has happened?"

He opens his palms to show the futility of the question and his inability to answer. He says: "He is behind us and going gud, gud, much gud, no problems. Then he sudden go quick, quick like hell and swing out of line. Much quick . . . like err," he searches for the suitable word . . . "like bomber, like bomber. He come past like bomber."

He is sobbing and tears stream down his face. "What he do? What he do?" His face is compressed in anguish, he has just witnessed a man die. "He was going so gud, no problems. What he do? Maybe he lose brakes, but he was going so gud."

Agitated police wave traffic on. "Mufe, mufe, yak, yak, yak." Hurry, hurry, hurry. They have hands on their gun holsters. "Mufe," they bellow. Nobody else is allowed to stop.

On the edge of the triangle is the tail of young John's trailer. It looks terribly bent and twisted. Searchlights on the police car light the scene. The cab can just be seen through the wall and over the edge—a tangled wreck, reduced to mangled, metal matchwood. Shattered concrete posts litter the ground. There is a hurried, urgent bustle of activity round the wreck. Now there are soldiers in attendance as well as police.

Nobody is allowed to stop, the police and

army have their hands full and will brook no interference or sightseers. The logistics of dealing with accidents when the only approach roads are themselves a hazard, and the space to work in is virtually non-existent, are formidable enough in themselves without the unnecessary intrusion of spectators.

The drop to Tarsus and Adana is interminable and curiously oppressive. Atmospheres permeate sections of the run and they are quite inexplicable. A serious accident subdues the entire road. Every driver senses it, the feeling spreads with incredible speed and trucks appear to move in mourning. Communication is telepathic and experienced drivers know from miles away when there has been a bad shunt just by the look and feel of the passing trucks. They can never explain it, they just know.

John's colleagues were sick. The older one explained in the wholly matter of fact manner of a man searching his mind for an explanation: "I can't understand what happened, a concrete block went right through his cab, his leg was twisted up so that it stuck through the cab roof. I tried to move him to get him out and his stomach fell out.

He must have gone over at a hell of a lick to do such damage."

He shakes his head, sighs and ponders aloud: "I just can't fathom what happened, it's impossible. I was talking to him on the CB at the time. He was perfectly all right, no problems. He said he was all right. I said, 'John . . . John?' Then the CB went dead."

The Blackburn men were detained to assist the police and Turkish authorities and the full extent of the tragedy became apparent the following day. A Turk had been parked on the triangle when John hit it, he was swept over the side in his car and killed.

Procedures in Turkey are tough and inflexible, it is not the best place in the world to fall foul of the law. If the death of a Turkish citizen is involved, penalties are draconian. A roadside court was convened, attended by the equivalent of the coroner, an examining magistrate, police and army chiefs and lawyers for the dead Turk's family. The family was the primary concern of the court—the Turk was 27 years old, married with children. The court took these facts into consideration and, on the spot, awarded the wife £75,000. A bond had to be put up instantly to cover the amount before reclamation of the cargo and wreck could be started.

Many people feel that they have been treated unjustly by Turkish law and Islamic law in general. It is usually not so. The difficulty is that the Islamic concept of justice is so different from that of Western societies. In the case of accidents, the Islamic view is, as previously stated, that if the foreigner had not been there, the accident could not have happened. No matter whose fault it is, the foreigner must bear some of the responsibility come what may. One thing is sure in every case: it is a very expensive process.

Almost immediately there was another fatality in the immediate vicinity. A driver for A-Line, travelling along the road from Adana to Kiziltepi at two o'clock in the morning, ran head on into an unlighted heavy farm tractor which was being driven in the pitch dark on the wrong side of the road. The fearful impact ripped the driving cab in half. The driver's legs were amputated in Kiziltepi cottage hospital, but two days later he died.

If anybody should doubt the risks involved in this journey, consider the fact that in the course of the one trip we are following, seven Britons died in accidents.

We are still only halfway through Turkey, there is half as much of it to cover yet—and rough country too. It is not so rough nowadays as once was, but it is still not easy. In fact just ahead lies Mardin, once the worst mountain on the route. It was called Bandit Pass, home of the outlaw Kurds who, armed to the teeth and violent with it, infested the area. Then, in 1978, there came the catastrophic earthquakes which killed thousands, shocked the rest of the world into sending massive aid, and removed the mountain completely. The roads were destroyed and the Government had to open the military road to all users.

For sheer visual drama and romance, this little known part of the country cannot be surpassed. It is the home of the truly magnificent Crusader castles which are quite the most unexpected and remarkable military structures to be seen anywhere—though the greatest castle ever built, Les Chevaliers, is over the border in Syria.

Turn left out of Adana and there, on the right, is a castle which surely can only have a place in a vision inspired by Walt Disney. It sits on top of a hill rising abruptly from flat land. Sheer, towering rock faces jut straight up from the sand, craggy and unscalable. Hills, surely, cannot exist naturally like this! Nor, surely, is it possible for man to build such a mighty stone castle topped with battlements, encompassing keeps, towers, inner strongholds and a supporting village all surrounded by soaring outer walls which conjure up every nursery dream you ever had of knights in armour, deeds of valour and mortal combat. And there is not just one single castle but a string of them, proudly standing sentinel on their hill tops as far as a day's drive will carry you. Those Crusaders walked from Europe, fighting battles all the way, then dallied awhile and built these fortresses, solid as the rocks they surmount which have stood through the centuries splashed with wild, flame-red sunsets and the outrageous hues of Asiatic dawns. Now the hunchbacked juggernauts, their tractor units level and trailers hoisted at an angle behind, drive past them in silhouette on a crusade of Mammon.

The old road over Mardin Mountain used to wind up a series of the tightest hairpin bends to be found anywhere. It formed a remarkable geological formation: on the left was sheer rock face and stepped terraces on the highest of which sat Kurdish tribesmen, draped in bandoliers, grenades, scimitars and toting long rifles.

On the lower terraces stood Kurdish youngsters holding rocks half as big as themselves over their heads in a threatening gesture. They would balance the enormous missile in one hand and gesticulate for cigarettes (two fingers held in a V-sign) or money (thumb and forefinger rubbed together) or food (fingers to mouth).

Such was the formation of the mountain that, if the passing driver did not oblige, they could run across the top of that particular outcrop and meet him coming up the other, higher leg of the hairpin. They were always fair, they would give him a second chance to oblige, if not they would hurl the boulder either through his windscreen or onto his cab roof. Drivers have been killed by such boulders.

Things got tricky when the children's elders, but by no means betters, became bored by sitting in the sun and would organise impromptu shooting practice with trucks as the target. This cost more than a few cigarettes and some loose change, often the price was everything the driver had and sometimes the load as well. A few drivers were brutally murdered.

Towards the Iraqi border the road runs along a wire fence dividing the two countries. It is a curious sight, it looks like fencing which might surround a playing field, it surely doesn't have the clout to divide two sovereign states. The road is crowded. The war between Iraq and Iran rages intermittently whenever either side can muster enough spares and ammunition to have another crack.

Since the Iranians destroyed Iraq's only port of Basrah, all Iraq's supplies have had to come in by road. This is a monumental undertaking. It involves not only all heavy goods but all types of refined petroleum products because the Iraqi refineries have also been wiped out.

This is bonanza time for truckers of all nationalities. Nothing makes the cash flow more freely than a war. Everybody is running to and from Baghdad as quickly as they can, grabbing the money while it is going. In the heart of a severe economic depression, this road is laden with every conceivable type of commodity, most of it being ferried to the war. It is a sobering thought that, but for the

Iraqi-Iranian war, the depression in Europe and the West would be even worse.

A road gives a remarkable insight into the affairs of countries. A gutter-eye-view often reveals far more than the cosmological vista from the crow's-nest of diplomacy. There are three dominant types of traffic on the road at this point: tankers and fridges, which take priority and stream down the left hand side of the road to be allowed through the border first; tipper trucks; and Turkish Tonkas loaded with pipes.

For hundreds of miles the tipper trucks have been running toward Iraq in convoys of 20, 50 and 100—that is an awful lot of tippers. They are bright yellow Mercedes, exact replicas this time of Tonka trucks. There is some international skulduggery about them, a fiddle is on the cards. The plates show that they have been exported from Germany to Bulgaria then re-exported from Bulgaria to Iraq, but so hurriedly that often both sets of plates have been left on. The happy Wombles drive them down and take with them their own coaches to ferry the drivers back home. It is very good business.

But why? It is easy to hazard a guess which will not be far from the truth: Germany has no oil of her own and wants to keep well in with all oil-supplying countries. She does not want to be seen exporting what might be considered war supplies to Iraq and therefore offend Iran and a potential source of oil—so Bulgaria is used as the third party. The deal cannot be concealed in any way, hundreds of miles of bright yellow tippers cannot easily be hidden. There are enough tippers to move one half of Iraq to the other half and back again. Nobody has ever seen so many tippers.

All over the Middle East they are building pipelines, mammoth pipelines which are quite beyond the ability of man to visualise in their entirety. It is hard to imagine 1,000 miles let alone 1,000 miles of pipeline. Our visual limits at sea-level to the horizon are approximately nine miles and that is not enough. So it is impossible to conceive of the quantities that go into a 1,000 mile pipeline. And there are several such monumental pipelines being constructed in Iraq and Saudi Arabia.

The pipes, two to three feet in diameter and 40 feet long, are piled at twice and three times the height that would be allowed in Europe. They are transported by weight, so much per ton and painted black on the outside, brilliant white on the inside. The pipes do not stay on the trucks, they topple off at every corner. For hundreds of miles— yes, hundreds of miles—there are stacks of spilled pipes on every mountain corner. They are too heavy to put back on the trucks so they are just left there.

A thought crosses the mind—what will happen when the engineers reach the other end of their pipeline or, since they are building from both terminal ends, when they realise they should have met in the middle? They will be thousands of pipes short. We give up counting spilled pipes when we have clocked up 1,260, by then it is dark.

An M & C British truck flashes us down. The driver says with a laugh: "I don't want to put you off, but that queue at Zacho is 36 kilometres this side and 18 kilometres the other. Or put another way, four days' sitting. Have a nice day."

12

TURKEY is the land of the dog—the splendid Anatolian Karabash dog. It is bigger than a German Shepherd dog, a terrier in shape, reminiscent of an Airedale but sturdier, standing four square on powerful legs. It has a thick coat, big bones and muscles and stands with a high, proud head and tufted ears. This is a very fine, pure bred animal, so good that the breed has recently been recognised by Crufts and registered at the Kennel Club. It is here in numbers, both wild and domesticated, and it is impossible to tell which is which. Every village has its pack of between six and a dozen who hunt, or scavenge, together.

The wild dogs are timid, though the idea takes some getting used to. They will block a path and stand their ground until the very last moment when they turn and scatter with great fleetness of foot. Locals assure strangers that they need not fear the dogs but it needs faith to put that to the test and walk directly at a pack.

Near Adana, Mike Pearce, asleep in his cab one winter's night, was disturbed by blood-chilling screams, yaps, growls and sundry animal noises coupled with the rattle of over-turned refuse bins outside the restaurant. Scavenging wild dogs, he thought and when the racket had lasted half-an-hour or more, he decided to chase them off. He climbed from his cab, shone his powerful torch and in its beam saw great, big, brown shapes. They were massive, shambling mountain bears bigger by far than a standing man and 10 times as heavy. He dropped his torch and cleared the height into his cab in one bound. The torch remained on the ground and threw its beam into the darkness of the park until the batteries died.

The next day the café proprietor explained: "In winter the mountain bears are hungry so they come down to the towns at night . . . verr fierce, verr dangerous."

"You might have told me that *last* night," said Mike.

Dogs, donkeys, geese, camels, all types of livestock roam free near the roads. So they are often run over. They replace the humble hedgehog, rabbit and cat of Britain's thoroughfares as nature's casualties and they lie spattered from here to the end of the road. Donkeys are killed and rigor mortis sets in, they roll on to their backs with stiff legs sticking up into the air like toppled nursery rocking horses. Camels do the same. Dogs and geese lie where they have been felled as if asleep in the road. They are all big animals and can seriously damage anybody who runs into them. Nobody moves them, they lie until they decompose and in summer are covered in dense clouds of flies with attendant carrion birds.

This is, naturally, an offensive sight and turns the stomach, but you had better get used to it. This is no place for sensitive animal lovers. The habit in these parts is to flog a weary, reluctant beast half to death, the whacks and squeals of anguish can be heard half-a-mile away. The grinning owner will stop the thrashing to scrounge cigarettes from passing drivers, then return with renewed gusto to the methodical, nonstop torture of his scraggy, underfed animal. Locals will take great amusement from a foreigner's horrified protestations.

We are now waiting to cross the border into Iraq at Zacho. Our friends in the M & C truck were not exaggerating, the queue to the border tails back a full 36 kilometres—22 miles. That is the equivalent of queuing at Luton, Reading, Guildford, Maidstone or Basildon to get into London; or at Leamington or Stafford for the centre of Birmingham; or Buxton, Huddersfield or Widnes for Manchester. It is a long way and a long wait in an unbroken line of trucks stretching to the horizon. We are stationary for most of the time, a couple of hours waiting then a couple of kilometres drive to shuffle nearer to the crossing. (By March 1982, the time of writing, the queue to the border post at Zacho had stretched to 240 kilometres—149 miles.)

There is time to walk up and down the line, to renew acquaintanceships and socialise, time for coffee and dinner parties, time to watch the sun come up on the left and sink on the right. Time to reflect that perhaps the human race was born to queue, for nobody loses patience or temper. In fact, everybody is quite jolly and gives the impression that they will be sorry when the queue is over and they have to leave such pleasant company.

At Zacho the landscape is beginning to deteriorate into part-desert. The lush, ordered acres of olive groves are less frequent, great tracts of uncultivated land surround the productive areas. The houses and villages are those of a desert peasant people, more mud-hut than cottage variety. From the cab we watch the unremitting grind of peasant daily life, the women assembling to go to their work in the fields, the tedium of driving flocks and herds from one barren place to another. Tufts of lifeless, light brown grass and desert shrubs are the fodder these animals exist on—nothing—yet it suffices.

All day long, all night, these people are subjected to the influence of modern technology and modern life yet, for them, it does not exist. The truck and drivers are not there. But the wheeling, dealing, mercenary kids and their mothers are out in droves from the crack of dawn until midnight. School doesn't exist here, or if it does, nobody takes any notice of truancy. They are slick, agile little robbers—all the trailer elastics are stripped in a half-minute raid. These are foot long, half-inch wide rubber bands attached to the tarpaulin which are stretched over hooks on the trailer sides to keep the fabric taut. What use the little thieves put them to except as catapults is hard to see, but they treasure them. At £1 apiece, it is an expensive irritation.

Yvonne Keeghan has not quite made the necessary adjustment from surburban life in prosperous, salubrious Southport. She has made the mistake of comparing these children with her own 13- and 11-year-olds at home and, being a naturally gregarious and maternal lady, she has befriended them. The wisdom of experience forbids drivers to do this beyond a strictly limited measure. It always, without exception, backfires. Attitudes must be adopted here which would put a social worker in a welfare state into permanent shock. These children came off the breast as mature, dyed-in-the-wool, miniature villains and have been nurtured and schooled in the arts of villainy ever since. The Golden Rule is: keep them out of the cab. "Show them who's boss", "Keep them at arm's length", "Make them show respect", "Never be familiar"—unfortunately these reactionary sentiments are the only safe course of conduct. The newcomer to the situation thinks the others are behaving cruelly, until experience rapidly changes his viewpoint.

Yvonne, in the privacy of her cab, changes

into her comfortable clothes, including her off-the-shoulder jersey top which, by its very design, shows a bit of cleavage when she moves. She also puts on a skirt with a slit side, a wholly attractive and decorous outfit for Lord Street, Southport, any Sunday morning. She opens the cab door to speak to one of the "children" she has befriended and lets in a nightmare.

The cab is besieged by screaming, ranting youths. With an enormous struggle and by hammering clutching fingers with a spanner, Albie manages to get the cab door closed and locked. The kids clamber over the whole truck until it is thick with them. They hammer on the windows, they pull at the doors. The windscreen is a mass of contorted, yelling children's faces, so many that they block out the light.

"Ficky, ficky, missee, ficky, ficky," they shout. And they gesticulate accordingly as they work themselves into a sexual frenzy. In terror, Yvonne climbs into the back bunk and draws the curtains. But still they hammer and scream. A mass sexual hysteria drives them on to greater clamour. Albie is powerless to do anything, fearful that the windows might break.

The frenzy only ends when a woman from the village, disturbed by the din, emerges from her house and sets about the struggling mass with a stout broom handle, cracking heads with swinging clouts. The woman says nothing. Whether she is old or young is impossible to tell under the full chador. That she carries some authority is undoubted. The village men take no action but stand in menacing groups with the youths at a distance. Until the queue moves, Yvonne has to lie in the bunk, out of sight, in the darkened cab.

Sexual repression and frustration is so acute in these Muslim countries that it leads to widespread homosexuality and the curious sight of Arab soldiers walking hand in hand along the streets. Arab truck drivers press to go to Turkey for virtually no wages in cash but the promise of a woman once they arrive. Their educated employers joke about the fact that they can get their work done for virtually nothing because of the sexual fantasies of their employees.

Those Arabs with whom it is possible to communicate and establish a genuine relationship, usually Jordanians, Yemenis and Egyptians, who are the wandering workers of the "Arab Nation", look upon the situation with amusement and contempt. They complain that this sexual obsession deprives them of work and good wages.

Jordanians say: "They sit for weeks or even months dreaming about this encounter like men in a trance. They are going to Turkey and they will have a woman and when they come back they will tell the other young, unmarried men of the village about it and they will be men above men."

The Arab attitude to sex means that Arab adolescence is unduly prolonged. And in the stricter countries it leads to the most appalling sex crimes followed by more appalling punishments. Of all the many taboos in Muslin countries, sex, not drink is the most strongly enforced. Some countries ban drink and the ban is very widely reported and commented upon in the world's media. However, all countries ban sex books, girlie magazines are at the top of the prohibited goods list. Inside Arab countries they are sought after with the fervour of a junkie seeking his next fix.

Such is the quite improbable power of sex books over the Arab mind that the European director of a £100 million project in Iraq overcame the difficulties and acute shortages caused by the war with the aid of two smuggled copies of *Hustler* and *Knave*. One of his suppliers had forgotten to remove them from his luggage and the customs had missed them. They were gratefully seized by the expatriates in the mess, the locals heard from native workers in the European compound that the magazines were there and the place came under virtual siege. The director confiscated the copies fearing trouble if they were left lying around. Then he came under pressure from high officials who suspected that he had access to the forbidden goodies and wanted to buy them from him.

At the time difficulties in obtaining permits for supplies to be released from customs, now under military control, had become so acute that the job was frequently brought to a costly halt. The director, a shrewd man and well-versed in the Arab mentality, made photostat copies of the magazines and gave them page by page to officials, with the promise that they could have the full-colour originals when the documents were signed and goods delivered. Suddenly there were no more delays, drivers could arrive in the morning, be cleared and tipped by mid-afternoon.

The irony was that the director himself was a strait-laced, gentlemanly member of the professional classes who deplored porn and found it abhorrent. He was a man who had worked with Arabs for 25 years and had repeatedly returned to the area either because his company wanted somebody who knew the field or because of his own fascination with it. He said: "You can have the Arab mind and culture explained to you in the most meticulous detail until you think that you understand every facet of it, the trouble is that you can never *feel* what is in their minds. That was the trouble with Iran. Every so-called expert and Arabist thought he understood what was going on and that progress and enlightenment would triumph, but not one of them was able to *feel* what was happening in the Arab mind, so the ghastly mistakes were made."

The first lesson to learn about the Arab mind is that time is a different dimension and a three day wait is inconsequential. It is called "the Insh'allah syndrome"—God will make it happen when he is ready and I can do nothing about it. It is also known as the "IBM factor"—Insh'allah, bu'kra, ma'alish—

when God is ready, tomorrow, what does it matter?

So now as we drive at last into the border post, the waiting may just be beginning. We will get through—insh'allah.

Bobby Brown decides to stage a "Bobby Brown Spectacular" in the customs post. Mr. Brown is a man of many parts, expert truck driver, haulage company proprietor, farmer, all-in wrestler/comedian of high professional standard and fitness freak who does his rigorous bends and press-ups every morning. In his wrestling days when he appeared on television as Vincent Randell he dyed his hair honey-blond, carried a spangled handbag and vanity box and adjusted his make-up in the ring with powder puff and lipstick before getting down to the rough stuff. When he first began to run to the Middle East he still had blond hair and caused a mild sensation at the borders. His hair grew out to its natural brown in the course of time and nobody recognised him so he gained no advantage in the queues. He bleached it again and the doors re-opened.

Today at the customs post he puts on his Max Wall funny walk act with bottom sticking out, legs stiff but disconnected, and a whole repertoire of steps, knees together, about turns and shuffles all accompanied by drum beats and rolls. The Arabs sit behind their desks, eyes riveted upon him and mouths open in astonishment. Not only the Arabs, but the other drivers are fascinated by the performance which changes sequence and tempo with limitless variations. The drivers begin to beat the rhythm and mouth the rolls until the performance takes over the whole room.

So far the officials have been obstructive, refusing to stamp papers—a familiar attitude. The last stomping march takes Bobby alongside the officials' desks, he picks up the stamp and with his last six heavy drum beats—bump, b'bump, bump, bump, bump, he franks the documents lying there. The officials giggle in high pitched delight. "Let's go, lads," says Bobby, "next office."

As we pass from Turkey to Iraq changes come with startling abruptness. Imagine a lantern lecture with the voice of an old traveller speaking his commentary: "Ah, this is Iraq, and those chappies are Arabs, you can tell because a lot of them are wearing garments which resemble nightshirts—their jellabas. You get several kinds of jellabas, some are white, some grey and some are striped. And they wear head dresses, those in the white ones have been to Mecca. Of course, a lot are wearing their little skull caps.

"Now, the Arab is quite a different man from his neighbour, the Turk. Both are Muslims, but absolutely different breeds, different as chalk and cheese . . . the Turks regard the Arabs as the English do the Irish. They will spend a week happily telling you stories of Arab foolishness. But, of course, the Arabs have got the money and the Turks do the work for them. Turks have to go cap in hand to the Arabs to borrow oil, which they can't afford to pay for. So the Arab may be foolish, but he's also rich . . ."

Which makes it all the more saddening for the Turks who used to own and run Iraq when they called it by the much prettier name Mesopotamia. Iraq is still rich from its oilfields and the wealth created by the Iraq Petroleum Company, which adds insult to Turkish injury because that company began life as the Turkish Petroleum Company. Also galling for the Turks is the fact that the famous Armenian celebrities, the Gulben-kians, father and son, were granted a five per

340

cent share of Iraqi oil, hence the nickname—Mr. Five Per Cent. It made the family richer than the Turkish government and certainly more solvent.

Zacho, then, is the cross-over from poverty to riches, from need and want to plenty. But it comes as a terrible let-down, an anticlimax . . . Zacho is a hole, a sorry mess of a place.

Look at its architecture and buildings. Arab architecture and building techniques in the backwoods can flatteringly be called rustic, but that implies a certain primitive charm. More accurately they can be compared with the efforts of a beginners class in pottery—somebody has explained the general idea, but the application has proved difficult and the results are not exactly Wedgewood. Here the buildings are constructed on liberal principles with tolerances of two to six inches in places where things should join flush. A two feet lean in an upright is permissible.

At the end of the main customs hall is a window which is intended to be a Gothic arch with straight sides elegantly curving to a point at the top. This one could have been drawn by Picasso in a drunken moment. The doors have great originality, all being interesting trapezoids with no two sides parallel or equal in length, whoever installed them must have held the plumb line in a strong breeze. Surveying the interior, one driver who has experience in the British building trade, exclaims: "You'd pay money to go into a building like this on the Pleasure Beach at Blackpool or Coney Island. I can't work out how it stands up." The paintwork has the same unique quality of free expression: the man who painted the window frames obviously used a flat brush, broadside on. The paint is applied to an irregular six inch border of the window pane and smeared across the rest to look like windows in a new building in a Western town when the glaziers have splashed them with whitewash to show that the glass has been put in. But the Zacho paint is permanent.

On the other side of the border post is the passport office and it surpasses the constructional follies of the customs house by a wide margin. The doors are held to their frames by nails hammered through screw holes in the hinges. Locks miss latches by several inches and so are secured by chains passed through loops made by nails whacked into the woodwork and bent double. The whole shambles is held together by six inch nails. The passport chief's office has a window at the end which fills the wall. It is held in by knobs of putty about an inch-and-a-half in diameter squeezed into place by thumb. No attempt has been made to smooth the putty or force it into the gap between frame and glass; finger and palm prints of the workman's hands are left as dried, permanent mementos of his work. A quarter of the glass has been cut away at the bottom and an AEC air-conditioning unit inserted, but the air-conditioner takes up only one-third of the window width so the gaps either side are plugged with Kelloggs cereal boxes. These do not quite fill the gaps, so yellowing, screwed up newspapers have been rammed in as well. The wires for the unit dangle under the window sill; wires hang all around the room and in the corridor outside; unattached wires protrude from walls or are tied in a knot and slung over a nail. Plaster has fallen from the walls, which are a uniform black colour shading to dirty grey at shoulder height. They are slimy to the touch. Dust, litter and rubble cover the floors.

This is a new building, put up three years ago to handle the increasing traffic. The air of dilapidation is all pervading, the squalor is absolute.

The truly horrifying thought is that this wealthy nation, while manifestly showing an abysmal lack of basic skills, has in its hands batteries of complex Sam missiles and armouries of sophisticated weapons. And, in Baghdad, until the Israelis blasted it sky high, they had a nuclear reactor.

Back in the customs house, the official has glanced at the papers and estimated that charges would be 224 Iraq dinars, which seems a lot. Playing around with Iraq dinars is not playing with peanuts, it is an expensive currency at the rate of roughly £2 sterling to one dinar. The trouble is that, since the outbreak of war, it is only held at that value internally—nobody outside wants to know it except at a huge discount. So, buying at the Iraqi bank on the border you are buying at an excessive premium. If you were coming back from Kuwait, the Iraqi currency could be bought half as cheaply and paid for in hard currency in any of the money shops at a discount of 50 per cent buying, 60 per cent selling.

Clearing the papers is a lottery. The clerks sit, bored out of their minds, in a glass-fronted office next to the bank. Passports and papers are piled on to the counter outside the glass panel. When they have mounted to an unmanageable number, a section of the panel is slid open and they are scooped inside and stacked on a desk. Depending on how the clerk picks them up, shuffles and stacks them, yours can be at the top or bottom of the pile. That can mean a difference of two or three hours. In the meantime another pile may have been scooped inside and dumped on top of yours. On odd occasions it is possible to be lucky and, by fluke, be dumped on top of the pile. The clerks flick the pages and stamp all day, there is no visible end to their labours; the pile stays just as big all day long, all night long too. They flick and stamp a life away and get bored. After four hours your papers are coming to the top, you can see them—two more, then me.

Our customs man is agitated, he drums the desk with his fingers. "Moment," he says and goes to see the chef in the next office.

"Moment," he says on his return and places the papers in his in tray before leaving the office again.

"Moment," he says on his return half-an-hour later.

Two more trips from the office, a dozen "moments" more and an hour later he struggles for the English to string together a sentence. "Is good . . . you pay less? Is good . . . company . . . pay less? Is good . . . yes?"

"Yes, is good pay less."

"Good, give me money. Dinars two hun'red."

He counts the money with a flicking action of his thumb, slices off a wedge and puts it in his top left-hand drawer, which he locks before going to the chef's office again, papers in hand. Splendid, we think, now we might be away before 10 o'clock and get a few kilometres under the belt before midnight, which will help in getting through Baghdad before the rush starts.

He brings back the papers which he puts into his tray and retains for a further 25 minutes while he chats to friends who come in. Then, without taking his eyes from his friends' faces, he extends his right arm, picks up the documents and passes them across the desk. They are franked and receipted for 124 dinars with an additional receipt for 16 dinars clipped to the top—an insurance permit or some such thing. So there are 60 dinars lying in his desk and that, we rapidly work out, is £120; The logic of where the benefit comes to us, or the company, is somewhat obscure.

A bi-lingual driver is sitting in the customs hall and listening with interest. He wanders in when the customs man takes another of his little strolls and confides: "Bandits. Always mucho monies, always mucho problems."

"Tell this little punk that we are not leaving here without a receipt for 200 dinars or the money back."

The driver relishes the job but adopts a curious stance to do it when the customs man returns, he stands like a schoolboy on the carpet before his headmaster, looking at the floor and mumbling. The customs man stares at a fixed spot on the ceiling and says nothing. Positions become entrenched, customs staring at the ceiling, offended parties staring at the floor. Nobody moves.

It could be a long night. But the customs closes at 1.00 am, so we mutter about "commandanti soldiers". "Here, driver, where do we find the commandanti soldiers?"

At 12.59 the customs man unlocks his drawer, takes out the roll of dinars and flings it to the floor, spits in disgust and stalks out into the night.

All other European drivers have paid about £150 in taxes and dues. Now we have 84 useless and unwanted dinars in the purse. There is nothing to buy with the money in Iraq, we are full up with fuel, so we cannot spend cash on that. Mr. Moment has effectively rolled us for £60, which will be lost on exchange rates, the only satisfaction is that he has not got his sticky little fingers on it.

The days of waiting are forgotten. Like pain, they are obliterated from the mind the instant they are over. The psychological uplift of movement renews the spirits and brings on a euphoric feeling of freedom. Underfoot there is the comforting drumming of the motor and the lovely, reassuring roll as the truck takes the bumps and cambers of the road in her stride. It is all systems go and she is running like a queen; the old girl loves to be motoring and bowling along.

13

IRAQ is the most contradictory of societies—a laugh a minute followed by a shock at every turn. A country under Socialist leadership whose specialists in free enterprise beaver away unhindered along the roadsides and in the bazaars; an oil producer on a big scale whose people queue all day for a fill of diesel; a society housed in tin shacks which is spending thousands of millions of dollars installing the best of high technology.

It is a country of private traders and free spirits strangling in its own red tape. A nation where it is a security offence to own and operate a typewriter without a permit and all unlicensed typewriters are chained to prevent their unauthorised use. A society whose civil service with rocket blast rubble round its feet and the smell of cordite in its nostrils, will say: "What bomb damage? There is no bomb damage." Officially there *is* no bomb damage and it is treason to admit that there is.

Bobby Brown knows a little place down the road from the border which he insists is worthy of inclusion in Egon Ronay and an honourable mention in the *Guide Michelin*, so we pull in there for a meal.

The restaurant is set in the grey, dusty sands of the desert behind a barricade of worn out tyres, concealed man-trap holes, rusting old iron and is quite salubrious for the area. It must be posh because the proprietor sits behind a table at the door where he takes the money and yells at his menials while he keeps an eye on the spit of chickens rotating outside. Occasionally he bellows at the chef to turn the handle or put on a little more charcoal. It boasts a washroom which is an open alcove off the dining room. There is a pee corner and a squatter loo with a torn curtain which does not quite cover the hole so that, pulled one way, the squatter's strained face is exposed. Pulled the other, his rear end comes into view. A high tap stuck on the end of a loose pipe hangs over three brown basins. The loose pipe is a good idea because you can pull it towards whichever basin you are using. A packet of Tide washing powder on a shelf is provided free by the management for ablutions.

The proprietor himself comes across to sort out the tangle when the waiter, between fits of giggles, fails to convey what delicacies he has to purvey. The boss has a menu which is in Arabic.

We point at the top line. "What's that?"

"Chicken."

Line number two. "What's that?"

"Err, err, hmm . . . good chicken."

Lines three and four. "Chicken . . . err, hmm, err . . ." This calls for a conference with friends near his personal table.

The problem is resolved. "Big chicken," he demonstrates with an evocative rounded gesture of the hands, "little chicken," he cups his hands. Then he goes to the serving counter, picks up several pancakes of unleavened bread, waves them under our noses and says: "Egbek, chaud, chaud, chaud."

The big chicken is a whole chicken served just as it comes from the spit. There is no fuss, no frills, the boy takes it by the legs, brings it over and drops it on the plate. No knife, no fork, we just tear it to pieces. If it is too hot to handle, wrap a piece of floppy, flexible egbek round the bit you fancy and hold it in that. Coke? Seven-up? He drops the bottles on the tables, you wipe with a

Kleenex, and drink from the neck. But chi does come in glasses.

"Look at the chickens," says the smiling Bobby with pride, "plump and with meat on them, not your average emaciated, Twiggy Arab chickens, but Raquel Welches with bits of breast on them. Ahmed here actually feeds his chickens before he kills and cooks them. I told you this was Egon Ronay class. I'm starving, let's have another portion."

We signal to order more—little—cup the hands to show half a chicken. The whole restaurant stands to clap our order, one calls something that sounds like "Bravo, good." Well, it is a rough approximation to that.

The proprietor swells with pride that his cuisine is so appreciated, elbows the cook to one side and selects the second portions himself. He splits the chickens with a cleaver and, one in each hand, carries them over. Then he wipes his hands on his bottom.

"Egon Ronay, I told you so," mumbles Bobby, gnawing a leg and mopping the streaming fat from his chin.

The bill comes to £6 per head, which is expensive hereabouts, but Iraq is pricey.

Magic names once more appear on the

signposts again—Nineveh. The modern town is Mosul, but Nineveh is here. So it is Nineveh—Mosul—by the Tigris river to Baghdad. Which, when you are driving, goes to prove that John Masefield was a better poet than he was a geographer

> "Quinquireme of Nineveh from distant
> Ophir.
> Rowing home to haven in sunny
> Palestine"

Nineveh used to abut the Tigris until the river changed course by three miles. The quinquireme, an ancient ship with five sets of oarsmen, must have rowed down the Tigris which flows in the opposite direction away from Palestine into the Persian Gulf. There are 500 miles of desert between Nineveh and Palestine. The Suez canal was not built then, so Masefield's rowers would have had to pull down the Persian Gulf, all the way round Africa and back through the Mediterranean—no wonder they needed five sets of rowers.

On the outskirts of Baghdad, the army has just knocked off for the night and is walking, hand in hand, down the streets. The Russian automatic rifles they carry get in the way of love's young dream so one slings his gun over his left shoulder and the other totes his over the right shoulder. The one on the left has a nicely turned pair of ankles in his tight fitting jump boots, he lolls his head on his taller companion's shoulder, he is very smitten. We switch off the spots and dip the headlights, it is so embarrassing playing gooseberry.

This is the parting of the ways. The Baghdad truck boys turn into the city centre to the customs compound, the Gulf boys run straight on to Kuwait and the Neutral Area. We have come a long way with Bobby, it is sad to see him go. It is possible to become quite maudlin at this roundabout. Goodbye, too, to the Dutchman who has been running six hours behind us and pulling in for a beer, Coke or spliced coffee whenever he has caught up.

The Dutchman suffered some of Iraq's non-existent war damage in Baghdad. And he was disappointed by it.

He says: "I was sleeping in the truck park near the Airport hotel when the cab shook and I thought it was tipping over. All my gear was thrown about and my mug with the naked woman on the front rolled off the shelf and shattered. I miss that mug. I can't find another like it.

"I thought it was an earthquake and I

thought, Great, an earthquake, I've never been in an earthquake, that's something to tell them back home.

"Then they said it was a pissy bombing attack. Two minutes later all hell was let loose. The army had got out of bed and began shooting anti-aircraft guns and 45 mm cannons and Sam missiles, but the enemy was 200 kilometres away by then. There were only seven aircraft in the attack but the Iraqis kept up the barrage for a half-an-hour. There were no aircraft about, but I suppose it made them feel good. They were saying, "We'll show you, if you come back." More people were hurt by shrapnel than by the bombs.

"But I hoped it was an earthquake. If you tell folks back home that you were in a bombing raid they look at you like, so what? Everybody gets bombed. If you tell them you were in an earthquake they get interested and excited and ask you what it was like. Everybody is more afraid of earthquakes than bombing."

"Tough, Dutchie, better luck next time. See you next trip. Take care."

Then the finality of the parting roar of engines, the puffs of grey exhausts, flashes of lights. Some are heading west and then home again, others east, and further east; there are still a few thousand kliks to cover.

It happened during the hours of darkness, now the unending yawn of desert lies in all directions as far as the eye can see. It is not desert on the grand scale of the Rub'al Khali or Sahara, but a mucky, dismal desert, scrubby, flat brown desert slung with electricity pylons performing feats of uninterrupted perspective. A good, metalled road runs to Basrah and there is at least a touch of magic on the map—Babylon. Not a lot of people get to see Babylon though everybody has heard of it.

Tonkas, tankers and juggernauts line the other side of the road in shuffling, higgledy-piggledy queues to the nearest filling station a couple of miles away. They are waiting their fill to get back to Turkey, or to Kuwait and other oil suppliers in the Gulf. Supplies are better south of Baghdad but most of these drivers have blown their diesel in getting to Baghdad.

With a war on, the army is very conspicuous, throwing its weight about at check points and patrols on the roads. They site their guns in a curious way, prominently on the tops of hills (where no British officer would ever put a gun) and in positions under pylons where, if the 45 mm cannon were ever fired, they would surely blow to pieces the very things they are protecting. That is the way it looks to the observer. And on bridges over the River Tigris the cannon look as if the most likely outcome of opening fire would be to blow their own comrades to kingdom come.

"It's their war," say the old soldiers among the drivers and there are several. The trucking life attracts ex-toughies of the Parachute Regiment and Commandos who know about such things.

Life for ex-patriots working in these countries is pretty comfortable as a rule. The big companies do them well. So well than an ex-patriot engineer says: "The trouble with this job is that you get so used to living well that you hate to go back to ordinary life, no matter how much you loathe the bloody place. And you get paid so much that you can't afford to go back to your old lifestyle. My problem is that my standard of living at home has gone up so much while I've been away that I have to stay out here to earn the money to keep it up. So I go home on leave and say to the wife, 'You've made this very nice, pity I can't stay to enjoy it.' Here, you don't lift a finger, you are waited on hand and foot, if you want a cup of coffee, you just flick your fingers and the servants bring it. They do your shoes, washing, make the beds, cook the meals, clean your rooms. It is a perfect lazy man's life."

Many drivers will not visit the compounds, they find the life there artificial. Drivers live close to the ground and are instantly integrated into whatever society they drive into—ex-pats take their home-town lives with them.

One Astran driver comments: "These people have never been abroad, they have been in a Boeing 727 and a Portacabin compound, got a sun tan, and they think that's it. Even though they do it for years, they've never really been abroad." Others, not quite such dedicated purists, leap at the opportunity of hot baths, a lie-in between sheets. European food, ironed shirts and cold beer.

Our first "tip", to unload cargo, is near Basrah. It is almost an unofficial tip, to deliver copies of urgently needed documents to contractors on a huge development site. Previous attempts to deliver the documents by airmail and airfreight have been unsuccessful because of delays in the Iraqi postal service or in the incoming censorship office. It can take months for letters to be delivered in Iraq and often they do not arrive at all.

In the head office of a world famous engineering company in England there are angry grumbles of annoyance.

"What the hell are they playing at out there? They never answer letters, they never reply to queries, they act as if they are a law unto themselves. I'll send them a rocket they won't forget in a hurry."

Send it, sir, the probability is that it will not arrive. Your men in the field cannot answer your letters because they do not receive them and the letters they write to you may never get out of the censor's office. Should they try to smuggle out an inter-office communication by an employee coming home on leave, there is no guarantee that it will not be seized at customs and held for censorship by somebody who can speak English.

In Britain, the export director exclaims: "They've been out there two years and they still haven't got the office working, I just cannot understand it. What the hell *are* they doing? Why haven't they got an office after all this time?"

They do indeed have an office, beautifully furnished, air-conditioned and comfortable with all the modern accessories anybody could want. But the typewriters are chained to the desks, with other chains padlocked round the keyboards to prevent them being used until authorised. It is the same with the copier and other equipment, because two years after applications have been made, still no permits for their use have been issued by the Iraqi government.

Exasperation rules at head office. "For God's sake, what *are* they playing at? Has the sun got to them? The second site we are developing there is only 10 kilometres down the road from the first one. And they send us a handwritten note saying that they cannot start work on it until they get new bull-dozers, diggers, trenchers, Caterpillar tractors, cranes—you name it, they want it. They've got a mountain of gear at number one site. Surely somebody there must have the sense to move it 10 kilometres to site number two, unless they've all gone barmy."

Yes, they do have all that equipment, every item that could be needed on a complex, high-technology construction job. It is all neatly stored in a huge compound surrounded by a high, chain link fence with a platoon of soldiers guarding the gate. That equipment was imported, at a cost of £1.5 million, for use on site number one, so it belongs to that site in the eyes of the Iraqis and there it must stay, never to be removed. Even though the machinery belongs to you, you cannot move it without a Government permit, the soldiers will prevent you. If, in desperation, you persist and try to drive it through the gates, they will shoot you.

Hundreds of such compounds exist all over Iraq; dumps full of beautiful machinery in perfect working order which cannot be moved from the site for which it was ordered. Almost new equipment stays impounded until the summer humidity of 100 penetrates its guts and rusts them away.

It is the Iraqi system: red tape, the rigid application of the rule book with no flexibility or goodwill, all allied to a distrust of everybody and an acute spy fever. As a recipe for complete frustration try mixing the Iraqi attitude with the Japanese mentality . . . and stand back and wait for senility to set in.

The Japanese are in Iraq in force. The Toa

Harbor Company's development south of Basrah is the biggest and most sophisticated of its type anywhere. It is for manufacturing protein and fertiliser from oil. The oil is piped in from the oil fields at one end and the packed goods roll off the lines straight into ships at the other. This is excellent business for the European trucking industry which brings in great quantities of materials, all the more since the war closed Iraq's only port, Basrah. It is not, however, the most pleasant of places to tip. The site is on the Shatt al Arab, the waterway up to Abadan, Iran, and Basrah. Three miles across the estuary is Khorramshahr, where lies the front line and the war-desolated city of Abadan. The city is under constant fire and reciprocates with artillery and rocket fire.

Battle lines extend their influence far afield, the tension spreads across the surrounding area and the atmosphere is heavy like that before a thunderstorm. The way down to Toa Harbor bristles with missile sites. Batteries of rockets are angled skywards, cannon and machine guns stand in sand-bagged emplacements and sinister radar discs rotate without stopping. War jets scream overhead at radar-mast height. The only time you see them at such low altitude is if you catch sight of one accidentally. Usually you only know they are there by the thunder they leave in their wake. We have gleaned the rules: Migs and Mysteres, OK—Phantoms, duck. In the distance can be heard dull thuds and reverberations as rockets explode, but work goes on.

The idiocy of Iraq's war is all around. This great industrial sea terminal is almost finished. Ships line the quays, they have been there since the outbreak of war. Other ocean going ships of all nationalities lie marooned by the dozen, in the muddy waters of the rivers and seaway. The channels are completely silted up. Until the war is over, no ships will be able to come to this terminal. The Shatt al Arab has become Dead Man's Gulf.

More dramatic evidence of the war is close at hand. Huge sections of the new buildings have been blown to smithereens. The whole roof of one enormous shed has been lifted by blast and the interior of the shed has been reduced to a tangle of twisted steel. A 100 yards from the bomb's point of impact, holes have been punched by shrapnel through three-eighths of an inch steel girders. More than 200 men were working on the site when the bombs struck, but only one was killed. An Englishman working on the roof was blown 100 yards. He landed on his feet and walked away unharmed.

The Cleveland compound is almost on the Shatt Al Arab. It is formed by spacious Portacabins grouped round two courtyards with the mess and dining hall taking the whole of one side of the rectangle, the other three sides are living quarters, bathrooms, laundry and guest rooms—Fort Cleveland, they have named it. Indian stewards cook and run the place—they are helpful, lovely people with bright, white smiles and laughter.

After days in the truck cab, it is a joy to sleep in a bed with clean sheets. The disappointment comes at two o'clock in the morning when the wind rattles the windows and wakes everyone up. The desert is a breezy place and a breeze can turn into a fierce blow at any time.

The Indian stewards never seem to sleep. "Pradesh, find me some pegs to wedge the windows, the wind is rattling them.' '

"That is not the wind, sahib, that is the bombard-menting."

Flashes bright as lightning light the sky,

reflecting from the clouds. In the courtyard the crump of landing shells is heard more clearly than indoors.

During the day, Pradesh scuttles out into the courtyard at the sound of aircraft and gives a running commentary. "Three Migs, three Mysteres . . . two Phantoms very low . . ."

"Thank you, Pradesh. Is it safe to come out now?"

The big bumps, Pradesh patiently explains, are anti-aircraft ground to air missiles and not aimed at us. He says: "The pilots now are clever at avoiding missiles, the missiles miss and land on the mudbanks and shore."

"I don't find that very reassuring, Pradesh."

Says Pradesh: "Lots of noise, lots of shouting, few people ever killed. It is fun to watch it all."

Of all things that can go wrong with a truck, the ones that bring on universal gloom come under the heading "electrics". Drivers who know and tinker with every nut, bolt, sprocket, gear, shaft, pipe and compressor in the machine go glassy-eyed and dumb at the mention of electrics. Electrical faults are hell to deal with.

The ammeter on our truck has begun to show a charge of 30 amps, dropping only to 22 amps. That is hot enough to melt steel. The ammeter should flick momentarily to 11 amps and drop immediately to zero otherwise too great a charge is being pumped into the batteries. How long she has been blowing 30 amps into the batteries is hard to tell, but they are cooked—burning hot to the touch and giving off acrid fumes. The chances are that the plates inside have buckled under the heat, it is impossible to say at a glance.

Overnight, she has cooled and, astonishingly, holds sufficient charge to start the motor first flick. But still she is pumping out 30 amps. The regulator must have packed up. There is a spare but that doesn't work either. The answer is to start up in the morning and once she is running, disconnect the electrics and motor without them during the hours of daylight. Meanwhile the batteries have run almost dry and require topping up with distilled water. "No problem," say the Cleveland men, "we'll pop down and see the Toa Harbor people in the workshops."

Toa Harbor run a vast workshop housed in

big inflated tents, they have enough equipment to build a vehicle, let alone repair one. What is needed is two litres of distilled water. In the Toa Harbor store we are relieved to see vats of the stuff. But the Japanese store boss is perplexed and frightened, he dare not give us any water. It is against company rules to give supplies to non-employees of the company.

"Just two little litres . . . the dregs from that vat would be plenty and the vat is being thrown away."

"No, it is not possible, go office and apply for requisition."

There is no budging the man, so we went to the office to be formally introduced to the office hierarchy and explain that we need two litres of distilled water, please, the dregs from the vat would be ample.

"Ha, so. I will write requisition, you must sign."

"Great, where do I sign?"

"Ha, so. Now you must come office at two thirty o'clock for signature of office director. Two thirty o'clock, be punctual."

At two thirty on the dot we arrive. "We dare not be late," says the Cleveland man, "they go spare if you are a minute late."

"Ha, so. Have you manifests for delivery Toa Harbor or sub-contractor Toa Harbor, you put manifest number on requisition."

We explain that we have delivered documents which required no manifest since they were carried in the cab and were not cargo as such. The man retreats to the office director's sanctum.

He returns to say: "Without manifest number, the requisition must go to project director for sanction. Please be at project director's office at six o'clock."

At six o'clock our little delegation arrives at the project director's door. He is pouring over our requisition through thick glasses, looking every myopic inch the traditional caricature of a Japanese. He delivers a speech to his henchman from the general office. It is a long speech, far too grand and fluent for two little litres of distilled water. The henchman turns to us and says: "Director say, without manifest and proof of delivery to Toa Harbor Company or Toa Harbor contractors water cannot be supplied. Japanese water is for Japanese vehicles only, that is the company rule and it cannot be broken."

So the Cleveland men scrape every ounce

of dried ice from the deep freeze and fridge in the compound. When that isn't enough, we all pee in a bucket and use that. It turns out to be good stuff, it carries us for another 7,500 miles without a hitch and holds the charge beautifully.

Basrah has become sand bag alley with its face hidden behind piles of protective barricades. For a "non-war-damaged" city it has a battered similarity to parts of London during Hitler's blitz. At 11 am the centre of the city empties in a headlong rush to the outskirts and further. An Indian worker says: "They leave at this time to avoid the bombing which starts every day between 11 o'clock and two o'clock."

Yet, in his government office, the civil servant looks fixedly ahead at the wall and says: "Nobody is leaving the city, there is no bombing." Outside his window the cacophony of car horns from traffic streaming out of town drowns his words.

He adds: "The Iraqi Air Force does not allow the enemy to bomb the city." Finally he says: "Excuse please, I must leave now, you must come back tomorrow." And he rushes to his car.

The city streets are left to the scrutiny of the beady eye of the leader, President Saddam Hussein, whose face peers down from 10,000 posters. His is the only face allowed public display in Iraq, so it looks from hoardings, walls, shop windows, café walls, government offices, lamp posts and the back windows of cars. It is an offence to deface President Hussein's face.

"Nobody would want to deface the President's posters, the posters are there because the people love him," the civil servant assures us.

However, it must be some disaffected reactionary who has punched a jagged, defacing hole through his features on one large poster displayed in Baghdad. It must be somebody since it could not have been shrapnel—President Hussein insists that there *is* no shrapnel damage in Baghdad, none at all.

From Baghdad, it is half-an-hour to the Kuwait border, to peace and plenty, to the staggering profligate riches of Arabia.

14

TRUCKS entering Kuwait from Iraq are assembled outside the border itself in a huge desert corral. On a given signal, they are moved into the customs point parks for examination, passport checks and taxes. Then they are herded into a convoy to run under military escort to Kuwait City and into the main customs compound there. The convoy leaves at about 10 o'clock in the morning and arrives in Kuwait City at noon—half an hour after the whole customs facility has closed down for the day. So Kuwait is a two day job at any time.

There are a lot of trucks in the corral and the main customs compounds are packed. A driver for Leo Smith's firm says: "They cancelled the convoy yesterday and didn't give any reason. Trucks have been piling in ever since. It'll be a shambles when we all reach the city customs." The sand of the corral is compressed into fine white dust criss-crossed with intricate patterns of tyre ·

treads. It seems a pity to spoil the effect by stepping on them.

Here the British influence is pronounced. The guards are well turned out in British style military uniforms with British badges of rank. They walk in the square-bashed, upright stance of the British Army and they do not slouch or shamble about. Being Kuwait, the privates are probably paid as much as a British Field Marshall on retired pay and could well afford to keep servants to look after them—but they look good.

They have smart surroundings to work in—by comparison with Iraq. The uprights of the buildings are indeed upright, the angles are at 90°, curves and arches match on both sides and the paint is mainly on the wood where it is supposed to be. There is a semblance of order. As much order, that is, as the desert will allow because the desert is a sneaky adversary and creeps back to destroy order whenever it can. The sand creeps over retaining walls and blows in through open gates to re-establish itself on top of metalled roadways and concrete structures. It forms ridges and ruts, it squirts like water from the wheels of moving trucks and runs in waves over itself. In every angle and corner, the returned desert lies in small, fluid piles defying all efforts to sweep it away while its ally, the sun, burns the life from concrete structures and sucks the colour from painted surfaces.

The interiors of the trucks become a uniform grey-white. The dust penetrates everywhere. There is a way to reduce it, the pliable plastic covers of margarine tubs fit the air intakes of most trucks perfectly. So press them over the ends, keep the windows tightly locked and the air conditioning running. Nothing will stop the dust accumulating on the floor. It sticks to clothing and shoes, trickling off when the cab vibrates. It adheres to the skin, running off when perspiration dries in the air conditioned atmosphere. It blows in when doors are opened. It is tougher on nasal passages and lungs than a Los Angeles smog and sinus sufferers are badly afflicted.

In the main hall is the agent's office, when he sees us we all break into the old pal's act. His face creases into a smile of genuine greeting, he clears his underlings from the chairs and invites the honoured guests to sit. In a flood of explanation, information and tittle-tattle he tells us who has been through in the past week, where they are going, where they will be now, which route they are taking back, together with all relevant personal details, from the states of their livers to their love lives. No village gossip could hold a candle to this fellow, not a detail escapes him and his gossip covers several thousand square miles so that he knows, accurately, every nuance, every detail of every cargo and every problem it has encountered at every border throughout Arabia.

"My friend . . . no . . ." he wags his finger across his beaming smile, "no, you must not do that. I will tell you what to do, because there have been changes while you have been at home. Now if you take this road . . . and stay here . . . and see this person . . . and go the other way . . . then you will avoid problems and save much monies. Do you understand, my friend? It is better this way . . . for the time being. It may change later, it is always changing . . . but for you, at this moment, this, I think, is the best of things to do."

All the time his hand is wafting in the breeze to hand out glasses of chi and cigarettes, interspersing his instructions with more gossip and darting questions. "Mr.

Snow, I have not seen him for long time, is he well? And Mr. Frost? Where is the big man, Mr. Ellis, so tall, so big? There have been many problems in Kuwait City, you must be careful, you must watch what they are doing."

There are two types of traffic through Kuwait, the long-distance Europeans and the locals—if you can call a 2,000 mile round trip a local. These are the trucks running on Arab plates and working internals within the Arab states, driven by British, Jordanians, Yemenis, Turks, Pakistanis and sundry Arabs. Apart from the plates it is easy to spot a local because the truck is decorated Arab fashion, with pretty pictures and designs on every available surface, fairy lights all round, pretty tassled curtains at the windows and lethal, frightening attachments to the wheel hubs. These are bright, chromed stars which project beyond the wheel by about 18 inches and rotate at great speed like mincer blades when the truck is moving. In a close encounter they will saw through the side of a private car like a chain saw; they will chop a person to mincemeat. The Arabs love them, the more they can bolt on the better. They climb from their cabs during idle moments and polish their wheel stars with loving care.

Arab trucks differ from European trucks in one essential way, the engines stick out in front housed under a bulbous bonnet. They are made by the thousands by Mercedes who have a special factory producing only Arab trucks. Big, 100 tonners, they are universal. In all technical aspects they are the same as the standard Mercedes truck, but even tougher and better for the rugged life they have to lead. Mercedes, with Teutonic thoroughness, researched the market and discovered that no Arab likes to drive a flat-fronted truck, no matter what the advantages may be in visibility and handling. An Arab does not think that he is even in a motor unless he has a thumping great bonnet in front of him which he can flog and whip along like a war horse pulling a chariot . . . with Boudicca scythes attached to the wheels.

Mercedes won the battle for truck sales throughout Arabia, they are predominant even over the Japanese. In what was once the exclusive province of British Leyland, not a British truck is to be seen and a British car is unique enough to raise comment when it appears. The sad story of British truck decline is that in this 14,000 mile journey, from Britain to Arabia and back, we only saw 11 British trucks on the road.

When the whistle blows and the gate is opened for the locals in the corral at Kuwait to move into the customs area, the scene resembles an amalgam of *Ben Hur* and *Death in the Afternoon*. A roar of engines started in unison shatters the desert quiet and a mushroom cloud of blue diesel smoke erupts over the area. Spinning wheels churn the soft sand and fling it in a dense cloud from the treads in their tyres. It builds in a slowly rising fog from ground level until, embracing truck and trailer, it erases the sharp shadows thrown by the hot sun and blots out the light in a swirling, yellow fog.

Through this murk trucks swing and skid in a furious stampede to gain a front spot in the compound. Competition is fierce. Trucks rush to fill any gap that opens up. When one vehicle gains the advantage the others brake with a scream of compressed air, bucking and rolling to fall in behind. Pedestrians, unwittingly trapped by the unexpected opening of the gate, twist and squirm to avoid the monster machines. It is fatal to jump out of the way of one truck, another will be thundering up whichever way the leap is made. The only method of escape is that of the bullfighter, face the charging beast until the final moment then smartly twist aside. The most dangerous place to be is in the rear. The last trucks thunder across the back of the surging mass seeking an opening and are liable to swing violently at any moment. There are, as there are bound to be, terrible shunts. When the dust settles shapes of stranded and wounded vehicles emerge from the gloom—lonely stragglers left behind by the tide, floundering in a turbulent sea of sand.

After this spectacular charge comes a more orderly progress into the compound to park in neat lines facing the customs complex and await the assembly of the convoy. By luck we are part of a British enclave, six UK trucks must have pulled in and managed to park together. This isn't blind patriotism at work, merely a way to ease the language difficulties.

Alex Greaves, who runs four Volvo trucks in his own transport company and drives one of them himself, is anxious to examine the burned out wreck of one of his vehicles in the Saudi Arabian desert. He says: "Save me from Scottish drivers on this run, they have caused me nothing but trouble. That truck of mine was said to have caught fire, well, it did, but the grapevine has it that it wasn't entirely accidental. There was no reason it should catch fire, there were no mechanical faults, it was a newish truck. But it went up in flames. I got a whisper that maybe all was not as it should be. But how can you tell? What can you prove? I took on two Glaswegian drivers and they both lost their trucks, which I reckon is a bit careless of them . . . or worse."

The grapevine had the story all right, but it could never be substantiated that it was not an accident. A shrewd old boy from Lincolnshire who was the first British person to examine the truck after the fire said: "In my view, the English police would have put it down as arson in the first five minutes. In the first place, where was the cargo? No matter how inflammable a cargo is, there is always something of it left. That tilt was clean, all that was left were just the charred embers of the trailer, there wasn't even a covering of ashes from the cargo.

"I've seen enough burned out trucks in my time to know what they ought to look like and know when they look wrong. That truck and tilt burned from the chassis upwards. Truck fires usually start when a bearing collapses and gets white hot and that starts a fire around the axles. If a bearing goes—or a gear box—you know when it is beyond repair. If the metal has turned blue, then it is finished, it's brittle. I hammered all the black off the bearings on that wreck and there was white metal underneath them all. And it looked as if that fire had broken out at about five separate points.

"Nothing about it looked right to me. But it happened hundreds of miles out in the desert, how can you get a competent wreck inspector out to see it? He probably wouldn't even get a visa to get into the country.

"It is a bloody funny thing but if there is ever anything a bit funny about an accident like this, it has always happened where it is almost impossible to get at the truck. It's down the bottom of a ravine in Turkey or in the middle of a desert in Saudi. I am convinced that Alex was turned over and I'll bet that if you cared to chuck good money after bad and pay a visit to Glasgow, you'd find a bit of high living going on and a couple of new Granada Ghia's running about. OK, the insurance pays up, but it makes it worse for the rest of us and it bungs up all premiums, not just Alex's. These jokers are poison to the business."

There are few secrets kept from the grapevine, the chat travels quickly, particularly if something seems wrong—and it is remembered for a long time.

The sergeant in charge of the convoy organises the run with commendable efficiency. But any convoy is a problem, no less a convoy of trucks than a convoy of ships. Here the speed is restricted to that of an Arab 30 tonner piled to the sky with 88 tons of steel pipes and about to collapse under the strain.

The army, lights flashing on the roofs of their vehicles, move off and the bizarre train of multi-coloured trucks of every shape and size falls in behind them. Army trucks intersperse the convoy at given intervals. A corporal blows his whistle, flashes his lollipop and the Brits move into the line. Winding up a slight incline the line stretches away into the desert like wool being pulled from a ball, a bit kinky and erratic.

This is Kuwait, according to the World Bank it is the richest or second richest country the world has ever known. First or second, what does it matter when it has a million or two in the bank for every one of its citizens?

To prove its wealth, in the first sandy kilometre there are three abandoned Cadillacs left in the desert. There is nothing seriously wrong with them, just a blown tyre or dust in the carburettor. Cars like this have been wrecked by the sportive young bloods of the town who have rolled them at excessive speed, but most are left because of minor mechanical defects.

"The ashtray was full," the drivers say.

They are an aspect of life which makes the whole of Arabia the biggest rubbish dump ever seen. From here to Oman, the desert by the roadside is littered with wrecks of every description. Millions of pounds worth of expensive, luxury machines are dumped without a second thought and left until they rust into the sand. They cannot be moved by strangers, to take even a wing mirror from an abandoned vehicle is a criminal offence incurring stiff custodial penalties.

Kuwait is a flat of burning sand, 120 miles in diameter, arid, waterless, barren—with a modern city in the middle. There is nothing but sand and a city sitting on a sea of oil.

Soon the mini-palaces of the city appear.

382

They sit enclosed by high walls. The wall is the predominant feature of all Arab architecture, it keeps the family in and the desert out. Even within the boundaries of the city, the houses are enclaves set aside from the desert; in city streets the desert runs right to the walls of the houses.

The mansions bristle with television aerials of incredibly elaborate design. In recognition of the source of their wealth, the Kuwaitis construct their aerials in the shapes of oil wells, so giant drilling rigs in the shape of miniature Eiffel Towers sit on the roofs of the houses. Over each house is a gleaming silver ball, this is the water tank which draws its supplies from the enormous de-salinisation plant. The silver ball and the ornate television aerial—these are the marks of Kuwait's advance into the twentieth century.

The wide road opens out into an eight lane urban highway with fly-overs and under-passes and Cadillacs travelling at great speed. They hurtle en masse in one direction in the morning and in the opposite direction at noon. The city is closed to all heavy traffic at these times so that the headlong rush is not impeded. Only a brave man or a fool would wish to be out in the chaos.

The convoy swings from the main approach road to circle into the city customs compound and park for the day . . . or the week . . . or even the month. Kuwait is another tricky spot to get out of.

Mr. Zarrar Paloba smiles a resigned and sympathetic smile and says: "They change the rules every day. All the rules—the transit rules, the rules about duty payable, the rules about loading and unloading, the rules about tax, the rules about who can carry and who can't. They make them up as they go along. The art of business here is to know how to cope with the constant change and not to crumble under the strain."

His assistants emphasise the point. "Only Kuwaitis can hold official positions and all executives and senior officials are Kuwait nationals. It means that the man at the desk makes the rules. There is nobody above him to appeal to except a member of the royal family. There are no books or papers to consult, if the man at the desk thinks of a good idea and says, 'That is the rule,' then that is the rule."

Mr. Paloba is a handsome, non-Kuwaiti gentleman of relaxed disposition, charm and easy wit—all of which attributes are necessary in Kuwait. He plays cricket and is a member of a cricket club which, because of the climate, plays all the year round. So he is obviously a good bloke and a pleasure to deal with. He is a senior executive with Kuwait Maritime and Mercantile Company, who are our agents in Kuwait and as such responsible for the cargo which is to be unloaded here.

Kuwait Maritime and Mercantile are housed in the Gray Mackenzie offices, which is hardly surprising since an awful lot of business between Britain and the Gulf seems to have some connection with Gray Mackenzie & Company. Gray Mackenzie is to Arabia what Jardine Matheison is to Hong Kong, Singapore and the Orient, the East India Company to India, Unilever to Africa and the Hudson's Bay Company to Canada— it is part of the history of the place.

The immediate problem is that a quarter of the load is to be tipped in Kuwait, a cargo of luxury carpet tiles and supplies for the Kuwaiti Navy. That will be unloaded in the customs compound and cleared by Kuwait Maritime and Mercantile. The rest of the cargo is to be taken on to Saudi Arabia.

A week before we arrived, the Kuwaiti

customs chief responsible changed the transit rules. Now if you are actually unloading in Kuwait but have other cargo to take further, you must pay tax on the remaining cargo—a bail bond which will be returnable on application after a month. Three Astran trucks in transit the week before were required to stump up £12,000. For this cargo, they want a deposit of £1,900—which we have not got. We must telex head office and they, in turn, will have to telex back to authorise the payment of the money by the agents. This is late Thursday evening, tomorrow all Islam closes down, Saturday and Sunday all Britain closes down . . . we are stuck until Monday.

Paloba grins and says: "Just accept the fact that it will take at least four days to clear . . . probably more. There is nothing to be done about it."

That is a body blow. Nobody is allowed to stay in the customs compound, so sleeping and eating in the comfort of the truck is out, it means a hotel. Said quickly, that seems a good idea, put into practice, it is a shock. The Kuwait Sheraton advertises its twin rooms—without board—at 44 Kuwait dinars plus 15 per cent per day which is £101. The cheapest available hotel is 12 dinars per person per day, without food—£55. So without eating we are in for £110 minimum per day. And food is correspondingly pricey. It is a one hell of a place to be stranded—among the most expensive in the world.

Hell! Stuck in Kuwait, which is as dry as a bone, with no signs of any diversion. You cannot even go into the sea because it is shark infested.

Driving in from the gumruk—the customs—the first shop to be seen in the city centre sells Rolls-Royces. There aren't any cars to be seen, it is filled with Range Rovers—you are supposed to order your Rolls like a bespoke suit.

From the roundabout, the main drag runs right through the city to the old souk—the bazaar. On the right side of the street are six electrical goods shops stacked to the ceilings with hi-fi, stereo decks, videos and radios; two camera shops, also stuffed with their brand of wares; and an opticians brimming over with assorted frames and sunglasses. Further down the street, in exactly the same proportion, are similar outlets for consumer durables. And on the other side of the street, too. Occasionally there is a jewellers, a Paris fashion house, a furriers—in a city where the winter temperature is 98° and the full chador is obligatory for all home town ladies.

What is always referred to as the old souk is the old part of the city and has been left untouched in a town which is one vast construction site. Here there are narrow streets, pungent smells and a constant rabble babbling its business all day long. The vegetable and meat markets have stalls groaning under the colourful, tempting exotica of the East with proprietors as colourful as their own produce.

This is the heart of Arab life, the stuff of Arabian Nights, Aladdin's cave in the flesh.

The city has built new souks which can put any similar shopping complexes in Europe in the shade: vast and magnificently appointed structures, finished in the finest marbles and rarest of timbers with stainless-steel escalators linking the floors. It is sheer luxury just to walk in their opulence and revel in the design and taste of their expensive fittings—nothing cheap, shoddy, second-rate or inexpensive has been allowed to mar their excellence. This is what immeasurable wealth, wisely spent, can buy.

Sanyo have introduced their new stereophonic, twin-speaker portable radio. It is a sensation. Every Sanyo dealer is inundated with customers. So furious is the trade that dealers have not had time to unpack their consignments, they take the cartons from the crates and rip them open in the shop; cardboard cases are knee deep on the floor.

Down the street, a camera shop has a consignment of Hannimex cameras and lenses, the very latest to come from the factories in Japan. Customers jostle to lay hands on them as they are unpacked from the cases—zoom lenses, telephoto lenses, wide angle lenses, all are heaped into plastic carriers and the happy customers scuttle away in glee.

Shop windows along the street display television sets of every size from portables to 50 inch projection screens. Nobody is interested in them but in the car parks on sandy, undeveloped sites, excited crowds jostle around car boots where the latest novelty is being shown: a six-inch battery portable TV. The owner juggles the aerial to gain and lose a good picture to the gasps and applause of the crowd.

Kuwait is the electronic toyland of the world, a micro chip nightmare. A dealer proudly, and delightedly, says that this year Kuwait has imported and sold 11 televisions, 18 radios and 23 cameras for every head of population.

From £25 to £2,500, the goods sell like hot cakes; from £2,500 to £25,000, they never even have time to collect dust on the shelves. Says the Indian salesman in the camera shop: "I give you 50 per cent discount on this zoom lens, it is last year's model."

Driving home in their latest model Cadillacs, piled high with this month's model of electronic wizardry, to their mansions with the oil rig aerials on top, what have the Kuwaitis got to look at, listen to and take photographs of? The answer is not a great deal.

They have two channels on their television an Arabic and an English one. They have a half-hour reading from the Koran, followed by the most popular programme, the nightly one-hour cartoon show. They can pick up lessons in surveying, trigonometry, or geometry, a few ancient, soft American sit-coms, live sport by satellite from the world and the news. Radio Kuwait is just as scintillating with a diet of programmes about Islam and Arab culture.

A day in the life of a driver stranded in Kuwait: 7.00 a.m. rise, drink fruit juice at £1 a small bottle; breakfast—cereal followed by two fried eggs with selection of unleavened bread or crispbreads and coffee—£5; walk round radio shops until noon; lunch—soup, lamb, chicken or savoury Arab dish, dessert—£9; walk round camera shops, return to room and watch television, drink bottle of water, discover bottle of water is charged at £1, forego second bottle of water; wait for evening re-opening of shops and souks; walk round radio shops and camera shops and watch Kuwaitis scramble for new models; 7.00 pm dinner—soup, lamb, chicken—£12; a quick walk round radio and camera shops before the town closes down at 9.00 pm; 9.30, go to bed.

On Saturday morning the Kuwait load is cleared. The tilt is opened for unloading to reveal that the system has gone awry—the Kuwait consignment has been stowed midships. The cargo behind it will have to be moved, the sides of the tilt stripped down by removing the slats to allow access and the rest of the cargo redistributed, which, in simple terms, means humping nine tons about. Getting it down is easy, getting it back up is more difficult. And, even though it is winter, the temperature is in the high 80s.

There are assistants available to help but they have to be closely watched or the cargoes will become mixed. It is hard work but it goes smoothly; the agent's man rushes about organising papers and workers, the cargo disappears into the great cargo sheds, receipts are signed, import duties are paid . . . that's over. We are once again roped up, TIR tapes intact and plumbed, next stop Saudi Arabia.

Not today, however, as it is now approaching 11.30 am and the gumruk is closing for the day. Anyway, the £1,900 bail bond has to be lodged. Astran has moved speedily and the money is already at the agent's office. Tomorrow all we need is a receipt for the cash, the papers stamped and passports franked and we can be away, so the delay isn't as bad as it looked as if it would be.

The problem is how to fill in the time between now and 7.30 in the morning—walk round the radio shops, look for a camera bargain, what a good idea! But first, let's go back to the Bristol Hotel for a long, refreshing bath.

The hotel is built to a design common in Arab countries, a door from the main corridor leads to a lounge area serving a suite of two or three rooms. It is a large communal sitting room with the bedrooms leading off it. This is to cater for the Arab custom of travelling in tribes. This hotel has been built to high, though not excessive standards and all the fittings in it are high quality and solid. They have not stinted money on the job, even the plastics are super quality and good to the touch. When the contractors finished the building and handed it over it was completed to the standard of a three to four star European hotel. Then the Arab workmen got at it and set about their free-hand maintenance. All Arab workmen without exception distrust such devices as spirit levels, plumb lines, set squares or T-squares, they believe only in the eye. And every Arab eye has a built-in wobble and lean which probably comes from sitting on too many loping camels and peering at unsteady horizons shimmering in a heat haze.

Along the main corridors, nosegays of coloured electrical wires protrude from walls with their copper innards bared to the touch but flared out so that they do not touch each other. In the bedrooms, the bedside lights will not work because they are not plugged in, they cannot be plugged in because the plugs are a different shape from the sockets. The Egyptian handyman summoned to rectify the fault studies them with great intensity, goes away and returns with a heavy hammer with which he wallops the plugs into the sockets. Amazingly, the lights come on. He holds out his and hand with commendable frankness says: "Flous"—money.

The bathroom is large, tiled floor to ceiling with heavy, rather beautiful tiles. It has a king-sized bath, wash basin, loo and bidet; the fittings are heavy and thickly chromed. Good, substantial stuff at the top end of the price range.

A maintenance man has knocked a hole in the tiles where the combined shower and bath mixer taps are attached so the assembly hangs free. When the lever is turned to hot it produces a weak trickle of cold water, turned to cold it produces a thinner trickle of warm water.

The Egyptian handyman returns with his heavy hammer, hits all the taps and pipes thumping whacks and holds out his hand: "Flous."

When the loo is flushed everything stops—dead.

Then the awful secret weapon of the bathroom is revealed, turn on the tap of the bidet and a powerful, penetrating, high-pressure jet of water explodes like a tropical rainstorm inundating the whole room, drenching the walls, soaking towels, under-clothes and loo-paper, floating slippers toward the central drain and getting hot, hotter and hotter still.

Yet water of any kind is a miracle in Kuwait. A few short years ago the idea of running water on tap would have been classed as the wild imaginings of a deranged mind. Now, here it is in the houses, in fountains in the streets, in ornamental ponds and swimming pools in the hotels.

Whatever the follies of the place, the Amir and his family have spread the wealth around for all to enjoy. The Amir, against frightening odds, is turning a blistering wilderness scorched by intolerable heat where most men found it all but impossible to exist, into a comfortable, advanced city state.

However, by dragging a primeval society into a condition of affluence and indulgence he is suffering the consequences of too much too soon. Much has gone sour on him.

Kuwaitis take the simplistic view that the objective of being rich is not to work—work is for the poor and is degrading, so they don't and won't work. Which makes the cynics say: "From camels to Cadillacs and back to camels in three generations."

The refugee Iraqi in the agent's office comments bitterly: "They are all too rich, the young people are given too much money which makes them believe that they can stay stupid all their lives. They spend their lives acting foolishly and thinking childishly. Others make their wealth for them while they play silly games."

While the mullahs wring their hands in despair and preach their ancient beliefs every night on the television, the kids go out and wreck Cadillacs for the hell of it.

There is nowhere to go, nothing to do, this is a totally segregated Muslim community devoid of female society in public . . . deadsville after 9 o'clock at night. Which is why it is not safe to be out on the streets after that time. That is the time the bored young bloods bring out their Cadillacs, Ferraris, Porsches and Mustangs and turn Kuwait City into Monaco with a round-the-houses Grand Prix. They do circuits of the city and thunder down the coast road, racing each other, at breakneck speeds. When they shunt or roll their expensive cars, if they get out alive, they come up laughing. It's a joke. "We'll buy another one tomorrow when the shops open."

It is saddening to sit and watch it. It is even worse to observe them watching foreign television programmes with rapt attention. They cannot understand a word spoken and the actions and nuances on screen are completely alien to their culture and incomprehensible to them. Our hotel neighbours watch an obscure American sit-com with plenty of cleavage on show. The plot, such as it is, is to get the girl into bed when she is tiddly, it is the sex war being fought with 1930's Hayes Office innuendo rather than 1980's full frontal attack. Sub-titles are infrequent, there is one to cover five minutes backchat on the screen.

"What does that one say?"

The Kuwaiti with a grasp of basic English says: "The lady is going to do her shopping and the man will help her."

Actually, the man has suggested that there are easier ways to afford a mink coat than working for it—it is that sort of sit-com, accompanied by loud laughter from the studio audience after every weak joke. Whenever the studio audience laughs, so too do the Kuwaitis.

On the table in the hotel room lies today's edition of the *Arab Times*. It carries a front page headline stating: "Man Jailed for Grave Sexual Assault". The man, a Kuwaiti, had, after a party, gone into his sister-in-law's room and "placed a hand on her shoulder". He was charged with attempted rape and jailed for five years. The court was told that all the Kuwaiti members of the party had been given alcohol in one of the European hotels by a visitor who had been deported. They were all fined several hundred pounds, including the alleged victim of the attempted rape.

The way the man on the television has just handled his co-star would have got him life down here.

Two beautiful Indian girls were eating in the café in the new souk. "Don't look at them, don't stare," said an agitated driver who was working internals and knew the full score, "if you want an ogle, do it through the mirrors. You will get nicked for looking at women down here. The police will grab you and you will be inside. The mullah or the police will tell the court that you were looking at the woman in a sinful way and you will be locked up."

"Rubbish!"

"Well, if it's rubbish," said his companion, "I can't think why I spent six weeks in the cage. I was looking at this Kuwaiti bird who hadn't got her veil up and trying to work out how old she was. I didn't wink or smile, or anything and they whipped me in and banged me up. It took six weeks to get me out."

The Koran says: when a man and a woman are together, the third person present is the Devil.

The Palm Beach Hotel, on the seafront, is the most popular with European drivers, but it has raised its prices and many people are seeking economies so they find cheaper accommodation. However, the cheaper prices soon catch up. Owner-drivers say: "You don't want to blow £1,000 of the profit on the run for the dubious pleasure of parking your arse in a Kuwaiti hotel armchair while the customs piss you about."

Andrew Wilson-Young, well connected ex-public schoolboy, ex-turkey farmer, ex-maggot-breeder, non-smoker, non-drinker, who declines even tea or coffee because it means he has to stop for a pee on the way, the only person who has never been known to utter an oath stronger than "golly", breaker of records for time out and time back and a living legend in his five years on the run—he solved the accommodation problem in Kuwait.

But he has the manner, the voice and the connections to do it. Impounded in Kuwait customs, he took his bivouac tent from the cab and pitched it on the lawns of the British Embassy. He told embassy staff: "I won't pay these outrageous hotel prices, the quicker you sort out these Kuwaiti johnnies, the quicker I can leave, so get to it." So saying he closed the flap of his tent and went to sleep. He was cleared by ten o'clock the following morning. Lesser mortals have to sit it out and suffer—not in silence, but still suffering.

Along the seafront are the banks, the commercial offices, the Palm Beach hotel and the impressive Royal Palaces guarded by soldiers dripping gold braid. Being near the Royal Palaces is another danger in Kuwait, to stay alive you have to stay alert. The nine o'clock evening "Grand Prix" is as nothing to the Amir and Crown Prince's sorties into the town. They come like thunderbolts from a clear sky.

The entourage of royal limousines and motor-cycle escort plus five or six support vehicles sweep from the palace grounds and hit the public highway at 60 mph on the turn. Then, in perfect formation, they thunder at ever-increasing speed toward the city centre. The traffic miraculously parts before the approaching phalanx and the formation roars intact to its destination leaving a trail of shattered nerves and springs behind. Experts say the reason the royal party moves at such speed is that it reduces the chances of an assassin taking a pot shot, they quickly add that no such thing is even remotely conceivable since the royal family is loved and worshipped by the populace. All kings, princes and sheikhs of importance throughout the Gulf States travel this way—a sheikh's chauffeur could be a good job for a retired Formula 1 racing driver.

Everything else in the area moves more slowly, particularly paperwork and officials.

At 7.30 am we assemble at the Gray Mackenzie offices and head for the new gumruk building. The new gumruk is slightly out of town and built to the scale of

London Airport departure lounge, floored in marble and furbished in onyx, mahogany, cedar and walnut. The offices skirt three sides of the great assembly hall. Benched seating is available in the centre of the hall for the waiting public. Opening hours are from 7.30 until 11.00 am but that is nothing to go by.

The sheikhs, or relatives standing in for them, attend when the fancy takes them—or not at all, as the case may be. Crack of dawn in the customs hall begins with optimistic enthusiasm, chatter and glasses of chi— "today's the day, I will get my papers, the chef promised"—and wanes to a desultory mumbling, a shifting from side to side in the chair, a quick stroll to stretch the legs as the sun rises higher in the morning sky and the required sheikh doesn't appear.

Occasionally one does arrive, surrounded by his supporters, and his party is immediately mobbed by anxious supplicants while he stalks imperiously through the crowd, his retainers clearing his way. He slams his office door in the face of the mob and immediately telephones his uncle for a long, long family chat.

Our man arrives and our Iraqi agent's

assistant is much sharper than the rest, he scuttles like a startled rabbit across the hall. We are a bit put out because he is running away from the sheikh and not joining in the ruck. But the clever lad has run to the sheikh's office, darted inside and squatted cross-legged on the floor in a corner where he cannot be seen. After the sheikh has slammed his door, made his obligatory telephone call and demanded his chi, our lad pops up like a Jack-in-the-box from the corner and slides the papers under the sheikh's nose.

There is a heated argument and much flicking of pages, it goes on for 22 minutes until the sheikh rises abruptly, stalks from his office, calls on a brother sheikh down the hall and together they depart in the second sheikh's Cadillac with our man's Cadillac in close attendance behind. That is it for the day, the sheikh is finished. Call again tomorrow.

The sheikh will not stamp and sign the documents because "there is a new rule, it concerns transit and the papers are not correct". He has forgotten exactly what the new rule is but he will inform the agent's assistant in the morning. A sad-eyed supplicant, a mournful, all but beaten Arab, says: "There has been a new rule every day for a month. I have waited a full passing of the moon for it to be explained."

The following day the performance is repeated.

The day after that the sheikh suggests that the only way out of our dilemma is to write to the Under Secretary for Trade in the Government who will decide upon our application.

Mr. Paloba explains: "That will take a week for the letter to reach the Under Secretary and a week for him to reply. But there is possibly another way open to us. The sheikh may want a present."

He grins widely and says: "I will take advice, I will consult our . . . PR man." He lays emphasis on PR.

On the third desk down from Mr. Paloba's office sits a worldly, cultivated Egyptian gentleman, he is immaculately turned out, with well cut grey, wavy hair, beautifully manicured hands and a knowing air about him. He is the official present giver. He smooths out problems and eases the path of commerce.

He listens attentively to all the details of the case and says: "I will make discreet enquiries,

I know the sheikh very well, he is a friend of mine, I am acquainted with his family."

He returns to the office within the hour and tells us all: "It is a great problem for the sheikh and causes him much worry. I think he would appreciate a present in consideration of the trouble he has gone to on our behalf. By discreet enquiry, I think I know the very thing that will please him most and I will make more enquiries about that. I am sure I can find the very thing for him."

We arrange to meet again at 7.30 am and go mob handed to see the sheikh at the gumruk. Which leaves another 18 hours to be killed as best as can be arranged in the social whirl of Kuwait society.

The Sheraton bookshop looks good and is as plush as its surroundings but is sadly lacking in reading matter. There is a selection of coffee-table books—*The Flora and Fauna of Arabia, Desert Wildlife, Wildlife of the Arabian Peninsular, Arab Art and Craftmanship, A History of Oil in the Gulf States, The Arab Economy in a World Context*—lots of full page colour pictures and short paragraphs set in an ocean of glossy white paper.

"You must have *something* to read, what about a Harold Robbins?"

A wry smile. "Sorry, sir, that is proscribed."

"Jacqueline Susann?"

"Sorry, sir, that is proscribed."

"OK—I'll have the *Sunday Times*—that's this week's issue, isn't it?"

"Two dinars, sir."

"Four quid! Give me the *Sunday Telegraph* instead, that's half the price." There are black deletions in the text obliterating offending words and phrases, you can drive yourself mad trying to work out what they were. Some naughty English journalist must have written bum, boobs or knickers.

An oil man standing at the counter remarks: "I've only ever seen one copy of the *Guardian* out here, that had so much black ink over it that it looked as if the whole paper was a crossword puzzle. Particularly the arts pages."

On an old alleyway leading to the new souk is Kuwait's finest little shop, a sort of Arab take-away. The man has a pressing machine into which he inserts up to a dozen fresh oranges to squeeze one drink. He has slivers of spit-roasted mutton hanging on a spindle and looking exactly like the rag-rollers in an automatic car wash. He hacks them off onto a pat of unleavened bread until they pile an inch high and slaps another pat of bread on top. It is the best, and tastiest, quick meal in Kuwait. However, be careful to eat it with your body inclined forward and neck extended because the fat runs out in rivulets.

At our friend Eric's truck we are joined by two "compounded" Brits who have almost run out of cash and have gone native to survive. They are staying in an all-Arab hotel near the old souk where they have rented a corrugated tin shack with two bunks on the roof. It is a tall building, one of the original new multi-storey hotels built when the boom began but now superseded by newer "down-town" developments. Tattered sun-canopies overhang the windows, half of which seem to be missing, and chunks of the yellow facing stone have fallen away.

On the long climb to the roof, doors are open on each landing, the rooms contain a minimum of 10 guests, they sleep rolled in their blankets on the floor. Half the lavatories are Western style bowls and half Arab squatters, the bowls are stained black and they all stink. The stench of lavatories and blocked drains rolls like a solid cloud along corridors and down strairways. To reach the tin shack is a delicate operation, stepping over sleeping figures rolled in blankets who are thick on the roof. The astonishment is that the shack has an air conditioning unit installed. For this luxury, our friends are paying £11 a day each.

Naturally, in a country where an income of £1 million a day for one individual is not unknown, life can be very good for some. And there are enough about in Kuwait to support magnificent hotels like the Sheraton which tempts its clientele with glowing descriptions of the good life: "With a touch of Riccardo's own version of the nouvelle cuisine a completely new dinner menu has been devised by our master-chefs which will delight the gourmets of Kuwait with its wide selection of luscious, tempting dishes 'fit for a King'. The list of hors d'oeuvre includes caviar from the Beluga Sturgeon; Alaskan King Crab meat folded into paper thin Crepes; Smoked Salmon from the waters of the Norwegian Fjords; Pate de Foie Gras and tender Smoked Duck Breasts served with a Pear Salad; New England Rock Lobster and the Gulf's finest Hamour which can be cooked and prepared to your choice. The entrees include mouthwatering slices of Veal

Loin served in a Cream Sauce with White Truffles from Piedmont; Breast of Baby Duckling served with ripe Kadota Figs; Prime Sirloin Steak and Crown of Spring Lamb carved at your table."

The culinary masterpieces of the world, all washed down with fizzy Coke and sparkling fruit juices.

However, say what you will of the excesses of the oil kings, amirs and sheikhs, a salutary fact emerges: they have distributed their money far wider and more generously to the benefit of their peoples than coal owners, iron masters, cotton mill proprietors, railroad barons or city merchant princes in the West ever did.

Morning, however, is a long time coming in Kuwait.

At 7.30 am we meet at the agent's office. The present guaranteed to please turns out to be a pair of Sheaffer pens. He'd asked for a pair made of solid gold at a UK price of £1,600 including tax—£900 here. Those he was *not* going to get. A gold plated pair, £76 at home, £44 here, was his lot, like it or lump it—the greedy swine.

"Better than another fortnight's delay," says Mr. Paloba.

In convoy we drive to the new gumruk and commence our vigil. Our man arrives early at nine o'clock, he is called Ali Abu; the derivation of his name is explained in detail by the knowledgeable Egyptian and the genealogy is vital to those doing business in the city because it shows exactly what pull he exerts. He is a large, very fat man whose feet protrude from under his white jellaba at 10 minutes past 10 o'clock and he flips them out when he walks. He walks leaning slightly back to balance the weight of his stomach and his jowls and neck hang loosely round the collar of his dress. He wears a thick, black moustache and surveys the world through sad, brown, heavily bagged eyes.

As he crosses the marble floor towards his office, he moves at quite a speed and our contingent is pushed to keep up. The urbane Egyptian puts in a couple of little skip steps to keep pace and retain his urbanity without being seen to hurry. The slender, but shorter Iraqi breaks into a trot to make sure not to have the office door slammed in his face; he is clutching the box with the pens inside closely to his chest.

Just before the door is reached, he makes a dash, opens it for the sheikh and Egyptian to

410

pass through, leaps through after them, and slams the door in the faces of the pursuing crush of other supplicants.

A long, intense conversation, interspersed with much laughter from our Egyptian colleague, ensues. The sheikh stands behind his desk nodding sagely. The Egyptian is waving his hand behind his back in a circling motion while still talking earnestly to the sheikh. The Iraqi gets the idea and slips the pen box into the rotating hand and the Egyptian produces the box from behind his back like a conjurer pulling a dove from his jacket. He opens it towards the sheikh with the expertise of a salesman tempting a client, then passes it over. We watch the charade unfolding through the plate-glass window.

No reaction, not a flicker. Could this be £44 down the drain?

The sheikh takes out the pens, weighs each one carefully, balances them in each hand for comparison. He does not like to be fobbed off with tatty gold plate, solid gold he has asked for and solid gold he wanted. With a resigned nod he slips them into his jellaba pocket, the clips proudly displayed for all to see, bravely hiding his disappointment with a shrug which indicates that he knows the English are mean and miserable sods and impoverished with it.

Unexpectedly the party leaves the office and hurries down the hall. They go to see another sheikh, but this one is a "black job", robed in the elegantly styled black jellaba of the big bosses. That takes a further half hour of frenzied discussion, then a flash of pen across the papers, a dash back to Abu Ali's office, stamp, stamp, stamp, a flash of the new gold pen across the stamps.

"Quick, hurry," says the Iraqi, "let's get out before they change the rules again."

Our truck has been eight days in the compound, now the stamped and signed papers can begin the rounds of the compound offices, the police and cab control—then the open road again!

The Iraqi begins his rush around the desks, the truck is run up to the police examination post. A large, fat sergeant is supervising operations with a squad of soldiers. This is not good.

They are searching an Arab Merc and are in the process of taking this truck to pieces. Or rather, they are making the driver take it to pieces. The sergeant sits in the driving seat, leaning on the steering wheel and idly drumming his fingers. The driver is unscrewing and disassembling the facia. He has already taken off the door panels, roof lining, interior side linings, removed the spare seat and floor covering.

Next, the sergeant instructs him to take his lights to pieces, then his wing mirrors. A soldier cuts a jagged hole in the diesel tanks, the oil pours out and they tip sand on to it. Bit by bit, the truck comes to pieces and the compound begins to look like a breaker's yard. Parts of the truck lie all around. The reflectors hang at the end of their wires, the radiator grill is off, laying the engine bare. It is a complete demolition job.

The middle-aged Arab, clad in grey and wearing a little skull cap, shows no emotion. His face is completely impassive, he says nothing and acts like a zombie, not a flicker of expression reveals his inner feelings. He takes the appropriate screwdriver or spanner from his toolbox, removes the required item and steps back.

The soldiers root and prod, pull and probe, nothing is revealed.

The vehicle designation, 2236, is missing from the right side of the bonnet and only the holes where it was originally secured are visible. It is intact on the left side. Stepping back and surveying the wreck, the sergeant strides to the truck and taps the bonnet with his swagger stick at the point where the plate should be. He shakes his head in a vigorous negative gesture. He will not clear the vehicle because that plate is missing. There can be no argument. He flicks his hand in a dismissive wave signalling the driver back to the waiting line. The Arab patiently begins the task of re-assembling his truck.

This is clearly an anti-Merc day. A new Mercedes 480 SEL private car with delivery plates on is directed over the inspection pit. The Arab driver, in direct contrast to the truck driver, is a smiling, garrulous chap. He slips from the driver's seat, beams at the sergeant and soldiers and greets them volubly. They ignore him, the sergeant stares straight through him making no acknowledgement of his presence. He signals to his troops. As a man, with well-drilled precision, they produce jemmies from leg pockets in their blue overall uniforms and advance on the car. They plunge the jemmies under the linings of the central door pillars and rip them out, they follow with the rear interior linings, then the front.

The driver stands in shock, dumbfounded. The sergeant instructs him to take out the facia but he doesn't know where to start, he doesn't even know where the toolbox is stored. The sergeant orders his jemmy men into action and they lever off the dashboard. The interior is now down to the bare metal with all the wiring exposed. Bits fall off and tumble into the pit below. The driver is dispatched to retrieve them. A soldier is working on the exhaust and it falls off with a clatter. The boot is open and ripped to pieces.

Then they come to the bonnet. The sergeant taps the engine with his stick and signals a rising motion with his upturned palm, he wants the engine out. The driver collapses and sits on the ground blubbering. He is saved by the arrival of the sheikh in command whose Cadillac roars to the main entrance of the police station. He wears a black tailored jellaba. Everything stops for the sheikh.

The shiekh's chauffeur has parked the Cadillac too close to the station steps and the door won't open. The shiekh will not move across to get out of the other door, the hell he will. So there is a shunting and reversing and the sergeant waves aside all volunteers to open the door himself.

Now it is our turn and we are feeling just a little apprehensive. The sergeant climbs into our cab. "'Ello," he says, and smiles, "Inglisi? Much come here often? I know trucks. You got nothing? Oh, you make coffee, good. Oh, you got Rothman's Imperial, good."

He shakes his head and sighs, a worried expression crosses his face. "Drugs, forbidden drink, mucho problems, mucho problems, they know it is bad but still they bring it in. They are fools, these peoples. There are bad men who sell them the drugs and drink and then the bad men tell the police so they claim big reward for information. I must search all Mercedes, it is ordered so.

"My friends, I must go. I sign your papers. Good trip. Kuwait now has good football team, you know that? Verr good."

A glow of satisfaction creeps through the bones, we feel relief and that old familiar surge of elation. There is the gate to freedom with one thin chain barring us from the open road. There is just the personal check for people leaving the compound—turn out your

416

pockets, a quick frisk over legs and torso, open your bag . . . and away.

But where is our Iraqi friend? The clock shows 11.17 am, we have 13 minutes in which to get away. Here comes the Iraqi, running. He is harrassed and clearly worried. Oh, God, don't count your chickens . . .

"Some fool in the office has missed two names off the fourth copy of the documents and the words 'in transit', the man won't stamp them."

"Hell!"

"Yes, yes, yes, it is only missing on the fourth copy, it is on all the rest."

Action stations. We run like lunatics across that wide square. No, the clerk will not stamp the documents, there are two names and an "in transit" declaration missing from one copy, they should be on all the documents, that is the rule.

To hell with protocol, vault the counter and beard the boss sheikh in his office. "What bloody nonsense is this?"

11.23 on the clock.

The sheikh flicks through the papers in puzzlement until the omission is pointed out to him with a stab of an agitated finger.

"Ma'alish . . . ma'alish," it doesn't matter,

says the sheikh. We grab the clerk's stamp thrust it into the sheikh's hand, pass his pen to him, rip off the document we require, vault the counter, break the 200 metres sprint record across the compound and gun the truck up to the chain. We leap from the cab with bags open, arms raised the legs akimbo for the personal check. Stamp, stamp, goes the official and we hurtle back into the cab.

11.29 and 30 seconds. The chain drops. We are through! The gates swing to behind the trailer.

The engine sings, the wheels rumble, the air brakes hiss, we cruise through six, seven into eighth gear. Rolling, rolling, rolling. Hallelujah!

15

*S*AUDI ARABIA! The land of everything, the country of nothing. From
north to south, 1,300 miles of emptiness
with a hostile, lethal climate so vile and cruel
that no one lived there, but for a handful of
scattered bedouin and eccentric pioneers,
until three decades ago. No white men had
known it at all until half-a-century ago,
indeed, Saudi Arabia did not exist as a
country until 1925. Yet from this
intimidating barren wilderness has come the
greatest concentration of wealth in the
commercial history of mankind. More money
per person, per year, per day, per minute
than ever known before.

Kuwait is immeasurably rich but Saudi
Arabia is immensely bigger and so wields
relatively more power. Money, money,
money—life here is all about money. The
problem is to comprehend the extent of such
wealth.

Let us take one example of a sheikh who
courts publicity, compared with those quiet

ones who maintain strict Islamic isolation and who scorn the West for everything except its money. Sheikh Mohommed Al-Fassi, who is related by marriage to King Khaled of Saudi Arabia, has been known as the Sheikh of Sunset Strip since he bought a million dollar mansion on Hollywood's Sunset Boulevard and painted it a livid lime green—to the horror and consternation of his neighbours.

"We only wanted the place to look more beautiful," one of his wives explained to outraged protesters.

His personal income from oil, property and other businesses he has floated is revealed as £1,700 million *a day*. Many of his businesses are private companies throughout the world and no figures are available for them. The sheikh discloses his living expenses as £1.5 million a month. This includes the up-keep of several houses in America, England and Saudi Arabia and fleets of Rolls-Royce and Lincoln Continental cars. His personal fortune is quoted, and not contested, as £3,243 million, which makes him a genuine six billion dollar man though not necessarily bionic. But who needs to be bionic with all that loot in the bank? As a teenager, his younger brother received an allowance of

£170,000 a month and proudly claimed to be "down to his last $80" by the end of the month.

Do such revelations distort the image of a country? If they do, it is in the interpretation that we ourselves place upon them. Western cities and pleasure resorts went out of their way to tempt Arabs to live it up with gaming and girls, encouraged them to buy into property and to spend, spend, spend. And then sneered at them for doing so.

But excess is a part of Saudi Arabia. After Kuwait City, the desert becomes more dramatic and disturbing, easy to become afraid of and wonder what would happen if you got lost or broke down. The sight inspires great respect, this is not for messing about in. Kuwait gives a false sense of security because it looks like a little Luxembourg on the map, somebody would be bound to find you in such a pocket handkerchief state. Saudi is as big as Europe.

From here, at Kafji on the border, we can mentally leap 1,000 miles ahead and remember a day in that appalling stretch of desert, the great, untracked, salt flat between Qatar and the United Arab Emirates. At that time, in the mid-1970s, no white man was

421

allowed through without bedouin guides. They squatted in the shade of their sand tractors and the desert looked serene, inviting and benign. Seen from the air-conditioned comfort of the cab, it could have been a brilliant summer's day on the beach at a grossly overblown Camber Sands.

It looked sublime enough through the windscreen to tempt you from the cab. Within 10 paces spittle dried and stuck to the palate; the tongue parched and curled to the roof of the mouth like paper shrivelling in a flame; a furnace scorched the inside of the nostrils and breath began to dry in the lungs. Vision blurred and thought became disconnected, only an insistent throb in the head said, "God, it can't be so hot, it isn't possible." And the heat began to smother and asphyxiate, to bubble in the veins and raise the body temperature to match the intensity of the desert furnace.

Ten yards back to the truck had become 10 miles of effort and the watchful bedu lifted you back into the cab and the shock of heat took an hour to dissipate.

And you were lucky.

Remember, too, the time when Alan Warner, Chris Bold, Richie Woods and Mike

Pearce were in this area, on the verge of this same desert and they had with them a fit, strong, young driver of 30. He climbed from his cab to mend a flat on the trailer. As he tried to fix the jack, his eyes glazed and he stiffened to rigidity, his face set and his mouth opened. Slowly he crumpled and sank to the sand. In the time taken to cover the 20 yards to where he lay, he was dead. His blood had boiled, he was past saving. There was nothing the cool of the cab could do to restore him. In two minutes, the heat had killed him. He left a widow and two young children.

Night falls as we run from Kuwait to Saudi. The crescent moon and evening star appear with startling brilliance and the reason for crescent and star emblems on so many national flags east of Suez becomes immediately apparent.

Along the desert road the lights of the truck throw curious, dancing shadows which give the illusion that the road is bordered by tall hedgerows. Rocks on the verges catch the beams of light and throw shadows, tiny pebbles on the road cast enormously magnified shadows. So you move through a valley of shadows. The sense of loneliness is overwhelming. You are moving, the road is rolling up, rushing toward you when you look down at it. But peering ahead to the limits of the light beams there is no sense of movement, only an illusion of being in a vacuum. Like the enormity of Saudi wealth, the intensity of the desert confounds the imagination.

The border post with Saudi Arabia emerges from the night like a string of pearls on a black cushion in a jeweller's darkened window. Even when the post becomes more clearly defined, and when the truck rumbles into the compounds to stop under the brightly lit canopies, the darkness beyond is absolute. The Kuwait-Saudi Arabia border posts are rich men's back doors leading to the servant's quarters. They are neat by Arab standards but the Arabs are not a tidy-minded race, the concept is alien to their nature. Arabia is one gigantic rubbish tip from beginning to end, every village and shack is surrounded by piles of refuse, discarded household goods, old cars, foundries full of tin cans, oil cans, old iron, mounds of used, worn out tyres, bones and unidentifiable debris.

Saudi Arabia paid an Anglo-American company, Saudi Pritchard, £10 million a year to keep the cities of Riyadh and Jeddah clean and this lucrative contract kept 3,000 British and Pakistani workers employed in each city. They were called in just in time to prevent the cities drowning in a deluge of litter resulting from their own super-affluence.* The Arab way is: if it's broken throw it away or abandon it where it breaks down. At Kafji, the same rule applies though there is not much to throw away in the border post itself. It is in the settlement which has grown around the post the litter begins in earnest.

From six o'clock in the evening until a quarter to seven, the place closes down for prayers. There will be five shutdowns every day, Fajr (dawn), Dhuhr (noon), Assr (afternoon), Maghreb (sunset) and Isha (night). For

* On the very day of writing this, Saudi Pritchard lost the cleaning contract in Riyadh. Their tender for its renewal after five years was undercut by a couple of millions. That is the way of things in all the Gulf states. Western companies do the pioneer work and establish the system, then Korean, Pakistani or Philippino companies, paying very much lower wages to their workers, move in and take over. Their incursion has devastated European and American civil engineering contracts and Western companies have lost huge sums in the process which is why they now concentrate on high technology. But it is not as simple as it seems on the surface, with big business handling the sort of capital sums the Saudis are paying, there are wheels within wheels. Some of which will become apparent as the tale continues.

this is the heart of Islam, the land of the forbidden cities of Mecca and Medina and the observance of Islam is obligatory in every detail: no alcohol, no pornography, no women, no pork, no products of the pig at all.

"Everything you fancy is forbidden. God, I miss my bacon and eggs for breakfast. The others, I'm glad to get a rest from them," comments one notoriously randy driver.

The luck is running well. A soldier signals us straight into the customs inspection bay, there is no wait in the compound. Nothing will happen until the morning, but it is a good start.

Now is the time to seek out the agent responsible for handling our business, who lives with the rest of the clearance agents in a row of lock-up shops just beyond the barrier. They are all cheerful "foreigners"—Yemenis, Sudanese, Jordanians and the like—so we can sit drinking our chi and have a giggle with them. (But whisper it, because laughter in Saudi is almost a sin and is looked upon as the voice of fools. The Saudis are not a fun-loving race.)

The agent sets about his business on our behalf. The main task is to work out how much money we will have to collect in customs duty when Riyadh is reached. We will have to collect the cash from the customers and bring it back here to the customs.

That is the Saudi system. The truck driver leaves his triptyches, the temporary import/export papers for the vehicle and trailer, at the customs post and they are returned to him when he hands over the money he has collected for his load. Only then is he allowed to leave.

For us this means a minimum extra journey of 930 miles from Riyadh back to Kafji to hand over the cash and collect the papers—a five minute task. Then we must turn round and head back to Riyadh and the Jordan border—unless we are diverted to Doha or the Emirates, which is a possibility.

On this subject, the border is agog with the story of an English "internal" driver who has "pulled a flanker" on the Saudis and "done a bunk", driving his cream coloured F10 Volvo clean out of the country and getting away scot free. He deposited a false set of triptyches with customs at the Selwa border coming out of Qatar, went to Riyadh and collected 30,000 Saudi Riyals (£4,400 at the time) in duty and then drove to Al-Hadethe on the

427

Jordan border and headed back to Britain. By the time that it was apparent that he was not returning to Selwa, he was half way to Europe.

There is anger among the European drivers because he has left a colleague at Selwa who is suffering the wrath of the Saudis over the affair. The agent at Selwa has had to make up the missing money out of his own pocket and the authorities have cracked down on all European drivers.

Stealing from the government is the most heinous of offences in Saudi Arabia and is treated as treason. "That's a hand-chop job, probably a head-chop job, if he's ever caught," the drivers agree.

Back at the truck, night has settled in and domesticity prevails in the compound. The atmosphere is relaxed and friendly and our Jordanian neighbours in the next truck invite us to a party. They spread their carpets on the ground under the star-flecked night sky, light enormous butane gas stoves to boil heavy iron kettles for the chi and summon their friends to sit and smoke.

The butane stoves are fun. Nothing at all like their functional European counterparts, they are huge, highly chromed and polished spheres which reflect all the people sitting cross-legged around them and spin off the flickers of the burning gas like a glitter-globe over a ballroom floor.

Since it is an improved open air tea party with the guests contributing assorted goodies, nuts, chewy seeds and various sticky goo, we supply the sugar and, with fitting delicacy, teaspoons. Ahmed skilfully wets the slender glasses with rich brown chi to about a quarter full. The teaspoons baffle him, he discards them, plunges both hands into the plastic sugar container and with a remarkable movement projects a stream of sugar into the glass until its contents reach the top. Then, flexing his cupped hands, he shuts off the stream until he is poised over the next glass. He does not spill a grain.

A remarkable fact that science has so far ignored is that real Arab chi will absorb twice its own volume of sugar before expanding. The liquid comes out at the consistency of liquid honey or golden syrup. We supply another kilo of sugar and continue drinking chi just to watch Ahmed perform his feat of dexterity and defy the laws of nature.

The Jordanians are humping steel, 90 ton a time, up to Iraq and doing it at half the economic rate for a European. Even at that low price it has made them rich men by Jordanian standards. The truck is earning them between £1,200 and £1,800 a month. With good luck and an exceptionally quick run through customs posts, they can sometimes earn £2,400 or £3,000 over a five week period. There are three or four of them per truck, members of the same family, so they all live together when at home. That sort of income was unheard of in a working class family before Saudi Arabia got rich. The Saudis may be funny people but like the Kuwaitis they do spread their wealth around.

Vast amounts of the Gulf oil riches are siphoned off to poor Third World countries in return for labour. Gulf wealth is, in fact, the mainstay of many desperate Third World economies. This is a fact not often recognised by Western economists and governments and which only becomes strikingly apparent when you confront the Third Worlders toiling by the hundreds of thousands in the Gulf.

Nevertheless, the Arabs are baffling, infuriating, arrogant and plain stupid as well as being intolerant. The noble, fascinating Arab is a myth created by T. E. Lawrence in his

Seven Pillars of Wisdom and Edward Fitz-gerald with his translation of the Rubaiyat of Omar Khayyam. The real romantic desert Arab was a scruffy individual who never knew better than to live in a filthy tent and died by the thousands from starvation when the rains failed—for the truth of that, read Doughty's *Travels in Arabia Deserta*. Doughty was one of the two odd-balls who roamed Arabia before any other white men were allowed in, he died in 1926, a year after Saudi Arabia came into existence as a unified kingdom.

The curtain goes up on the Kafji pantomime at seven o'clock in the morning. The bedu and the sheikhs arrive, flanked by their respective escorts of Pakistani labourers who will do all the work while the Saudis look on. They will strip every truck and unload each individual item for scrutiny and then reload it all if they are satisfied with their examin-ation—a state of affairs which cannot be taken for granted no matter how innocent the cargo.

This can happen on any border into Saudi, and with disastrous consequences. At Halar Ammar, on the road from Jordan to Medina, a mistranslation from the English to the Arabic on Dave Anderson's manifest caused untold trouble. As part of his cargo for the Oman Defence Department, he was carrying a batch of runway flares used for night flying from airstrips. They were oil cans with a long spout which was lit at the end to make a flare, similar to those used to indicate road works at night. By error, runway flares had been translated as "rifle spares", and it is forbidden to transport armaments through Saudi Arabia. Explanations were useless, argument was to no avail. "Everything off," the guards commanded at rifle point. So great drums of electric cable, machines weighing two, three and five tons each and all the odds and ends were levered off the trailer and tumbled into the sand. Crates were smashed open and packages ripped apart. Then, satisfied, the customs officers altered the manifest and cleared the cargo. Fork-lift trucks and a gang of labourers had to be brought from Amman to get the stuff back on to the trailer.

At Turayf, the old Saudi border on the Trans Arabian Pipeline, and across the desert from the old British fort, H4, Mike Pearce completely forgot that he had a 2 lb pack of Wall's best back bacon in his fridge—forbidden fruit in Saudi Arabia. The offending contraband was lifted from the cab by a soldier using a pair of tongs so that he should not be contaminated by the dreaded pig. A fire was lit in the sand and the package dropped on to it so that the still desert air was scented by the succulent aroma of sizzling bacon. European drivers quit their cabs and stood, mouths watering and dribbling, in the smoke of the fire. It proved to be an expensive fry-up—Mike earned a £200 fine for "attempted smuggling of forbidden goods".

At Kafji the customs set to work with less than a vengeance, the Pakistanis could not be accused of rushing about. But, then, it was hardly inspiring work. The six trucks in front of us in the bays were Arab vehicles loaded with four inch diameter steel pipes, 40 feet long. They were stacked, in the usual Arab fashion, 10 to 12 feet high on the trailers, double the height ever seen in Europe.

The loads were ordinary, empty, steel pipes, open at both ends and laid in alternate layers with the flanges at opposite ends so that the loads stayed flat and level. From the back of the trailers they formed a honeycomb pattern of circles and rectangles with concave sides where the pipes rested on each other. Looking through them from the back, they made quite pretty patterns against the light of the sky. The full load was clearly visible from whichever angle it was surveyed. However, the bedouin sheikh customs officer insisted that the cargo be completely unloaded.

Rattle, clang, clang . . . with maddening regularity the pipes clattered on to the concrete floor of the bay. A labourer lifted each individual pipe to eye level to allow the sheikh to look down it. Clunk, he dropped it to the floor again.

Rattle, clang, clang . . . clunk. The monotonous noise went on all morning. Eight hundred and sixty-four pipes per truck, 5,184 clank, clank, clunks in all.

With the back of the tilt open, the tarpaulin turned back and the cargo exposed, boredom can rapidly become alarm. The manifest lists 781 packages and maybe this gink is going to insist on opening every one. Let us try to convince him that the 641 identical four feet square boxes, all contain identical parts for circular filing cabinets. They are all well-packed and sealed with staples and strong adhesive tape exactly in the condition they left the factory and no one back in England has secreted a bottle of Scotch in any of them.

Tell him that English factory workers do not go giving away £6 bottles of Scotch or gin, or vodka, rum, martini, brandy or champagne for that matter, as a whim to corrupt Islamic morals.

OK, let him open half a dozen.

"What do they do? Well, they are for putting things in . . . files. Yes, I agree, most files are square and big. But these are special files and they have to be assembled . . . put together . . . made . . . built . . . all sam, sam . . . oh, for Christ's sake show him the instruction leaflet."

There is no percentage in doing that, he reads it upside down.

Every item must be described in detail and he checks it in a huge Arab dictionary. File is in the dictionary. Yes, yes, that's it. Success.

Hell! "Reprographic equipment" isn't in the dictionary, nor is "kello fishke reproduction templates". If only those bright technological whizz-kids back home would stop inventing smart words and use only those in the dictionary. "Dry ammonia . . ." No, that is wrong, signals the sheikh. The dictionary says that ammonia is a wet, pungent liquid. He is no fool, this stuff is dry and hardly smells at all.

"Reprographic equipment—microfilm. Oh, no, sheikhy, please no, please don't open it. Please don't pull out every sheet to look at it in the light. Very well, if you must, but please seal it up again with official blue customs tape and mark it "opened by customs". Even then, the chances are that the customer will not want to pay for a consignment of ruined goods. Why should he? Would you? There is bound to be trouble—and problems—when it reaches the microfilm company in Riyadh, they won't pay and we will never get out of Saudi Arabia. These inoffensive little packets have travelled 5,000 miles through hell and high water only to be ruined on the doorstep of their destination. It is like being away out in front in an egg-and-spoon-race and dropping the egg an inch before the tape.

The Austrian driver watching the proceedings is laughing, the cheeky bastard, he's a typical Alpine Turk, a menace on anybody's road. He produces a thermos flask and pours a cup of iced coffee, maybe he isn't so bad after all.

"I am laughink so that I am not weeping,

my frent," he says, "I haf four 10 kilo sacks of special furnace cement aboard, very special material. It has to be used within 24 hours of being opened, or fini, useless, zat is zat. For a year, we haf brought eight ton to Saudi Arabia, only two tons delivered in good condition. All the rest torn open wiz ze knife. Fini. Now we haf the sacks printed specially in the Arab language, still they open them."

The next task is to explain the workings and function of a highly computerised embroidery machine programmed to produce identification badges for the Saudi police and army.

"Well, it is a . . . and it does . . ." Forget it. Just say that the explanation started at 2.35 pm and ended at 5.20 in a state of exhaustion.

A consignment of contraceptives from the London Rubber Company once caused problems for Harry Robinson. The Arab customs officer could not understand what they were, he thought from the manifest description that rubber sheaths ought to be gloves. But they had only one finger. An intricate mime commenced with the customs man indicating five fingers and asking if they were gloves.

"Nix gloves," said Harry with a negative

shake of his head, "contraceptives . . ." But it was clear that the customs officer did not comprehend. The problem was how to explain contraception.

Now it was Harry's turn to mime the intended use of the goods. "Ficke, ficke?" he demonstrated with clenched fist and forearm.

Yes, the customs officer understood that. So Harry pointed to the Durex packet and mimed rolling a Durex on to his raised arm.

"Now—ficke, ficke . . . nix bambinos." To emphasise the latter point, he outlined a pregnant stomach with his hands, crossed it out with a gesture and repeated: "Nix bambinos."

The customs man carefully considered the packet, frowning intently. He summoned a colleague who had the barest smattering of English and they conferred at length.

Eventually the colleague asked: "Ficke, ficke . . . nix madame?"

After two hours' argument they settled for the translation: "Medical, for ladies' health."

A watching driver remarked: "You played the part perfectly, Harry—you looked a right prick sorting that lot out."

There is an incident which those who know

but wish still to be taken seriously are disinclined to recount.

A crate of rubber goods was broken open at customs and beneath the legitimate goods were three layers of life size, blow-up sex dolls, which the cartons said came from Hong Kong. They would not have been noticed but for the design of the cartons which came well within the Saudi definition of pornography. It was explicit to the degree that it explained that the dolls had pubic hair "so real you cannot tell the difference".

It was enough for the immediate confiscation of the whole cargo and the arrest of the stunned driver.

The dolls were inflated and—the big joke for many who later retailed the story—on the orders of the local mullah, they were taken outside, stood against a wall and shot.

This was not so funny for the unfortunate driver who spent many a long week festering in a Saudi Arabian jail until it could be established that he could not possibly have known the contents of the crate and was an unwitting dupe in the whole affair.

Eric Barker, who as a driver working internals with his own truck has more to lose than many, has a point when he insists: "It's all very well belly-aching and laughing about the way they keep ripping the truck cabs to pieces, but they still keep finding the stuff—booze, porn and drugs. Some people think they can fool them with impunity and they scream when they get caught."

It is not just anybody who walks freely into Saudi Arabia, they are pretty choosy about who they let in and it is difficult to get a visa. Only people with business in the country or doing some good for them are admitted. The most important document the would-be worker in Saudi Arabia can have is the "Non-objection Certificate" which is a paper to say that they do not object to you being there.

The Saudis keep a black list, blot your copy book once and you will never return to the kingdom, your name will come up on the computer and you will be barred. It is not a tourist paradise. Nor is a valid visa a guarantee of getting into the country once you arrive at its borders. They want to know the why and when and wherefore, and if too many of your category have recently arrived you must turn round, go home and wait for the next quota. Argument will get you nowhere.

A driver who had done the run many times

was promoted in his company, but he still drove a truck if the need arose. He arrived at Turayf with his new passport bearing the proud inscription "Company Director". "Sorry," they said, "no more company directors this month."

Police control in Saudi Arabia is an ordeal if only because the police look like children. They are in their early teens and their faces are contorted with the anxieties of extreme youth if they are confronted with a problem. And youth makes them arrogant and determined to show their authority. Not one on the border at Kafji has yet felt the need of a razor, nor are they any too bright. A difficulty is knowing exactly what kind of police they are, there are so many: army, civil, security, traffic and religious—unless you are fluent in Arabic, you will never know.

"In transit, valid for a number of journeys for six months" stamped on the visa utterly confuses the lad. He is a stickler for accuracy: "You stay Riyadh unload—not transit. You must have entry visa and also exit visa. Transit no good."

The Saudi dare not be allowed to lose face, so the officer must evolve a formula to clear the situation. He, in turn, must see his superior who will amend the visa to say it is in transit to Riyadh and then in transit again back to Kafji, and then in transit to Al-Hadethe, then honour will be satisfied and if other changes are then required they can be done in Riyadh. It only takes three hours, which is but a fleeting second on the Arab timescale.

Night has fallen again, all is well. Alex Graves says: "Through in a day, bloody good border this."

The open road is here again. And a pretty ropey old road it is by Saudi standards, soon it will improve.

There is a chicken and chi shop in the village just down the road. It is Arab tat with friendly heaps of rubbish piled high. We eat a disconcerting meal. A bedouin tribesman in full bedu gear stands one-legged, leaning on a shepherd's crook, three feet from the table, expressionless, without the blink of an eye, he stares straight into our faces. He does not respond to smiles, gestures or offers of food and cigarettes.

He has been at the hookah pipe and is probably stoned out of his mind.

Outside in the rutted, pot-holed sandy

street are old cans, olive oil cans, lubricating oil cans, fruit juice cans, tomato juice cans, Coke cans, exotic food cans, plastic water bottles and liquid detergent containers. Every can, bottle and container used in the course of a restaurant's business—and there are several here—is thrown outside to rest in perpetuity with the rotting tyres and old exhausts.

On a pole across the street is a solar-powered telephone, its nest of solar cells placed at an angle on top of the pole, the loud-speaker phone installation at head level. You can call anywhere in the world from here. And anywhere in Saudi Arabia free.

It is a dark night but with brilliant stars overhead, so big and so luminous that they look ripe for plucking. Now the desert is lying empty and vast on either side of the road. But there is no real black of night in this area for this is the land of eternal fires.

Great tongues of flame leap from the desert and loll on the evening breeze, they flicker and light the night sky casting weird shadows and turning the desert red while reflecting pink on the billowing clouds of their own smoke. Not a soul is to be seen, not a movement, just the dancing flames. They are burning off the gases from the sea of oil under these desert sands. There are no oil derricks to be seen here, the oil wells are three feet high. Just a capped pipe plunging into the ground with a valve on top and a horizontal pipe carrying away the black juices of the earth.

An oil well, by rights, ought to be a little Eiffel Tower over a hole, or at least a rocking-donkey in the Californian style. Here it is a black stump in the sand—a stump you can sit on and feel the life blood of the industrial world flowing under your bottom.

However, you do not sit for long on your oil well, the soldiers may come along at any moment and they do not like people too near their oil wells and pipelines, they may start shooting.

This red-tinged, shiny road leads to "Watford Gap", the drivers' desert junction, and also to the ancient and historic oasis of Al-Hofuf. Before Al-Hofuf comes Dammam. And Dammam is a name that should be written large in all modern history books. For this is the place where in 1934 a small group of "wildcat" engineers from SOCAL—the Standard Oil Company of California—bitter, disillusioned men who were crucified by sun and pestilence and at the end of their tether, sank a test oil well on the Dammam Dome and hit the biggest gusher ever.

They sank the well that changed the world.

16

WE park at The Triangle overnight, not Watford Gap, because it is night and night driving in Saudi is not to be recommended. Often it has to be done, but nobody is happy about it. Terrible accidents happen at night, there are inexplicable head-on collisions. The reason is well known to the foreign drivers. The Arab drivers are either exhausted or stoned out of their minds. Some work all day without a break, covering hundreds and hundreds of kilometres for 10 or 12 consecutive hours; others relax in the traditional way with a hookah pipe and take to the road in a dazed, soporific stupor. The roads do not help, they run for a thousand kilometres without a bend and the dazzle reflected from their surfaces is exhausting. Arab drivers will cut across deserts where the incessant, pounding noise of driving on sand keeps them awake and as soon as they come on to a smooth main road they fall asleep.

Apart from those hazards, our lights now

are not too hot. At the border we had to take off all our spots, their use by foreigners is forbidden. We have diced through a couple of tricky police check points without trouble, but to try further would be to push our luck. Our main headlights are illegal in Saudi Arabia where quartz halogen lamps are banned on foreign vehicles, though allowed on Arab trucks and cars. At the last police check point, hundreds of smashed and confiscated headlamps were strung on wires outside the post. If the police spot a quartz halogen lamp, they smash a hammer through it. If they did that to us we would be blind since Scanias can only use these kind of lamps, others will not fit. This rule was introduced because a powerful prince was dazzled by a foreign truck as he drove home one night.

Safety regulations are non-existent. On any drive you encounter at least a dozen broken down trucks with snapped axles caused by excessive, monumental, overloading. Loads are secured in perilous ways so that they overhang the truck by several feet. Lights may be on or off, red at the front, white at the back or vice versa. It is not uncommon to find a 12-year-old schoolboy at the wheel of a powerful car or tractor. And all night long the camels and donkeys stray across the road. During the day they are a menace, but at night they are lethal.

The next morning it is still a fair spin into Riyadh and there is a lot of traffic about. But we will still drive for miles without seeing another vehicle. We are now at a crossroads. The road to our right runs northwest along the tapline, the Trans Arabian Pipeline, and leads to Jordan on the other side of the country; to our left, the road runs southeast to Al Hofuf and Qatar. Our route lies almost due south to Riyadh. It will take us past Ain Dar, the huge oil installation and pumping station.

These roads are meant for business, there is little or no pleasure traffic about in Saudi, and they carry some colossal loads. The oil company drags drilling derricks along the roads, huge transformers are trundled along on 50 and 60 wheel low-loader trailers. They fill the width of the carriageway which makes for a very hairy situation indeed when you meet them and there is only soft sand at the side of the road.

A most spectacular and horrific accident involving such a load and a passing vehicle occurred at Ain Dar. A couple of huge American Kenworth tractor units were hauling a drilling rig when an articulated, 60 foot long petrol tanker, driven by an Arab, approached from the opposite direction. Eye witnesses, the few who survived, say that it looked as if he was asleep at the wheel. He did not slacken speed as he approached and he hit the rig and ripped out the side of the tank. Tanker, rig and the surrounding area were engulfed in a fireball. It burned so fiercely that it melted the road. Bulldozers sent to assist in rescue work also caught fire in the intense heat. It was a holocaust.

We have got to make fast time into Riyadh from here. It is important to reach Riyadh early this evening to get a quick start in the morning to try to complete our business before Friday. Otherwise we will be stuck again when the city closes down for the religious holiday.

Already the trade mark of desert driving is all too apparent—blown tyres. Thousands of blackened, disintegrating tyres lie by the side of the road in a continuous, jagged line—tyres of every size and shape with gaping holes and rips in them. The line will stretch from here right into the heart of the city, and from the city along the roads to the far boundaries of the country. Interspersed with the tyres, are the wrecks of cars, trucks, tankers, caravans; old and new, they will stay until they dissolve into the landscape.

The tyres and wrecks spell out a story of death and mayhem. The road is the culprit, straight as a die and flat. It is psychologically impossible not to be tempted into excessive speed with nothing except a straight, open road in front of you. The sheer tedium urges speed.

Inside the cab it is cool, the air conditioning keeps a steady temperature. Outside the sun is beating down at a temperature of 150°, the road is too hot to stand on, the tyres are burning from the sun and friction. If a steering wheel tyre blows when the speed is high death is the most probable outcome for there is no room on this road to manoeuvre. If something is coming the other way, you hit it. If not, you hit soft sand and roll, and 40 tons of rolling metal does not allow much leeway for survival.

Another hazard is dust. Dust settles on Saudi Arabia like gloom on a manic-depressive and it produces the same symptoms of anger, frustration, despair and futility. There is no way out of the dust, there is no escape, the dust is forever. You take every precaution yet every day dust will still settle one-eighth of an inch thick in the cab. It will penetrate clothing and shoes, it clogs the nostrils, the eyes, the lungs.

It blows on the road in a swirling fog and obliterates all vision. Dust is an unpredictable danger, it falls from a clear sky and rises from an empty road to engulf all moving things.

And then there is the wind which rolls unimpeded across a thousand miles of nothing to buffet man, beast and vehicle continuously. The desert is seldom a still place.

Make no mistake, Riyadh is a magnificent and wonderful city; a miraculous combination of ingenuity, skill and courage has created civilisation out of a hostile wilderness. It is a place of grandeur, style and, above all, space.

In a remarkably short time—10 years—it has become a resplendent capital city.

However, it is a Xanadu without a pleasure dome. Islam does not allow much pleasure nor does it cater for it, the boredom lies as

451

thick and heavy as the dust. Behind the expensive marble facings, the stainless steel fittings, the rich velvet drapes and fine, matured timbers there is an oppressive atmosphere. No foreigner ever feels comfortable in Riyadh and usually with good reason, for every stranger is suspect and closely watched. Not one foreigner will ever say: "I am here because I like it." They say: "I am here because of the money."

In Riyadh we stay with friends who have taken a villa. They are paying £12,000 a year for it, but behind its walls they have found some degree of privacy, security and social life. Relationships with Saudi families are rare for the system inhibits sociability.

Our villa is a product of the private building boom. It is expensive—and jerry-built. Which means that it looks good and is actually well constructed for the area. But no insurance company will give cover on it for more than 10 years, and that only at a push. With all its modern materials and fittings, the villa is as traditionally Arab as a mud structure in a remote desert village. It is built inside-out from a European home. The wall is the dominant feature, an eight-foot high wall completely enclosing the structure with two security gates let into it, one for people the other for the cars.

The European builds his house with living rooms on the outside to take advantage of the light and the view, the Arab builds his home with the living rooms in the middle, away from the light and often windowless, to keep out that all-searching, blinding sun. He also divides his home on the Upstairs, Downstairs principle with the women's quarters as sharply divided from the main house as the servants quarters are in an English mansion. It proves to be very useful to Europeans, who have to share villas because of the expense—they don't get under each other's feet.

Through ornate wrought-iron double doors lies the main hall and a large vestibule forming an L-shaped room. The vestibule has six wash-basins side by side with large mirrors over each basin. Enclosed showers and squatter and pedestal loos are at the end. Green, heavy wash-basins are the feature of the room. Out of context, away from the bathroom, they look an attractive and presentable furnishing. They act as a functional celebration of the presence of clean, running water in an environment which may never see rain for 15 years. They are joyous things, you are grateful and happy that they are there, there is no greater pleasure in the world than to turn those taps and feel the hot and cold running water on your skin.

Without doubt water is the greatest single benefit the wealth of oil has brought to the Arabs. The water from the tap in Riyadh is perfectly drinkable—in the short term. Europeans do not drink it because it is so rich in mineral deposits that, over a period of time, it causes liver and kidney complaints. A glance inside a kettle shows the strength and variety of the deposits, however, they do not affect the Arabs who have drunk the water all their lives.

We live in marbled halls: mauve marble with delicate traceries of deep purple, peach marble with red and black patterns, black marble with white and grey markings, the staircase itself is marble. The overall effect is marred by the fact that it doesn't quite fit, there are irregular gaps between the slabs and holes where it doesn't meet. Ugly, rough concrete shows under the elegant stairs. And the electrics . . . oh dear, the electrics . . . a tangle of multicoloured spaghetti.

Of course it is wrong to expect Arabs to have the building skills which are inherited and basic in Europe—they have never needed them in the nomadic life they have led for centuries. Nevertheless, their introduction to Western techniques does produce curious side effects. The first carpenter to arrive in Saudi Arabia to teach them Western skills with wood was brought in by Aramco in 1936. He was left-handed. To this day, left-handed Arab carpenters abound in the country even though they are naturally right-handed.

If an Englishman's home is his castle, an Arab's home is his fortress within the barricades of his high walls. That is a tradition of the country, intrusion and trespass are alien to the Arab character—a fact that stands foreigners in good stead. There is safety within the confines of the home.

The national social occupation of Saudi Arabia is illicit drinking. Because it is forbidden the ex-pats pursue drink with the frenzy of flappers during Prohibition, and they run the same risks. There is ample booze in Saudi Arabia but the genuine stuff prices itself out of the market even with the inflated wages paid there. Most people baulk at paying £60 to £80 a bottle for Scotch, except the sheikhs. There is at least one alcoholic sheikh in the city who consumes two bottles a day and uses powerful smelling herbs to disguise his breath when the need arises.

Excellent wines are made, some are first class, and good beer is brewed, but the hard stuff comes in the form of sidiki. Sidiki is a distillation of pure sugar and it can be powerful. Used as a mixer, it puts a distinct and very acceptable kick into Coke, Seven-Up and fruit juice.

Sidiki is a tricky beverage to make. So the best suppliers are the "big boys" with access to the necessary equipment. This has led to serious diplomatic incidents involving companies which are household names throughout the world, whose staffs have used available technical equipment to make illicit sidiki. Temperatures are critical in the distillation process. At exactly 74° Centigrade, drinkable ethyl alcohol is produced. At temperatures higher than that, within very narrow limits, methyl alcohol (wood alcohol) is made. And that can result in madness or death for the unhappy consumer.

So the first sip of sidiki from a new supplier is taken warily. Supplies nevertheless manage to adequately satisfy a large demand and to oil the wheels of social intercourse sufficiently to make a party possible. And, with little else to do—particularly for women—there are many parties behind closed doors.

Inside the walls all is free and easy, English hospitality. Outside the repressions of Islam are rigidly enforced and the unacceptable face of feudalism grates on Western nerves. First, there is the igtalla, the identity card with a photograph which every foreigner must, by law, wear clearly displayed. All visitors must carry their passports for immediate production. Any Saudi citizen, from a schoolchild upward, can demand to see your identification at any time and it is an offence to refuse to show it. The police are everywhere in their many varieties and it is still difficult to tell which is which.

A British official warns: "Be careful what you say and to whom you talk. Arabs can be very touchy about sensitive subjects and can quite easily take offence at a remark which seems innocence itself to you. Whatever you do, don't talk freely in taxis. The majority of the drivers are members of the political police, the secret police to you. Many of them speak English as well as you do, but they will never let you know, and they will report back to their superiors exactly what you have said and where you have been, so watch it. This is a very security conscious country."

The universal Arabic madness of the main road is prevalent here too. They have built the roads to accommodate it, all are at least four-lane roads, very many are eight-lane roads in both directions. Being so new, this is the first city created for the car. "Give it space," the authorities commanded, and space it got.

Traffic moves in spurts and crawls because the roads are criss-crossed with speed-ramps a foot high every few hundred metres. These are spring-wrecking lifesavers put down to curb the lunatic speeds Saudis drive at. This is equivalent to main drainpipes being cut in half and laid across the road every 100 yards down the Embankment, the Strand, Park Lane, the Mall and Oxford Street in London; it cuts the speeds but makes for a bumpy ride. The Cadillac in front of us just went airborne over the ramps, he hit them at about 70 mph and flew.

Traffic lights are tricky because nobody seems to obey them to a pattern, sometimes half the traffic stops and the other half crosses against the red, sometimes nobody stops. An American friend we know from the villa (one has to be circumspect in writing about friends and acquaintances and not name them for fear of repercussions) was faced with a dilemma at these very lights. They were red, he was stationary and a policeman was standing by the side of the road. The rest of the traffic in adjoining lanes surged by, the din of hooters behind him became deafening, so he slipped into gear and moved forward. The policeman arrested him. He spent three days in the infamous, vile main jail before his company could find him.

The police do not notify anybody when they make an arrest, nor do they willingly disclose where the arrested person is. It is incumbent upon friends to probe and press for information otherwise the prisoner will just rot. The holding jails are even worse than the central prison, they are not just inhuman they are subhuman. In fairness it must be said that efforts are being made to improve them as the building boom progresses. However, the thought of them is as bad as the fact of them.

An English friend once failed to turn up for work and after three days of persistent enquiries the police conceded that he had been arrested for a traffic infringement and was being held at an out of town surburban police station. Another day went by while the necessary papers and permits were arranged giving permission to his friends to see him. At the old-fashioned, mud-walled police station there was not a sign of the man or anywhere he could be—all the rooms in the station could be seen from the entrance and so could the walled yard outside. A heated argument ensued with the sergeant about the validity and meaning of the papers, he insisted on telephoning the main police station and discussing them with his superiors. Three hours went by and it became apparent that the prisoner's friends were, in the eyes of the police sergeant, as suspect and culpable as the prisoner himself. If he had his way, they would all be incarcerated with the prisoner, wherever he was.

"Where is he?" the friends asked the Sudanese interpreter, an employee of the same company and a very nice man.

"They will not say," said the Sudanese.

The sergeant sat in his large, brass studded armchair behind his desk and rapped out his orders to subordinates with autocratic disdain; they jumped when he spoke. He regarded the "prisoner's friends" with scarcely concealed contempt. The arrival of a senior officer from headquarters broke the stalemate.

Eventually the sergeant stood up and tilted his chair backwards on hinges which bolted the back legs to the floor. He pulled on a metal ring set in the floorboards and lifted a flap to reveal a barred grill. He lifted the grill. There, in a hole three feet square by seven feet deep was the prisoner. He was immobilised by cramp, covered in insect bites and soaked in his own urine.

Eventually it was agreed that he should be released into the custody of his employers and a due sum of money changed hands. Outside he said: "Oh, it wasn't too bad. It was a bit awkward if you dropped any of the food they passed down to you. There wasn't the room to bend to pick it up. But it wasn't too bad."

"What did you do? Why were you arrested?"

"I didn't do anything. Some bloody sheikh came across the lights on the red and ran into me. His bumper was jammed in my doors, but they nicked me."

Geoff Frost, the Astran driver, was

motoring into the centre of Riyadh when he was stopped by the police because of some hold-up ahead. The young policeman stood by his cab door shouting and gesticulating but Geoff could not understand him. He wound down his window and leaned out— smiling. The smile did not last long, the arrogant young lout in uniform, a whipper-snapper of a kid, produced a four foot length of heavy duty electrical cable from behind his back and laid it in a fierce whiplash across Geoff's face.

"I wasn't standing for that", says the quiet Geoff, "I don't take that treatment from anybody."

He is a big man with forearms like ham shanks. He climbed from the cab with a great, livid, red weal swelling down the left side of his face. The infant policeman was unsling-ing his gun. Geoff helped him, took it from his hands and flung it into the desert. Then he took the cable. Next he thumped the policeman and knocked him into oblivion for a couple of hours.

At the police station the Saudis fumed: "You are very bad Englishman."

And Geoff replied: "And he is a bloody bad Saudi."

"No. You must admit you are a very bad Englishman."

"OK, I am a bad Englishman as long as he is a bad Saudi."

A conversation like this can go on for hours, but finally the evidence of the ugly weal across Geoff's face coupled with the implement that caused it was too much for even Saudi law to ignore. With company and consular officials contributing to the argument, Geoff was grudgingly released after 24 hours.

So we pick our way carefully into the city centre. The road runs by a fun-fair, a genuine fun-fair with roller-coasters, helter-skelters, coconut shies, bumper cars, ferris wheels and blaring fairground music. It looks like fun for all the family, a day out, a treat. But one half is reserved for men and their children and the other half for women and their offspring. There is a tall dividing canvas between the two halves and separate entrances.

The depot we want is somewhere in the city so we drive along boulevards lined with palm trees and marble-faced palaces. Workmen are busily drilling holes into marble blocks on many buildings. A new city ordinance has decreed that all marble shall be plugged and bolted to the main structures of buildings. There have been problems with marble facings on Riyadh buildings. Architects had not made sufficient provision for the extremes of temperature and half-ton slabs of marble have been falling like autumn leaves from trees. Which has been something of a headache both for architects and passers-by.

Two English ladies from Kent, young wives whose husbands are working in Riyadh, stop and stare in unconcealed amazement to see an English truck, with English plates and the GB sign, in a main street in Riyadh. They wear the black chador over their European dresses to save trouble in the streets.

"You can't have come all the way from England," they gasp. "How on earth do you do it? We never thought it could be possible."

They are excited and happy to see new English faces, chattering and asking for news of home as well as trying to be helpful with directions. We must try to come round for a meal, they long for new people to talk to. We are in the cab, they are feet below us on the pavement.

Suddenly their faces cloud and the smiles

464

die. They say hurriedly: "We'd better fly or we'll be arrested. There is a policeman coming over, he will charge us with talking to strange men in the street and they'll put us in jail without any questions. Remember the telephone number." With that they are off skipping down the street as fast as fashion-sandals will allow them to go, clutching their chadors round themselves.

The policeman stops and takes our number—or pretends to take our number because he cannot read or write English letters. You soon tumble that dodge.

The girls might have been arrested and flung into prisons as bad as the men have to suffer. Nobody would tell their families where they were. Distraught husbands and employers would be badgering hospitals and police stations for information and receiving a blank denial of any knowledge of the women—until several days had passed.

The vivacious and charming Nurse P suffered that fate and found herself in a curious situation. We met her at a party on one of the lavish compounds run by European companies for their staffs working in Riyadh. On these compounds life is indeed luxurious and full compensation for the hardships endured during the working day. They contain splendid accommodation, luxurious swimming pools, their own TV and radio services, first class restaurants and every convenience it is possible to provide. People live their entire expatriate lives in them, venturing out only when absolutely necessary or on sight-seeing trips. On a good compound it is possible to insulate yourself completely from the Saudi way of life. And that is a good idea if you find the way of life offensive—or frightening—especially if you are a white, free-born woman, over 21 and not prepared to be ranked as a chattel or third class citizen.

Nurse P was being driven back to her quarters at the hospital after an evening with friends at the compound. They ran late and it was exactly three minutes over the curfew when they arrived at the hospital. The doors were closed. She was wisely travelling in the back seat while her English male companion drove. Women are not allowed to drive and the Saudis do not like men and women sitting side by side. The policeman examined their igtallas and because the names did not match, he arrested the woman. Nothing her male companion could do could prevent her being taken away, nor was he allowed to accompany her.

Four days later she was arraigned on an immorality charge and duly convicted, her papers were marked and she was ordered to be deported. But—Catch-22—nobody can leave Saudi Arabia without an exit visa. And her employers declined to authorise the issue of an exit visa—they insisted that she should stay until the day her contract expired. There she was, branded a Scarlet Woman, a prostitute, an immoral person, desperate by now to get the hell out of it, but unable to leave. The getting out can be tougher than the getting in. The little piece of paper in your hand and the stamp in your passport can be as valuable as life itself.

The way things go, when the luck runs against you, it keeps on running against you, and the Arabs will help it along. John Martin, Chris Bedder and their crew ran into trouble driving from Riyadh to Doha in Qatar. Chris developed mechanical trouble and blew his gear box near Al-Hofuf, so they decided the best thing to do was to ditch the trailer, drive on to Doha, where there were repair facilities, fix the tractor and return for the trailer later. It is safe to leave anything in Saudi Arabia, there is no thieving, thieves have their hands cut off and, despite what enlightened Western criminologists say to the contrary, it works in as much as there is virtually no thieving in Saudi.

Outside Al-Hofuf is a huge truck park, acres and acres of it, a little desert on its own with a security fence around it. It was empty, so they chose a spot at random and wound down the trailer legs. Chris pulled the tractor away and the trailer began sinking, the left leg went down, and down, and down. They watched in numbed, helpless amazement. Still it sank down until it rested on the main girders.

Apprehensively they shambled over to look into the gaping hole that had appeared, treading warily for fear of what might be under their feet. The leg had gone through the water main supplying Al-Hofuf and the precious, scarce liquid was bubbling away into the desert sands.

"What a bloody silly place to put a water main," said Anderson.

"What a bloody silly place to park a trailer," said John.

"A whole bloody desert to park in, miles of it, and we have to stick it on a water main.

Would you believe it? What shall we do?" Chris Bedder asked.

"Well," said John, with grave deliberation, "I fancy there'll be problems about this, mucho, mucho problems, knowing the way the rag-'eads' brains work. So I think we ought to fuck off, before they catch us with mud on our boots. Then we'll come back—or *you'll* come back, Chris—all innocent and say, 'Fancy that, the leg's gone through the water main. It was all right when I left it, and it is an official truck park.' So get in the cabs and shove off, a bit sharpish."

After a day in the workshops at Doha the gear box was repaired and Chris went back into Saudi Arabia to sort out the water main problem. He arrived at Al-Hofuf to find a gang of workmen and engineers with lifting gear surrounding the trailer and an atmosphere of excitement which accompanies any Arab working party.

When Chris introduced himself they were quite nice about it. They were, however, going to find the contractor who laid the pipe and fry him alive for burying it two feet higher than the plans specified.

Chris apologised for the inconvenience he had caused, thanked them nicely for lifting his trailer out, climbed into his cab and drove back to the Saudi-Qatar border.

"No," said the Saudi border guard, "you cannot go out, you have used the visa to go out already. Now you must go out by Turayf."

"But that is the other side of the country." He explained about the breakdown and leaving the trailer because he couldn't tow it, and going back to pick it up.

"No," said the border guard, "you must go out by Turayf, the visa says so."

It seemeed the trailer could go through because that hadn't gone out and come back, but Chris couldn't. He argued, so they arrested him and sent him under guard back to Al-Hofuf where they lodged him in the hotel under house arrest. All he had with him were his shortie shorts, a T-shirt and his flip-flops.

For a week the argument went on: no, he could not go out into Qatar, no he could not catch an aircraft either to Qatar or London, he had to go out via Turayf and how he got there was his business.

In the hotel restaurant he had befriended a Pakistani doctor who had trained in London and was fluent in English since he had lived there most of his life. At the end of the week the doctor asked: "What are you like at being ill? If they think you are ill, they'll ship you out of here like a flash. If you can throw a wobbler in the restaurant and make it look as if you are suffering, I'll certify that you are sick and they'll deport you—I promise." By this time funds had come up from Qatar, so he was able to pay his hotel bill and collect his passport.

He put on a very good performance in the restaurant and frightened the life out of the staff and the Arab owners who are not good at dealing with illness. The doctor swore that he was severely ill and it could be anything from bubonic plague to cerebral palsy. In no time at all an American-style ambulance, siren blaring and lights flashing, arrived to transport him to the international airport at Dhahran where he was hurriedly placed in the charge of British Airways with instructions to get him home—quick.

He arrived at London Airport at seven o'clock on a January morning. It was a bleak, wintery day with a leaden grey sky and the airport was white with a covering of snow. Chris entered the terminal clutching his passport, a carton of duty free fags and a bottle of

Scotch wearing just his shortie shorts, T-shirt and flip-flops and wrapped in a bright red blanket loaned by British Airways.

Ron Prankerd was astonished to receive a telephone call saying: "This is Chris. I'm at London Airport. Don't ask any questions. Get me a shirt, 17 collar, a suit, 42 chest, 33 inner leg, a pair of socks, shoes size 11½ and an anorak. Don't ask any questions yet. And Ron, get them here quickly, please. Everybody is looking at me as if I'm a nutter."

Riyadh. Did we say clear by Thursday night?

Here we are on the merry-go-round again. This is the headquarters of the electricity company, we have a valuable load for them, but the guard is threatening to shoot us if we try to go in. It takes a long time to locate the man who will deal with us but when he does turn up, he is a delightful Yemeni gentleman with a mouthful of smiles and white teeth. We have to take the load to the new depot, in the desert outside the city. A guide will take us there. The guide is a young Arab boy who, for some reason, is petrified. He sits with his arms wrapped round his body and occasionally flicking his forefinger vaguely in the direction we should be going. But always too late, he signals after the turning, so we progress like a game of snakes and ladders. He takes us past the old university, a new, grand and elegant building but now replaced with a newer, bigger and more splendiforous edifice further out of town. This one is still used and at noon the students are leaving. They rush to their parked Cadillacs and Buicks while their European tutors hurry to Datsuns and Mazdas. Nobody ever looks backwards when they reverse, they shoot out blindly and dismiss collisions with a laugh. What does it matter? Ma'alish, it doesn't matter. There are huge showrooms all over town waiting to supply a replacement off the peg.

Our guide is not clear where to go. We have passed the same point three times and the experience is making him more introspective by the minute. Somebody has told him that Englishmen eat young Arabs for breakfast. In the fullness of time our destination appears on the horizon. It is sited on the rim of a hill and marked by a massive, spherical, water tower on stilts, brilliant as a second sun in the bright sunshine. It stands next to a new power station with chimneys, cooling towers and the glittering paraphernalia of industry shining silver against a cobalt sky.

We approach along a new eight-lane highway, one side of a dual carriageway which has not yet been marked in lanes and so looks like a major airport runway. But between us and the depot is desert sand of purest saffron. The boy jerks a finger in the direction across the desert. Surely this cannot be? This is soft sand, we'll bog down—but he nods an emphatic affirmative. We stop, climb down and examine the surface. The boy looks glummer and even more terrified. He is almost ill with fear, what *have* they told him about Englishmen? This is a track of sorts, it has been used by Caterpillar tractors, earthmovers and geophysicals as the tyre marks show. He is insistent, and he is the guide.

Over the bank of sand and rock heaped during the road construction is a moonscape, a boulder-strewn swathe running across hills of fine, egg-timer sand. The rocks are white and razor edged, this must be the Asmari limestone the oil men talk about; they are scattered like the debris of a giant explosion. The track drops into a deep wadi and we are at the bottom of an escarpment which is steep enough to require careful consideration, so we quit the cab and scramble on foot to the top. It is impossible, the angle is as sharp as the lip on a golf bunker; if we get the tractor over, the trailer will bottom and sit there rocking like a see-saw. But there is no way back and no room to turn without sinking in the sand.

The boy is now visibly shrinking into his white robes, just his nose, eyes and hair are visible and at the other end his skinny ankles. We smile encouragingly at him, poor lad, but he thinks we are baring our teeth for the first bite.

The answer is to jump her over. If we can jump her far enough then if she does bottom, the centre of gravity should be far enough over the ridge so that the rest can be dragged over. If only those close-cropped, be-spectacled engineers from Scania could be here to see their brainchild in action in adversity . . .

A cloud of dense, pure white limestone dust explodes from under our thundering wheels and the front of the cab rolls it forward like a giant snowball. It shrouds the whole operation like a white dream so, thank God, we can't see and we do not know when we jump. The trailer hits ground with the crash of a thunderclap, she bounces up. It feels as if the wheels are grounded. We are rolling—we're over!

The rest is easy. As easy as coming down Snowdon on roller skates. The gate of the depot is ahead, we crash and bang from the desert toward it and roll to a shuddering stop on a smooth, new six-lane highway which winds across the desert dunes, a svelte black ribbon, in the opposite direction from which we have come. It is the access road to the power station and depot, especially built at astronomical cost.

The boy has disappeared from the cab, we know not where.

It seems that every item of electrical equipment ever made anywhere in the world has been secretly spirited to Saudi Arabia and dumped in this depot in the desert. It must be so, never was there so much electrical wizardry in one place at one time: reels and reels of mighty cable rolled on 10 foot diameter drums, crates of switchgear from England, Germany, Sweden, Japan, whole transformers, dynamos, insulators racked and stacked or tumbled in heaps beneath the desert sky. And it is all in a shambles.

The smiling Yemeni is here with his

equally smiling and happy Egyptian—
Yemeni counterpart who speaks English,
French, German and Arabic. His Egyptian
grandmother lived in French-speaking Syria,
his Yemeni grandfather worked in a German
colony in Africa, his mother worked for the
British in Egypt and his father worked at the
British base in Aden and conversations at his
home were held in four languages as a matter
of course.

"What a shambles," he laughs, "we had no
idea you were coming."

A furious American is raging that a team of
Yemeni workmen has been detailed to unload
us. They have been taken from the work they
should be doing for him. He calls us his
English brothers and tells us: "I have been
here since Monday. I have been seconded
from my company of consultant electrial
engineers to try and sort out this Goddam
mess."

He waves a despairing arm at the mountains of equipment and repeats: "Mess . . ."
For a moment words fail him completely. He
has with him a Saudi sheikh, an executive of
the electricity company, who stands with his
hands behind his back and stares fixedly
ahead as he replies to the American's

complaints with a standard remark: "I will raise the matter at our next discussion."

The American has more degrees than a protractor, they are listed on his business card: science, arts, electrical engineering, economics and psychology . . . plus Harvard Business School. His business card is a four column acronym.

He says: "Look, fellas, this is nothing against you, but I got promises and contracts and the workforce must do as I tell them, I gotta sort out this Goddam shambles. Soon as I turn my back, they swan off someplace else. I spend my day from 7.30 am hunting these Goddam people in this Goddam . . . mess."

The sheikh says: "I will raise the matter at our next discussion."

The American says: "The next discussion. We already had 1,000 Goddam discussions. Look, sheikh, there comes a time when we gotta stop discussing and get down to sorting out this . . . mess."

He sits on a crate, puts a hand on his forehead and explains: "There are seven Goddam contractors on this project of seven different nationalities. They have to lay 500 metres of cable, so they drive in here and take a mile of cable, and that is the last you see of the cable, there are miles of cable lying all over Saudi Arabia and not an inch indented for. Can you understand that, fellas? Somewhere in this heap of junk there are 14 transformers, but can anybody find them? No, sir. So wadda they do? They order three more transformers—from your country. Now those transformers cost 500,000 bucks apiece and that is good business for your country, but it ain't good business for the electric company and it ain't good business for the consultants."

The sun is beating down and the flies are thick. There is no point in swatting them, it just raises more sweat. Hard lumps are beginning to swell where they have bitten. The Yemenis are busy unloading our tilt and puffing our cigarettes. It was easier to give them half a carton rather than dish them out individually, they had formed a polite queue to collect their individual ration and it was holding up the work.

Scrap is piled everywhere, broken bits of that, dented bits of the other. Piled high in a corner behind the office shack are hundreds of broken circular filing cabinets of the type we are unloading. The Egyptian—Yemeni storeman bursts into peels of laughter. "They could not understand how to assemble them, so they proclaimed them faulty and smashed them up, now a man has come to show them how to do it."

The American's frustration continues to echo like small arms fire round the depot.

The Egyptian—Yemeni frowns and says: "He had better learn to cool down and think about insh'allah or they will take him to the funny farm. OK, Inglisi? Is that not true? Inglisis do not worry like that, do they? Inglisis go back to the mess for a Scotch and soda, I know Inglisis."

He laughs and says in an aside: "The American will be better next week, his wife is coming. He will be so busy with her during the nights that he will forget the work here. All the wives come here and stay for a short time, then they go home to have their babies."

The Yemeni from head office has brought the tax money with him, he counts it out on the bonnet of his car, 23,000 riyals. But nobody will sign the customs form. Surprisingly, there is no trouble with the microfilm, the recipients shrug their shoulders, smile, sign the forms and hand over the money. An English engineer has been flown out to assemble the embroidery machinery. He is an experienced man and half-expected his goods to arrive in a wrecked condition, so he is pleased to find it comparatively unscathed despite its customs ordeal.

Arabs are notorious for wrecking machinery, they have not yet quite got the hang of it though they love and respect its power. Like the sheikh in Doha who was thrilled to take delivery of a vastly expensive 300 ton Coles crane. A beautiful machine, as good of its type as any available. It has been a hell of a drag to bring it down to Doha from Europe and it was delivered with justifiable pride. The sheikh and his men were given hours of instruction on the intricacies of operating the crane. It was so versatile that it was fun to demonstrate. Time and again the demonstrator went through the procedures and drummed them into the sheikh's mind.

Twenty minutes after the demonstration team and the drivers had returned to their rooms in the Gulf Hotel—or, more accurately, to Room 501, the most famous room in Arabia, but more of that later—the sheikh and his men arrived in a state of consternation. Something was wrong, the demonstrators must return to the crane immediately, already it was broken. What kind of a machine was this that broke within minutes of being received?

The crane was indeed broken. The sheikh had extended the jib to its fullest extent and tried to lift a 250 ton weight, but he had forgotten the basic rules and failed to put the outriggers out, so the crane had no support. It had toppled over, now its jib was sadly buckled and twisted, the cab smashed, and the side it was lying on bent beyond repair.

It takes us until Saturday morning to get all the necessary customs forms stamped and signed by all our customers. We have the money in hand, but without the stamped form the customs at Kafji will not return the triptyches.

Friday is a bad and frightening day in Riyadh. The faithful flock to the mosques and the grand mosque is crowded to capacity. The drivers, in their black-humorous way, call the piazza where the Grand Mosque is situated "Chop-chop Square". Friday is the day that Islamic justice is meted out. It is execution day and the crowds of worshippers gather to watch.

It is unwise to go near "Chop-chop Square" on Friday. The Muslim faithful take great delight in seizing all Europeans and gleefully pushing them to the front of the crowd to watch the proceedings.

This Friday a teenage boy is to be stoned to death for rape. A detailed account in the newspapers later reveals that his father had to hurl the first stone. The stones are provided in neat piles, each one the size of a half-brick. The city cleansing company have dustcarts and trucks waiting round the corner to sweep them up, clean away the blood and store them for future use.

A thief is to have his hand removed. This is not done with an axe but is cut off by a series of insertions with a sharp knife and then severed with a cleaver. In Jeddah, on the same day, they are beheading another teenage boy also for rape.

The law applies to all without discrimination as was witnessed by the stoning to death of a princess for adultery. This incident was the basis of the notorious television film "Death of a Princess" and caused a considerable diplomatic rumpus.

"The desert has eyes," comments our host at the villa, "you would think it a perfect place to commit a crime unobserved, but it isn't.

"Almost every crime committed in the desert is discovered and the criminals arrested. Four policemen committed a rape in the desert, in the loneliest spot imaginable, miles from anywhere. Then they murdered their victim and buried the body. Within a day, the authorities had found the body and arrested the men. A fortnight later they were all beheaded in front of the mosque."

Violence, judicial violence, is prevalent, there is little compassion and there are no half measures in Islamic justice. There is also a strong attachment to the whip. Arabs like whips and whipping things, their activities would never do for the European Court of Human Rights. When Arab children around the age of 12 skip church the Religious Police round them up and whip them to the mosque.

Three Western nurses, a British girl among them, flew in the King's aircraft to the Muslim city of Buraidah, where many mullahs are trained; nurses accompany the King on every flight he makes. The King was officiating at a religious ceremony. While they were waiting, the nurses were accommodated in the local hotel. They decided to take the opportunity to explore the ancient town and went out in their official, Western style, uniforms. But the wearing of the chador in this devout city is compulsory for women of all races. The local elders were outraged by the sight of women's faces, bare arms and legs, so they whipped them back to the hotel. The women bore the bruises for weeks afterwards.

From Riyadh to Kafji is 748 km, then from Kafji to rejoin the tapline road, 75 km, then from the point we hit the tapline again, 1,200 km to Jordan—this makes 2,000 kliks to a legal pint of beer, 1,250 miles. Working on the precept that there will be no delays, this is two days driving, maybe two-and-a-half without pushing it too much. We will not now be going to Doha or Abu Dhabi. We have been instructed by telex to return to Mersin, in Turkey, and load satsumas or nuts. Today we can reach Ain Dar and cut across the desert track in daylight to reach Watford Gap for the overnight stop. With an early morning start and a dash to the border to pick up our papers we'll have virtually a whole day along the tapline, the longest desert run known.

So this trip we will not see Ain Dar by night which is like going to the Arctic Circle and missing the aurora borealis. However, at Ain Dar the lights are man-made. They come from the great fires which burn off the accumulation of gases at the oil installation. These fires are spectacular, they account for the speed ramps placed across the roads here. For the fires have a hypnotic effect, they can mesmerise drivers at night; cars and trucks used to run off the road or ran into each other, so they put down the ramps to cut speeds to a minimum. Ramps are the single most effective method of speed control ever devised. The casualty rate on the Ain Dar road dropped dramatically.

A bedouin tribesman is nothing if not a rugged individualist. Roads are a new thing, a fad of the past five or ten years only, they are new-fangled notions and still very scarce. Hundreds of thousands of square miles of the country still have no roads. The Rub'al Khali, the Empty Quarter, is still empty. From the air the isolation is absolute, the ribbon of a road is a puny thread between communities.

If a Saudi tribesman feels that a new road interferes with his rights or lifestyle, he will dig it up. So roads are liable to have a ditch dug across them if the local tribal boss feels that it is necessary. The ditch will only become apparent when you are on top of it, fast brake and gear work is called for to ease the thud when you hit it. On a scale of 10, rate the road dangers in this order: Arab drivers 10, straying donkeys and camels 9, ditches 8, dogs 7, children in villages 6, sand storms 5, soft tar 4, police, army and odds and sods to make up the rest according to preference. You work on the fixed principle that every inch of Saudi road is a potential hazard and take it easy. The fast boys thunder past and, in turn, you will pass them when they come unstuck.

The ditch we hit at speed near Ain Dar has not damaged us, merely shaken us up a bit. It was all the worse because we are now running empty and 18-and-a-half tons lighter, so we jump about a bit. These machines ride better when full and heavy, then they reach the peak of performance for which they were designed.

Watford Gap tonight is a Little England. A squadron of Brits have arrived most of them Dohas and Abu Dhabis, a couple homeward bound; business is booming, there is a lot of traffic rolling down. It runs true to form, in a deep recession, specialist business booms.

Perhaps exporters try harder when home markets are poor.

To talk of taking load to Doha, Abu Dhabi, and the United Arab Emirates is to measure the recent advance of motor transport. Up to 20 years ago these were places at the end of the earth, the only way there was by sea or air. Overland travel was an inadmissable dream, there were not the machines to do it. The desert would always beat man and machine, man, in fact, would be the more vulnerable because of the machine. Now there are many vehicles which make mincemeat of the journey and haul heavy cargoes quickly to inaccessible places without loss or damage. The machines absorb all the hammering nature can hand out to them: Christer Wickman hauls glass from Sweden along the route we have followed and delivers without a splinter or crack in his load.

To the Middle East driver Qatar and Abu Dhabi are as commonplace and everyday as London and Liverpool. Yet Qatar, Abu Dhabi and Oman are hardly ordinary places.

Qatar is the land of the grand, imperious gesture. When the new Amir succeeded his father his first act was to pay off all his subjects' mortgages and give them their homes and businesses as an accession present. He visited the Gulf Hotel one evening, saw the Qatari taxi drivers sitting outside in their battered Chevrolets and bought them all a new Cadillac each so that they could sit in more comfort with air conditioning.

The taxi driver known as Charlie was sitting in his resplendent new car when his trucker customers asked "Where did you get the new chariot, Charlie? It's fantastic."

Charlie was a tiny man. Lifting himself up on the steering wheel to look over the bonnet, he said: "It's a present from the Amir, but it's too big. Now I'll have to buy a new cushion to sit on before I can drive it properly."

Such things are really the hidden fascination of the trucking job for most drivers, the chance to see the extraordinary, to observe a bizarre slice of life and to be a part of it and to wonder at the contradictions and contrasts.

If you are squeamish you won't relish sitting in the café at Watford Gap. Even if you are not you still lift your feet when the three-inch long beetles crawl across the floor. Watch them and marvel at their size. Also marvel at the monstrous super-cockroaches, lizards and scorpions. And for goodness' sake beware of camel spiders. The camel spider is a big thing and agile, but you will not know that it has got you because when it lands on its prey, it injects a local anaesthetic, then gobbles out an inch-an-a-half chunk of flesh while the victim is unaware. Not a pleasant fellow, the camel spider and unfortunately quite prevalent.

The desert is alive with wildlife and it is always a thrill to pick up the gleaming yellow eyes of a desert fox in the headlights or see a lofty eagle soaring and hovering to spot its quarry. And there are also snakes, the maipolon moilensis, better known as the sidewinder—the silver-creamy spotted terror of the sands, mercury-quick and with the unpleasant habit of flinging itself through the air like a whiplash to strike its victim.

So, sitting at Watford Gap or some similar place, watching a straggling caravan wind its way across the horizon, the goatherd, the shepherd, the man astride his donkey and the huddled black-swathed women crouching to enter their mud-walled houses in a remote village, you are quite right to think that nothing much has changed since biblical times.

Then a few hours later you motor into

Qatar, pull into the Gulf Hotel and savour the blessed cool of its vestibule lined in solid onyx. There you may stay in the 13-storey annex that Sheikh Al-Hufman built especially to house visiting football teams when they came to Qatar for the first time to play in the Arab Games. Players in the teams were, alas, mostly genuine bedouin Arabs unused to the sophistication of luxury hotel life. They lit their primus stoves in the lushly carpeted coridors and cooked their meals on charcoal braziers in the rooms and did hundreds of thousands of pounds worth of damage. The shiekh did not raise a single whisper of complaint knowing, in his wisdom, that it was not their fault and that they would need to be educated in different ways as the wealth of the country increased.

Here, of course, you will take the lift to the fifth floor, and slowly, with feigned indifference, though your parched lips and tongue may be urging your legs to hurry, you walk round the corridors until you reach the corner door to the left numbered Room 501—the most famous room in the Middle East.

Slipping your private key into the lock you will let yourself into a spacious and wholly civilised bar stocked with ice-cold lagers, the best Scotches and the finest wines of the world. Here you can relax, sipping your desired tipple while gazing at the enormous swimming pool below and the hazy, misty blues of the Persian Gulf. It's so nice, so civilized here, you can feel indulgent to the world.

A London accountant, flown out to investigate the soaring expenses of drivers "stranded" in the Gulf Hotel because of a monumental cock-up in paperwork between Oman and Qatar, arrived in pin-striped suit and bowler hat. Running a finger round his white collar over a blue shirt, he said: "Goodness, it is hot here."

Carefully he examined the hotel bills and asked: "What is this 'Paid et L'?" Checking the code on the back of the bill, he said: "L—laundry. You must all have the cleanest clothes in the Middle East, you have them washed every morning, afternoon and evening, and it is damned expensive."

"Yes," muttered the drivers rather shame-facedly, "it's very hot here, as you said, you go through a lot of clothes in a day."

They did not tell him that since drink is officially banned, it cannot be charged on the bill, so drinks are marked down as "laundry" and laundry proper is marked as "washing". For a week the poor accountant did not know there was a bar in the hotel, until the drivers took pity on him; after which he became as laundry conscious as the rest.

Gulf state hotels are remarkable in many aspects, they are among the finest to be found, luxurious and beautifully furnished. But when they are dry it takes much of the atmosphere away and emphasises how much a hotel depends upon its public rooms. Often they come as a shock, and none more so than the Al-Alaina Hilton. Leave the Emirates heading south towards Oman, drive into no-man's-land over rugged, untamed desert with the knowledge that it is a very rough ride into the mountains and wadis over to Muscat. Then, 200 kilometres out into the wild wilderness, is that an optical illusion? A mirage? It looks like a towering skyscraper in the middle of a mud-hut township.

It is the Al-Alaina Hilton. It has a doorman in frock-coat and top hat, a coffee shop, bell-boys, restaurants, head waiters, a maitre d'hôtel, soft lights and piped sweet music. And outside there are just mud-huts and endless desert sands.

Back in the mid-70s the local Emir wanted to book the Abu Dhabi Hilton on the coast for a grand wedding reception. However, like all the coast hotels in the Emirates it was full, these hotels are always busy catering for construction men and businessmen visiting the oil industries.

"Build me another one," the Emir commanded. And they did. He was no fool, his hotel now is always full with visiting firemen and it acts as an overflow from the crowded coast.

However, there are no Hiltons back at Watford Gap, only the café at the intersection of the tapline and coast roads. When dawn comes, the engines roar, air-horns blast their farewells, the dust rises in clouds and stays risen. Then the truckers are gone and silence descends on the desert.

17

THE business at the Kafji border post takes all of 10 minutes, we pay the money, collect the triptyches, say goodbyes—the proper taking of leave is essential in the Arab world—and we are away. There follows the curious sense of elation, like being let out of school early. Though why we should feel elated after having to drive the best part of 600 miles to collect two scraps of paper is incomprehensible, it's like having to motor from London to Wick, in Scotland, to show your driving licence to the police after an accident.

It is an hour's drive back to the tapline road. Among roads, it can lay claim to be considered extraordinary, if not remarkable. Common sense and logic say that it ought not to be there at all since it goes from nowhere to nowhere through nothing. It does not link great centres of population and industry, there are no hosts of travellers anxious to follow it for their betterment or to pursue their interests. It does not carry the wayfarer through scenery to illuminate the mind and lift the spirits. It is, in every way, an agony to travel.

The Saudis and Aramco, the Arabian American Oil Company, made it so that they could build the astonishing Trans Arabian Pipeline which, in itself, is a staggering feat of engineering. They completed it in 1950 and it has carried a large part of the industrial world's oil supplies ever since. It is so easy to take these wonders for granted, but this pipeline was a feat of imagination and human endurance as well as engineering skill. The men who constructed it worked in a hitherto impenetrable wilderness inimical to mankind, an inferno, a life-sapping, waterless natural death trap, a place of fear and horror.

The very thought of laying a pipeline across such a place raised the eyebrows of the sceptics and there were many who thought it impossible. But the oil company and the King agreed that it could and should be done—a brave and imaginative decision. If they had, for instance, taken the same view as successive British Governments about the Channel Tunnel, they would still have been prevaricating today.

Since it was completed, the road has grown

immensely in stature and got better all the time. The desert is a powerful adversary and a constant running battle is fought to keep it at bay, it is nothing for the desert suddenly to roll a sand dune across the highway. The desert is not a static, fixed phenomenon.

Desert can be compared with illness, it cannot be fully appreciated until it is experienced and it comes in several degrees: mild, severe, serious, critical, dangerous and fatal. The desert the pipeline crosses varies from critical, to dangerous, to fatal depending on the season. In summer, at an average temperature of 120° Fahrenheit in the shade, it is fatal. The few men who crossed this desert took a pregnant camel with them to ensure that they would have a supply of milk to slake their chronic thirsts during the arduous journey.

This desert runs into the Rub 'al Khali in the south. And few people cross that, even now. This is the Empty Quarter, the worst of deserts, where sand dunes can drift in mountains 3,000 foot high disappear in a day and spring up elsewhere just as suddenly. This is a land where the wind can whip the sand to a fury and black out the sun for days. It is the desert of the "singing sands", the wild, ethereal space music that fills the night. The music that has been heard by Philby, Thomas, Doughty and latter-day oil men. It occurs when the moving sands slide over other, firmer sands and the friction generates a strange, eerie sound. The bedouin mind is filled with "jinns" and evil spirits—no wonder when they live in the land of the "singing sands". The wind, too, produces its own distracting, disturbing ghost music all the time. The desert is a nerve-wracking place for an imaginative man to be.

The heat of the day is the killer. It is a heat unimaginable in a temperate climate and a heat which cannot be remembered when it has passed. Midday in the desert is the time to think that if what the prophets say is true, that God punished the world first by flood, next time it will be fire, then that punishment is beginning now. Those men who, only 30 years ago, made that pipeline and this road, endured and suffered it all while they worked a constructional miracle. Now they are taking water, fresh, clean, pure water through by building other massive pipelines. There is, after all, something to be said for the human spirit.

The road is straight, a line of perspective

drawn to infinity, as it runs ahead to an ever distant horizon. The speedometer needle is reading a steady, static 90 kph. But you cannot trust it because the truck does not appear to be moving. The road is rushing under the front of the cab when you look down, but is that an illusion? Overhead, the sun is tracking the sky in the slow arc of a shotputter's throw. The shadow the truck casts ahead is shortening and moving towards the cab as the sun gains. The shadow is the only thing that moves, the rest of the world has stopped dead in its tracks.

A speck far away in the distance increases the heartbeat. Is it moving? Is it there at all? Yes it is, another truck is approaching, it could be several trucks, they raise a mist of dust which trails off into the sands. They are fascinating these trucks, sometimes they disappear from sight, so there must be a dip in the desert, but you cannot see a dip, the road looks completely flat.

Why don't they come, those damned trucks? They have been out there for ages, they ought to have arrived by now. Perhaps they are stationary too. Perhaps we are in a dream, running on the spot and getting nowhere, reaching for somebody who is forever out of touch. The blasted trucks are still half-sized Dinky toys, maybe they are parked, but the dust is still streaming from them in a grey, wispy streak like the tail of a King Charles spaniel. Forget them, pretend they are not there, check the speed, the revs, the temperature, count the blown tyres along the roadside. Those tyres that at least prove that other people have been here before.

We are five hours into the road now and nothing has changed except the shadow. That thin black pipe is still running alongside, perched on its supports, its filling of precious black sludge moving inexorably westwards. It seems as if we are tied to the pipe by an invisible umbilical cord and will never be cut free.

The approaching trucks are now upon us. Hell, they are hogging the whole road and there isn't all that much to hog. No, they're not, they only look as if they are. Hold the line, keep her straight, just sit where you are and don't deviate. Keep that off-side wheel on the tarmac, it looks like very soft sand down there.

Suddenly the trucks look enormous and uncomfortably close. The approaching driver smiles and nods, he, too, is watching his line.

There comes a thwack of battered air as we pass with just 10 inches between wing mirrors. A shower of trailing dust sweeps upwards in swirls and eddies. Thwack, thwack, thwack, they thunder past. The truck rocks under the impact of sharply compressed air, then they are gone and all is quiet again save the throb of the engine.

Now there are tell-tale whiffs of streaming sand across the black tarmac, thin as a dancer's gossamer veils. They are snaking across the road as if alive and in a hurry. Over there it looks hazy, it could be low cloud, but you don't get cloud here. It is blowing up, the sand is lifting.

Out in the desert there is a herd of camels. What are they doing here? Who owns them? Where is he? One thing is sure, if you hit one, he will pop up like "jinn" out of the ground and it will prove to be the finest racing camel Arabia has ever known, a real Nijinsky of a camel and priced accordingly.

Will this bloody road ever end? Will it ever get anywhere, a hut, a hovel, a shack would do. This is preposterous, it is nearly teatime. This is definitely the last time, never again will I drive down this hideous, boring, intimidating road. From nowhere to nowhere through nothing, it is like driving in an abstract painting. There is no other road like it.

And now the sand is up. A dirty, yellow, smoky smog rattling and spitting against the windscreen. This is when another convoy of trucks will emerge and this time they'll be driven by hashish-crazed Arabs. The Mirrors should be coming up any minute, they will all have been in there, smoking their hookahs and dreaming dreams.

When The Mirrors comes it arrives with speed ramps and a police check and proves to be the centre point of the universal rubbish tip. Civilisation and sophistication have not reached this outpost except in the meanest degree. There is diesel here, served from antiquated pumps each with a pronounced lean, a shop, an Arab restaurant and shack village.

The place takes its name from the restaurant, a large establishment whose inner walls are decorated entirely with mirrors set between red pillars; the supporting pillars in the middle of the room are also hung, on all four sides, with more mirrors, so the room reflects itself and its occupants in decreasing images on all sides. Around the walls are stored a collection of hookah pipes, they run the length of the room and come in all shapes and sizes.

This is the social centre of the desert. At night, from that nowhere we have been in all day, the bedouin and the local shepherds all assemble in the room. An Arab musician plays high-pitched, warbling music, the pipes are lit, spiced mutton and chicken are served, the bread is heated and the atmosphere grows thick. As the contents of the pipes take hold, the babble of talk subsides. The smokers stay all night. Many of the men sleep here anyway. Outside on the ramshackle balcony are bunks, rough wooden frames with ropes tied across them, they sag alarmingly in the middle and the frames wobble; by midnight they are filled with huddled, slumped bodies. They sleep on the ropes with no mattresses and they are dead to the world.

Let's face it, nothing is going to happen on this road unless you fall asleep and run off, and the hundreds of wrecks are sufficient indication of how many people do. Some are the result of blown tyres, but it is possible to follow people down the road and watch them just run off. They are in front of you, trundling along happily, they hardly seem to be moving at all because they are going at the same speed as you, then suddenly they swerve and run off.

If they hit soft sand it clutches the wheels, stops them dead and they roll over. If they hit a hard surface they slide and bump and then roll over and over. Either way it is better if they are dead. Medical services are a long way away. From road level you are able to see the Arab character in a different way. For such a warlike and bloodthirsty a race they are not overfond of the sight of blood, they will happily watch an execution, but they will not get involved in a bloody accident. They usually go away and come back later hoping that the victim is dead. That is not quite as callous as it seems, an accident is an immense difficulty in such remote areas. Death is simple, and there are just not the medical facilities to deal with casualties.

British medical personnel are initially shocked by Arab attitudes. An eminent brain surgeon who had gone out to Arabia to supervise the building of a hospital looked at the existing hospital and insisted on its immediate closure.

He says: "It was a death trap. Nobody stood any chance of surviving who went into it. The place was infested. I insisted on a temporary hospital being flown out and assembled so we could work in a sterile atmosphere in that.

"Friday night out here is murder night. It is a holiday and they take out their cars and have accidents. It is a madhouse in a hospital. The first Friday I was here I was appalled, the staff left serious-looking cases to die. I saw a young boy with head injuries who the Arab doctor had said was too far gone for anything to be done. It was a nasty, messy accident but quite operable, so we operated. I dreaded the boy dying from infection, which was a major risk. But he survived and made a complete recovery to normality. The Arab doctor has never forgiven me, but they would have left him to die."

A mystery surrounds the enigmatic bedouin. Park 200 kilometres from anywhere, in a landscape devoid of any sign of life, without cover as far as they eye can see even through binoculars and within minutes the curious, staring, silent bedouin will be in attendance. Black-robed from head to toe, with only their deep eyes on view they will stand in a circle around the truck, at a distance, and they will stay as long as you do.

Deep in that fearsome desert between Qatar

and the Emirates, the mandatory bedouin guides would signal food and drink—fingers to the mouth and tipping an imaginary glass of chi. In the cab of the sand-tractor, they would shiver, flick off the switches of the air-conditioning, wind down the window and let in the scorched 140° desert breeze and head into uncharted desert. Over the twentieth high sand dune would be a cluster of black bedouin tents, full of their relatives. How they knew, no white Westerner will ever understand.

The light plays frightening tricks, there is no other explanation. Suddenly we are running across a causeway with sparkling lakes of fresh water surrounded by waving rushes and fringed by rustling palms. The waters flood across the road but the anticipated splash never materialises, the waters retreat in front of the truck. It is real enough to bathe in—solid, tangible thirst-quenching water. But it is a mirage.

People believe that mirages are a figment of the imagination brought about by thirst and heat and a wandering mind. If this were the case they would be individual hallucinations. This is not so, your companion sitting next to you will see them as clearly as you do. If you are travelling in convoy, your fellow drivers will see them and describe them exactly as you have seen them. You will all have expected the splash at the same point and have seen the swaying palm trees. Mirages can be very disconcerting. And you realise what torment they must have been for those first, tough, courageous desert explorers.

Time has become irrelevant. The day has gone, the night has gone, the day has come again and the sun is catching up once more. Reality only returns with the rumble of speed ramps under the wheels—Turayf. A little town with stone built cottages and a plantation of stunted palms in the middle of the road. There is the old customs house, the shop with its cold Coke. This is the end of the road. This is where, a few years ago, but not very many, you had to turn into the desert to run by the sun for 120 kilometres across to H4, the border fortress in Jordan. Now they have built a new road which sweeps down an incline, past a romantic sandstone fortress placed on a hill, into scrubland desert along to Al-Haydethe, the new border post with Jordan. This is the end of the Kingdom.

18

THE Turayf border is full of silly Saudis. They don't want to let us out. One particularly idiotic soldier boy is almost beside himself with anxiety to retain our services for the glory of the Kingdom. He seems to think that since we have come in at Kafji, we have slipped through the back door and are now trying to sneak out through the main entrance. "Bosche, bosche, bosche," empty, empty, empty, we tell him. He remains convinced that we have secreted aboard the Saudi Crown Jewels and blue prints of all the oil fields.

We are quietly working out plans to make a run for it when the shift changes and the second lot are too tired to bother about anything. We move in quickly as they come, yawning, to their posts and they stamp the papers with their eyes half closed. That is lucky, a Danish driver has been sitting under arrest for 12 days unable to move until money arrives from his company. The Saudis have discovered a box of liqueur chocolates in his food store which his wife had put there as a surprise. He had no idea that they were there and made no attempt to conceal them. The Saudis insisted he was trying to smuggle them in. They fined him £550 and would not let him go until the money was paid. He says: "I can't talk to my company from here, they are wondering what on earth is going on. They seem to think I must have a truck load of liqueur chocolates. Probably they think I have taken on an extra load without them knowing, they do not seem to understand that it is a £550 fine for a present from a wife. I will have to pay this from my own pocket when I return home, the insurance won't cover trying to take liquor into Saudi no matter how accidentally."

Now, again, is the time to enjoy a little bout of euphoria. Out of Saudi—and not arrested once, free from the Kingdom and never a feel of the inside of their abomninable jails. The thought of those jails is enough to make the blood run cold in a hot climate. The Riyadh jail has barred communal cages inside the jail walls. They are filled with as many prisoners as can be crammed in. There is no chance of avoiding the lice and whatever else is about. And the Saudis do not feed their prisoners, that is left to the goodwill of family and friends.

It is, the heart sinks, just as bad in Syria. Trevor Long once spent 10 days inside a Syrian jail in the company of 180 others in a small room. The Syrians kept beating their fellow countrymen and taking them from the room to spend a rest period in a hole in the ground in the prison yard with the midday sun beating down on them. Sometimes they "interrogated" them in another room and brought the remnants back to the communal room to recuperate. The British Embassy finally persuaded the Syrians that they had arrested the wrong man, and Trevor was released. In all, it was 10 days of misery—and a lifetime of experience.

We are running late and now is the chance to make up time, so we will zoom through Jordan which we can cover in hours. Jordan, the route we are following, is "mild" desert, though in parts it can be classed as "dangerous"—between H4 and Turayf, for example. The only stop will be at Rampha Rest House for old times' sake, and to collect the latest on the grapevine.

Rampha Rest House, in the early days, was the one place you could get a shower and, by the time you reached there, you needed one. Showers were, in fact, pressed upon drivers, particularly slim, young nubile ones, by the old boy—now retired—who had set up the place and ran it. That was because he was a raving old queer whose happiness was to watch through a peep-hole while young drivers were taking their ablutions. But he always gave himself away, when they came to wash their genitals he couldn't contain himself and uttered suppressed little squeaks and squeals of delight which sounded like mice, big mice, in the next cubicle.

"I'll catch the old bugger out," said a friend of ours. "I'll give him a real flash." He did, he turned full frontal to the spy-hole, soaped himself vigorously waving everything about until the squeals reached a pitch of joy uncontained. Then he peed through the hole and listened as the squeals rapidly changed note.

They sell a good drop of beer at Rampha and a lot of it is drunk. The bill is paid at the end of a session when the waiter counts the number of empty bottles on the table and charges accordingly. The Brits, true to the British tradition of fair play and honesty, always used to sit by a window and, as the

511

table filled with empties, dropped some through the window. The table top was always nearly full but never overflowing while a hillock of empties grew in the sand outside. Later the crafty Brits would move the pile to the back of the establishment where the beer crates were stored.

The old boy worried and fretted about how it was the British bill was always so little when they seemed to drink so much. Then he tumbled the game and had the windows permanently screwed tight.

"You rotten old sod," complained the aggrieved Brits, "now we'll suffocate in the poxy place."

Conveniences, in the delicate Western phrase, are not easily come by in the desert. The sand is good enough for anything and everybody. Chris Bedder relieved himself in the desert one boozy evening and then asked: "Why do those soldiers want to shoot me? Why are they pointing their guns? All I've done is to have a pee in the desert."

"Yes, Chris, but in the darkness you pissed against their bivouac tent and the flap was open."

A desert soldier's life is a dangerous one fraught with unpredictable risk. Such as a teapot being emptied through a truck cab when the corporal of the guard is passing, so the corporal spends the rest of his arduous duty with Tetley bags entwined in his camouflage netting.

In the village, the bright young Jordanian businessman who has established a small supermarket with a snack bar from his earnings in Germany, says: "I have finished with Germany now, there is no money any more in Germany, now there is much business in Jordan and plenty of money to be made." So the wheel has come full circle.

We pass into Syria at Derra—Dar'a on the map, but there are many spellings for each name throughout the Middle East. Syria has reaped enormous profits from taxes on vehicles in transit and the harder up she gets, the more tax she applies. She also applies an ingenious tax, the Syrian Drivers' Union surcharge, on the basis that Syrian drivers should drive all vehicles through Syrian territory, and if they don't, then they should be recompensed for not doing so. In theory, Syrian drivers should sit on their bottoms at the borders ready to pilot foreign trucks through their exclusive back garden. Not that any are ever on view and they will be very lucky if they ever see a penny of the money collected in their name.

We must have a record of the hassle, it would not be the same without an itinerary of trouble. Here goes: in three weeks the Syrians have upped the transit taxes from £60, empty, to £140, empty and they are demanding a deposit of £100 (Syrian)—£15 sterling—to stamp the clearance forms, allegedly returnable on leaving the country at Bab-al-Awa. But, we are reliably informed and will later discover to our cost, the Syrians say: "We do not give change on deposits, it is against the law." Sort out the logic of that, if you can. The police decide that they do not like "two chauffeurs, one cameon" so will not stamp the passport—OK, one of us will walk through when they are not watching. Or can one book in as a tourist—"So what, chef? I always go on holiday in a big truck, wouldn't use any other form of transport." It will not matter, one half of the outfit hasn't the foggiest idea what the other half is doing. All they really want to do is to collect a double ration of Syrian Drivers' Union dues, and sucks to that.

Yet Syria is a delightful place to visit if for one reason only. And his name is Mohammed

Ahmad Rashid Abu Al-Jazar, who is on the Ramtha side of the border. Though he is deaf and dumb he has been on the border since he was eight. Now 20 years of age, married with three children, he has become one of the best loved and regarded characters on the whole trip. There is not much scope for handicapped children in this part of the world but he has made himself the best customs clearance agent of all.

Out here, there is no education for a boy who cannot hear and cannot speak. But Smiler has made himself literate, numerate and an expert in the ramifications of customs law and tax in both Jordan and Syria. By sheer force of personality and the magic quality of charm he has won the hearts and trust of countless drivers. You can hand over all your paper work to Smiler with the complete assurance that it will be dealt with in the minimum of time at the minimum of current cost. And his boss, Mohammed El Khatib, knows and recognises his value. The drivers even leave their wives and girlfriends in his care when they are going on to Saudi Arabia, where unmarried women passengers are forbidden and wives are frowned upon.

Syrians have an appalling international

image and work hard to maintain it, with considerable success. The country is rubble and dilapidation from beginning to end; it is better to try and drive through it in the dark, but that is difficult. They like you to see the horror of the place so they organise convoys to ensure that you do not miss a speck of the general devastation.

Syria is a country at war. That becomes a litany in the Arab world, every Arab is at war with somebody. There would be no spice to life if they weren't. They march round all day singing at the tops of their voices or writing on walls: "Death to the filthy reactionary American imperialists" or Israelis . . . or Egyptians. It doesn't seem to matter as long as it is death to somebody.

Damascus, which is a city with a romantic, evocative ring to its name, is falling to pieces. Yet it is a busy, teeming place with life going on apace all round. There is a sight worth seeing in Damascus, the fountain near the city centre. The water comes out like a jet from a fire hydrant and thunders into the air, it is so powerful a fountain that the water doesn't tinkle back into the ornamental pool it crashes down.

Everywhere are young kids in uniform

toting guns. Waving guns at you, pointing guns at you, waving them over their heads, leaning on them, carrying them under their arms or slung over their shoulders. You can so easily become sick of the sight of guns. Everybody seemingly can afford to buy guns, they cannot afford food, or houses, or decent clothes, but they can always find the money for guns.

The road runs by the Golan Heights and the grim realities of Arab life and politics become all too obvious at night when we see what looks at first like sheet lightning. But this is not lightning, it is cannon fire and it is taking place spasmodically all the way along the border from Israel and Lebanon to Turkey. They are fighting in the Yemen, in Iran, in Iraq, in Palestine and in Syria. The Arabs are fighting everywhere, and usually themselves. This journey can be depressing and soul destroying—most saddening of all is that these child soldiers have never known anything else.

The young agent's tout on the border suggests a complicated and highly improbable way in which he can get a lift in a European truck out of Syria. He says: "I got plenty of money, foreign money from the drivers. If I get out, I can say I am student. If I have to stay they take me for army, then I am finish, I am soldier for too long."

The road to Bab-al-Awa runs through Homs, Hamad and Halat. We are running "bosche" so we travel alone. In Mons we met the night convoy heading south to Jordan, Iran and the Gulf states; this is a monster convoy of hundreds of trucks, it splits the town in two and takes an hour to pass. The army is in control and making a brave show in its jeeps and personnel carriers. They do not like to let anybody out of their sight in Syria because they are nervous and trigger happy.

A few days after we pass through Hamad on this trip, the army moves in and civil war breaks out. The government announces that it has rounded up and destroyed "dissident elements". Outside, half the world is baying for President Hafes-Al-Assad's downfall and the other half is condemning the "reactionaries". The radio war of words crackles on the cab's loudspeakers; sitting in the middle of it all, you do not know what the devil is going on, who is who, what is what, or why. In our small but wide-ranging world, these kind of events are a bloody nuisance because

518

they close the borders. Surprisingly, the combatants usually stop the war and let the trucks through because the trucks are carrying what they need most and bringing money at the same time. And money, more than war, is what makes the world go round.

When the rains come in Syria the whole country is bogged down, in particular the army. Wet weather confounds the army, it slithers to a stop and everything else stops with it. The roads are blocked by stranded tanks and army vehicles. Truckers call them the sunshine soldiers because they can do nothing when it rains. They add yet another risk to the already risky roads where a favourite pastime is to drive herds of sheep the wrong way along a dual-carriageway. It is quite common to see the flow of traffic break like the bow wave of a ship round some donkey cart trotting the wrong way, absolutely unconcerned about it.

Syria is a disturbing place and funny things happen. This is where Trevor Long was robbed at gunpoint in his cab. The thief picked the door locks, climbed in, pointing his gun at Trevor's head, and made off with £400. You might say that this is par for the course. But this happened 20 yards from the main gate of a large military establishment with sentries and military police on the gate and a constant flow of traffic in and out. Which says something for the nerve—or desperation—of the robber and the disinterest of the military. If you are stopped, from the driving seat it is difficult to tell who is genuine militia and who is a mugger. Both have guns.

Bab-Al-Awa, thankfully, arrives quickly. With luck, it is possible to get across Syria in five hours which is the only good thing about it. But, at this time of the night, the border will be closed, so let us do a "sneaky". There is a village a few kliks off the main road, where you can, as a driver from Lincoln put it: "Get a good fill of diesel if you pay in the right money."

The pump attendant clearly knows the score without asking. He takes one look at the truck through his dingy window and comes out armed with monkey wrench and spanners to get into the tanks without breaking the seals on the filler caps. "He's a good lad, this one," we say.

By the time we are ready to leave, the local schoolchildren are on their way to school all dressed like little soldiers, girls and boys, in military style uniforms of dull drill.

The customs man is monumentally bored and touchy. He gives the impression of working on a very short fuse and is about to explode at any moment. To cool off, he takes frequent strolls from his ill-lit, gloomy office to see the sunshine and sniff the dust and diesel fumes of the wider world outside. Then he returns to bristle and take umbrage at any unintended gesture, sigh or yawn from a hapless driver lounging in the waiting queue.

He matches the passport photograph to the face in the queue, waves the document fiercely in the direction of the offender and shrieks: "I have all day. If you want to wait all day, then you shall. I can work no faster, so why you sneer at me. You will go to the bottom of the pile." So saying he slips the offender's papers under the heap cluttering the table and takes another stroll to sanity. The culprit stands up, walks to the desk, takes his papers from the bottom of the pile and replaces them where they were originally. Nobody objects.

In another office, Mustafa Awad surveys the world through limpid brown eyes and smiles his Mona Lisa smile. His sharp, agent's brain is ticking away working out that the Government will take so much if it is done this way, but less if it is done another way, and the second way will, surely, be to everybody's advantage, my friend . . . and, by the way, you are bosche? It so happens that my cousin in Turkey has a load . . . if it can be moved quickly with no fuss . . . now that will be good for us all, will it not, my friend?

Mustafa Awad is a very honest man and as such has surprised many drivers. Those who have done him a service have always found their money waiting for them in cash when they have returned. But not all Mustafa Awad's wiles and knowledge can persuade the Syrian customs to return the £100 (Syrian) deposit (returnable on request). "No," they insist, "we do not give change, that is the rule."

They are stopping lines of trucks at the police cabin control post and this is the rear end of the queue. Suddenly, a soldier waves us into a rapidly emptying line. "Fast, fast, move up." His colleague speeds it up even more. We flash past people who were "processed" hours before. "Fast, fast." We are out without stopping.

19

ALL is forgiven. All is forgotten. Life is mellow again. We are back in Turkey. Avenues of trees overhang the narrow, pleasant roads. The orange groves are lush with ripe fruit, the fields are a mass of spotted gold and sacks of oranges and satsumas are stacked by the roadside.

You may think you know all there is to know about satsumas, or all you need to know, but you don't. Pick a satsuma from the tree, it will fall into your hand at a gentle touch, peel it while it is still warm from the sun. The skin comes away in one piece leaving the fruit encased in its soft, white pith. A gentle aroma rises to the nostrils. Split the pith and pull the segments apart and the scent becomes overpowering, activating the saliva glands in the mouth. Press the segments with the tongue and nectar trickles on to the palate; the whole fruit dissolves into a juice. It is young and delicate and only to be tasted straight from a tree.

Now lean out of your cab and pick a

handful of ripe nuts, delectable. And on this Mediterranean shore, the prawn are succulent. I wish I could tell you more about all the fantastic fish foods, so colourful, such fine, rare tastes, but their names are written in Turkish. There is *barbunya*, red mullet, and *kilic baligi*, swordfish. Also on the cold counter there is *imam bayildi*, which means "the priest fainted"—doubtless at the thought of aubergines stuffed with fried tomatoes, onions and garlic.

Dip into the bowls of natural Turkish yoghourt, and let's finish with a *tel kadayif*, which I know is a sort of shredded wheat stuffed with nuts in syrup. They call their sweets by seductive names like *hanim gobegi* and *dilber dudagi*, which means respectively "lady's navel" and "beauty's lips". Which shows the way a Turk's mind dwells on food and women. Which is how an Englishman's mind works, so we get on well together. Let's have another glass of raki, lion's milk they call it.

If we could hang around Mersin waiting for a load of satsumas, it would be great. But they have loaded all the satsumas that are ready and we will have to push off and pick up an industrial load Yugoslavia way.

We are thinking of plausible reasons for delaying the stop here but we know head office are not easily fooled. Drivers are inventive and original at making excuses. After all, they have a lot of time to think about it behind that wheel. But few have topped Terry Tott, the former Showaddy-waddy base guitar player and former Smokie player too. Now a driver.

He telephoned Bob Paul at Astran and the conversation went:

"I can't take the truck any further, Bob."

"Why?"

"The wing mirror's broken."

"Well," a pause and a pregnant silence with a sharp intake of breath, "get some glass and mend the wing mirror."

"I can't do that, Bob."

"Why?"

"The truck's lying on it."

Let us tick off the driver's log. We've done Turkey, we've done Bulgaria. This time we will make a left at Sofia and take the road to Belgrade via Pirot and Nis. At Nis we can pick up the motorway which runs straight into Belgrade. It will be soft motoring, once we clear Bulgaria. Well, maybe not so soft. *Truck* magazine wrote about this road under the stark headline "KILLER ROAD, Europe's most accident-prone road, 683 miles of it, exacts a terrible toll in life and misery. Yet it rolls inexorably on."

It is known to the locals as "The Raceway" which sounds more dramatic in Yugoslavian than it does in English. The police call it the "Gastarbieter Route". Drivers call it "Memory Lane" because of the hundreds of roadside shrines bereaved families have erected to their dead loved ones.

Somehow it just keeps claiming victims, all the way down from Radstadt, in Austria, to Nis, in Southern Yugoslavia.

We take it carefully.

Winter has settled on Bulgaria so quickly that they cannot catch up with it, so from Sofia to the border is a skating rink of black ice cunningly concealed under a powdering of fine snow. It leads to one of those events which, afterwards, the mind constantly replays in slow-motion.

Conditions, which were appalling, have now become frightening. It happens suddenly in this area. There is nowhere to lie-up so a cautious crawl is all that can be reluctantly attempted. A Bulgarian in a

Volkswagen Beetle is coming at us like a maniac, he is going to carve us up. Flash him—flash, flash, flash him. He's oblivious to flashes, he looks oblivious to everything. There is no way he is going to stop. There is no way he *can* stop. The only thing is to brake, not the best of things to do in circumstances such as these. The back begins to slide. When she goes, she will go with a snap quicker than a mousetrap. A split-second change down and gun the engine to try to spin her the other way. If the cab can be made to move at the same speed as the trailer she may pull level, but this is not the sort of lunacy to be playing at on a road like this. Slowly she slides sideways towards the Volkswagen and David sitting behind the wheel realises that the Goliath he has taken on is just about to roll right over him. His terror stricken face and bulging eyes stand out in the headlights, he looks stupefied and quickly passes from view as we glide past to sit awaiting the thud and rumble as he goes under the back wheels. But the thud never comes, only a crack like a twig snapping under the wheels. The truck is straightening up, ruts in the road are helping to swing her. The VW appears again in the mirror, we have clipped her front wing which has crumpled. The driver, too dazed to know what has happened, is limping along, crouched over his wheel.

Yugoslavia begins with a series of spectacular mountain passes with tunnels drilled through the mountain sides. It is a scenic road with exciting vistas built into every bend, above tower rock faces so high that they pinch the sky to a thin streak between their peaks.

It is a dangerous road, an extension of the brutal killer road and in itself it is sufficient justification, if any were needed, for every drink and drive act, breathalyser, stiff driving test and bloody-minded traffic cop that ever was. There is a simple truth that has to be stated: the locals are inexperienced, bad, silly, irresponsible and sometimes just plain drunken drivers. And the death toll on these Balkan roads is proof enough. If there were more cars on the road every day would be a national disaster. Kamikaze drivers are again the culprits. Official statistics record that 90 per cent of accidents are caused by Yugoslav bus and truck drivers and Turkish bus and gastarbieter car drivers returning from Germany.

The problems are the same as on every

other Communist Bloc road: underpowered, appallingly slow trucks, road trains with an underpowered truck pulling up to four trailers, unlit farm carts, tractors, horse drawn vehicles, suicidal bus drivers and drink, drink, drink.

The Austrian police in the beautiful Enns Valley have a dossier of death the final pages of which are written on tombstones in the graveyard at Liezen. One third of the people buried there are foreigners killed on what the police call "this accursed road".

They speak of Turkish gastarbeiters and Yugoslav drivers in the tones most people reserve for talking about terminal illness, quietly but with awe and regret. German and Austrian drivers and truck drivers make few problems, the others are an ever-moving menace. Take some of the instances the police record:

17 Yugoslavs pulled from the wreck of a nine-seater Ford Transit van of ancient vintage, the children travelling on top of the luggage;

an underpowered Lada with a top speed of 68 mph, overladen with seven passengers, attempting to overtake trucks travelling at 70 mph in a no-overtaking zone—clearly marked. The driver pulled into the offside lane of the narrow two-lane highway and ran head on into an oncoming truck and all were killed . . . that is one instance but it happens often;

a Turk travelling with a heavy brick wedged on his accelerator to save his leg because he was over-tired. He couldn't stop and flew off the road on a bend with severe casualties to his passengers in the overladen Merc;

another Turk who caused a fatal accident by blinding traffic with his powerful headlights and when questioned did not know there was a dip-switch in the car or what it was for.

It is not uncommon for Turks to allow their children to drive the whole way home. A ten-year-old-boy has been found at the wheel. The rural Turk sees nothing wrong in it; in fact, he is affronted that his son's skills should be called into question. He has lived in the West, happily taken the money, but he has not absorbed any Western ways or ideas since he has lived entirely in his Turkish ghetto.

The police say that the death toll in this

gastarbeiter route is twice that on any other of the country's major roads.

There is no need to visit a cemetery, the road itself is a cemetery and decorated as one which makes it a gruesomely distressing and unnerving drive to undertake. The length of the road is dotted with wreaths and shrines to those killed on it. The shrines are elaborately decorated with photographs of the driver, his vehicle and, incredibly, empty bottles of wine. At one stage so many shrines clogged the roadside that the authorities ordered a clean up and moved them, but the wreaths and mementoes return as the deaths continue.

The National Hotel in Belgrade is a great poste restante address for drivers and it is a trip down memory lane of an entirely different kind. All the sweet young things of yesteryear keep in touch through the National. The table in the vestibule is stacked with letters in distinctly feminine handwriting—and they are all read a sight quicker than the waiting telexes from head office. Some truckers have a quantity of fan mail a pop star might envy.

There is a moderately good meal to be had at the National, plenty of beer, they are friendly and reception is exceptionally helpful. But for the saucy boys, the stop is up the road at the motel known to drivers as The Trees. Built in a forest about 65 kilometres on the Belgrade side of Zagreb, the motel is actually built around the trees incorporating them in its interior design. There are also chalets provided in the woods.

"I wouldn't stay there, if it was laid on free," complained an older driver, "you can't get a wink of sleep all night. As soon as you drop off there's some brass or other knocking on your door. It goes on all night long, they won't leave you alone. The last time I was in the place, and I only stayed because the weather was bad, a young brass knocked me up at half past midnight. I told her I was too dog tired and all I wanted to do was get some sleep. Then she knocked me up again at four o'clock and asked me if I was feeling rested."

At first glance, it is a delightfully innocuous place. You could be lucky enough to arrive at the time when a favourite TV programme comes on in the early evening. Surely you could not fail to thrill to the stirring theme music: "Robin Hood, Robin Hood, riding through the glen . . ." Everything stops for

Robin Hood, staff and customers alike crowd round the box.

Outside in the truck park there is a more exciting live show as the girls—mostly happy amateurs—parade for interested drivers. Wearing nothing but fur coats and stockings they walk in front of the parked trucks. When an interested driver puts his headlight on, they open their coats wide, and twirl as fashion models do on a ramp, displaying their manifest charms.

"It's good here," says a young driver, "makes you feel as if you're a judge at a nude Miss World. I feel like leaning out of the cab window and saying, 'The winners, in reverse order, are the third blonde, the two-tone and the genuine raven-haired cracker.' "

There is a consensus of opinion among drivers that there is nobody lazier or more obstructive to be found than an Austrian customs official. They are so tired that sleep drips from their eyes all the working day and, by the end of a shift, they can hardly summon the strength to slam the shutter closed in your face.

Monumental rows erupt on the borders to shatter the general somnambulance when drivers explode from frustration. Tempers flare when drivers have been waiting for hours in a slow, orderly queue and the customs official, at the end of his shift, slams shut his window just as a driver's turn comes up.

Those two running mates of ours, the Dutchman and John Martin, caused an incident when the windows were slammed shut in their faces with the almost certain effect that, unless they could get immediate action, they would be "Weekended". Quietly, and in the approved Austrian manner they climbed into their trucks and shunted them across all the entrance and exit lanes—effectively jamming the border. They locked the doors and went to a bar where they continued to relax, with the support of various cronies, despite the uncharacteristic agitation the police were now demonstrating.

It is remarkably difficult to move two fully laden trucks from a confined, congested space particularly when other trucks have moved up close to back up the protest. The police threatened to send to Vienna for the Riot Squad. "Great," said John Martin, "tell them to bring a couple of HGV drivers with them . . . no, better make that a dozen, we'll all be pissed by the time they arrive, if they ever get through the traffic."

Eventually and not without very good grace, the police opened up the customs office and produced the requisite papers within the hour.

However two simple words can be guaranteed to galvanise Austrian officials into action such as you have never seen. A Liverpool driver, a Scouse through and through, and an ardent Liverpool FC supported, accidentally hit on the magic formula. After a six hour wait, his turn came and window was slammed in his face. But he managed to jam it and while the customs man, now supported by his colleagues, struggled to close it, the Liverpudlian hurled every insult and word of vile abuse he could muster until he quite ran out of vilification. Almost in tears with rage and fighting a losing battle against the press of officialdom on the other side of the window, he reached into the recesses of his mind and spat the ultimate curse.

"Youse, youse . . . Manchester United," he bellowed.

The effect was electrifying. As a man the customs officers let go of the window, the

Scouse nearly broke his arm. Then the office doors opened, and, fists flying, legs kicking, customs men poured out into the crowd seeking the Liverpudlian.

Naturally the waiting drivers, being what they are, immediately thought this was a little diversion laid on for their pleasure, so they all joined in and the battle spread throughout the hall. Curious policemen threw a few punches and beat a few skulls with batons which added to the general merriment, so the drivers politely reciprocated until the arena was filled with bloodied noses, black eyes, ripped clothing and missing teeth.

"Vat vas all dat about?" queried a grinning Dutchman, helping the Liverpudlian to his feet.

"I dunno," said the Scouse, "all I said was Manchester United . . ." And at the words the battle recommenced.

Later, bathing his wounds in the pub, the Scouse said: "They can't be all bad if they reacted to Manchester United like that."

The explanation is that Manchester United Football Club has played in Austria accompanied by a large party of their notorious, hooligan fans. The havoc and mayhem they wreaked can never be erased from Austrian memory and national consciousness. To imply that an Austrian can be related to a Manchester United fan is to imply that he is sub-human . . .

Do not be disillusioned about Austria, it is the most beautiful and breathtaking of landscapes to drive through and wholly civilised when it comes to good living. It provides, as a matter of course, fine wines, glorious beers, excellent food and accommodation. Hospitality is also high on the list which is why Ma's hostelry at Spielfeld gained such popularity and why it was accorded the five star accolade of the name Ma's. Any place which rates that designation in drivers' parlance must be good.

Ma's can also, however, put on a spectacle to rival the best of motor sport—a sprint start to knock that at Le Mans into a driver's helmet. On the stroke of midnight on Sunday, "weekended" drivers burst out of Ma's, all ages, shapes and sizes of them, and race as fast as they can to leap into their cabs for a flying start to be first down the road and first to the next border. It can save hours if you survived the initial strain.

A regular visitor at Ma's was Steve Goodman, one of the fastest and best drivers on the run who had worked for Astran for six years. Some can make the trip pay better than others, as it is in all other competitive businesses, and Steve was one of those, he could turn in a profit on every run.

For a time he had "opted out" from his life in England, he was divorced and wanted to keep his past life at home at arm's length. On his day he was a very big drinker and he loved an occasional gigantic thrash—anywhere, Zagreb, Belgrade, Budapest, Sofia, Istanbul, he had friends and girlfriends everywhere. Then he fell in love again. He married a Dan Air hostess who had worked for a time at Astran. It changed him a lot, he became a loving and devoted husband whose aim it was to get the run over as quickly as could be properly done and get home.

Returning through Austria he made an overnight stop and called at one of his favourite bars for a chat and a few drinks with the boys and girls. One girl, a known prostitute, joined the party. Steve told her: "Look, I'm not interested, but you are welcome to a few drinks, if you feel like it—as many as you want."

The girl sat and drank and chatted to him. The last thing Steve wanted was a hangover in the morning since he was anxious to be away quickly and make good time to the ferry for home, so he took it easy and quietly. Eventually he announced: "I'm off to bed, I've got an early start in the morning, nice to chat to you, see you next trip, probably."

At that stage the girl demanded to be paid for the time she had been sitting talking to him or at least a fee in lieu of her services.

"Come on," said Steve, "I told you when you first came over that I wasn't interested. But I said you could have a few drinks if you wanted to."

The girl was insistent, she wanted to be paid. People in the bar looked on with amused and bemused smiles, getting the gist of the argument.

"No way," said Steve, "I'm too long in the tooth to be taken in by a con like that, forget it. I'm going to sleep in the cab and then away. Goodnight."

He left the bar, the girl's pimp followed him outside, pulled a gun and shot him dead through the back of the head.

This happened in Linz, Austria's third city. But there is death in plenty throughout the route. Death and danger go hand in glove with guns and the risks are so much the worse when guns are in abundance. On this day of writing, Dick Snow, who has run the route consecutively for longer than anyone, returned from a trip having driven through Syria. He was forced to give a Syrian soldier a lift—you don't argue too much when they demand one. At a road block, the roadside soldiers signalled Dick to stop, the soldier in the cab ordered him to keep going. The army at the road block opened fire and blasted the back of his truck away. Of course, this is almost a commonplace in Syria. But murder in cold blood in an Austrian bar, nobody could expect.

Why drivers continue to do the job year in and year out is not easily explained. The journey is rough, tough, exhausting, dirty, uncomfortable and dangerous. But, like soldiers, they are not fighting all the time. And many men actually like to live dangerously. Winning gold medals in athletics, pushing the mind and body to the limits of concentration and pain is not exactly fun—but the sense of achievement afterwards is magnificent. Completing the round trip from England to Arabia produces a similar elation, this is the Olympics of truck driving.

So this is England again. And a driver with us on the ferry is going to drive to Birmingham, say hello to his wife, turn round and catch the midnight ferry back tomorrow night because an urgent load has come up. He must be mad.

Rub your backside and thighs as much as you like, by now you will be feeling saddle-sore and you will be thinking that the bottom half of your legs were invented for clutch, accelerator and brake. Next time maybe we can spend a few weeks running internals in the Gulf. We will go down through Midway Garrison to the Yemen war front. And what about a trip on the ro-ro from Abu Dhabi to Ayatollah land, Iran? We could land at Bandar Abbas, but the captain sometimes stops to visit relatives on Qeshm Island, if the mood takes him. That's a load of fun.

Just before you go, the new road from Pakistan to China, over the Himalayas, has been completed for a couple of years, but so far it is open only to military traffic. Every Middle East driver worth his salt is pulling every string he knows to be the first "commercial" to cross the roof of the world and take a cargo from Britain to China. Do you fancy it?

GUIDE
TO THE COLOUR CODING
OF
ULVERSCROFT BOOKS

Many of our readers have written to us expressing their appreciation for the way in which our colour coding has assisted them in selecting the Ulverscroft books of their choice. To remind everyone of our colour coding— this is as follows:

BLACK COVERS
Mysteries

★

BLUE COVERS
Romances

★

RED COVERS
Adventure Suspense and General Fiction

★

ORANGE COVERS
Westerns

★

GREEN COVERS
Non-Fiction

NON-FICTION TITLES
in the
Ulverscroft Large Print Series

No Time for Romance	*Lucilla Andrews*
Life's A Jubilee	*Maud Anson*
Beautiful Just! and	
Bruach Blend	*Lillian Beckwith*
An Autobiography Vol.1	
Vol.2	*Agatha Christie*
Just Here, Doctor	*Robert D. Clifford*
High Hopes	*Norman Croucher*
An Open Book	*Monica Dickens*
Going West with Annabelle	*Molly Douglas*
The Drunken Forest	*Gerald Durrell*
The Garden of the Gods	*Gerald Durrell*
Golden Bats and Pink Pigeons	*Gerald Durrell*
If Only They Could Talk	*James Herriot*
It Shouldn't Happen to a Vet	*James Herriot*
Let Sleeping Vets Lie	*James Herriot*
Vet in a Spin	*James Herriot*
Vet in Harness	*James Herriot*
Vets Might Fly	*James Herriot*
Emma and I	*Sheila Hocken*
White Man Returns	*Agnes Newton Keith*
Flying Nurse	*Robin Miller*
The High Girders	*John Prebble*
The Seventh Commandment	*Sarah Shears*
Zoo Vet	*David Taylor*

THE SHADOWS
OF THE CROWN TITLES
in the
Ulverscroft Large Print Series

THE WHITEOAK CHRONICLE SERIES TITLES
in the
Ulverscroft Large Print Series

by Mazo De La Roche

The Building of Jalna
Morning at Jalna
Mary Wakefield
Young Renny
Whiteoak Heritage
The Whiteoak Brothers
Jalna
Whiteoaks
Finch's Fortune
The Master of Jalna
Whiteoak Harvest
Wakefield's Course
Return to Jalna
Renny's Daughter
Variable Winds at Jalna
Centenary at Jalna

MYSTERY TITLES
in the
Ulverscroft Large Print Series

Henrietta Who?	*Catherine Aird*
Slight Mourning	*Catherine Aird*
The China Governess	*Margery Allingham*
Coroner's Pidgin	*Margery Allingham*
Crime at Black Dudley	*Margery Allingham*
Look to the Lady	*Margery Allingham*
More Work for the Undertaker	
	Margery Allingham
Death in the Channel	*J. R. L. Anderson*
Death in the City	*J. R. L. Anderson*
Death on the Rocks	*J. R. L. Anderson*
A Sprig of Sea Lavender	*J. R. L. Anderson*
Death of a Poison-Tongue	*Josephine Bell*
Murder Adrift	*George Bellairs*
Strangers Among the Dead	*George Bellairs*
The Case of the Abominable Snowman	
	Nicholas Blake
The Widow's Cruise	*Nicholas Blake*
The Brides of Friedberg	*Gwendoline Butler*
Murder By Proxy	*Harry Carmichael*
Post Mortem	*Harry Carmichael*
Suicide Clause	*Harry Carmichael*
After the Funeral	*Agatha Christie*
The Body in the Library	*Agatha Christie*